The Development of the Playhouse

The Development of the Playhouse

A survey of theatre architecture
from the Renaissance to the Present

Donald C. Mullin

University of California Press
Berkeley and Los Angeles 1970

University of California Press
Berkeley and Los Angeles, California

University of California Press, Ltd.
London, England

Copyright © 1970, by
The Regents of the University of California

SBN: 520–01391–3

Library of Congress Catalog Card Number: 77–84532
Design by Steve Reoutt
Printed in the United States of America

Foreword

In a work of this brevity it is manifestly impossible to include every theatre built since the Renaissance, or even to discuss every country and the contributions of its architects. For this reason, there are obvious omissions for which I hope I shall be forgiven. The theatres of the Orient are omitted entirely. The theatre in Spain is barely mentioned, and the Spanish popular theatre not at all. In other areas, famous playhouses are passed over completely because they are of little architectural interest or influence. Some theatres are included only because they are representative of a type, others because they are particularly well documented, and still others because they have been the subject of so much interest that their omission would reduce the value of this book. Since the purpose of the book is evaluative as well as historical, I intrude my own opinions and interpretations on occasions when I believe them to be pertinent. A mere list of playhouses has been avoided as much as possible, as have listings of statistics, except on the occasions where these may be of particular interest or relevance.

Illustration and comment has been restricted to permanent theatres, except for a few seminal temporary structures of the Renaissance. Some interesting festival, exhibition, and outdoor playhouses have been erected, particularly in the last generation. It was not thought appropriate to include them, however, because they have not yet had an effect on indoor, permanent construction.

Theatres erected for nondramatic purposes have been omitted entirely, because this is a survey of playhouses, not auditoria or stages. The word "playhouse" is interpreted to include buildings for dramatic entertainment, whether this be spoken drama, vaudeville, opera, or dance. Theatre project plans over the centuries have been influential in the development of new concepts and theories, and no student of theatre architecture can afford to omit them from his study of the subject. Projects have been omitted from this work only because of the limitations of space. Many are, however, listed in the Bibliography of Sources; the student is urged to consult them.

Since the ancient theatre is extremely well documented, and reconstructions are based upon the painstaking observations of archeologists, I have thought it unnecessary to repeat those observations. This volume begins with the Renaissance, because the theatre of that period still is not entirely understood, and because some controversy still exists over the merits of the theatres designed during that time. Detailed observations are presented as much as is practicable, widening into generalizations in later centuries as the number of theatres increases beyond a manageable figure. No attempt is made to give all the historical details about each period, much less about each theatre. Comment about modern theatres has been kept to a minimum, partly through space limitations, and partly because such information is readily available, even in modest libraries. This book is designed to supplement studies in theatre history for the student, and to give a clear, generalized portrait of past playhouses to the general reader. I regret that the limitations inherent in such a survey prevent the detailed observations in depth which would be of use to the specialist.

Every effort has been made to present correct data on each of the theatres mentioned. Dates, where given, and unless otherwise qualified, refer to the year of the theatre's opening and not to the year of the laying of the foundation stone, as is normal in discussions of architecture. Theatres are referred to as permanent when reference is made to their construction out of permanent materials (such as brick or stone), and bears no relation to the length of time which they were used.

Theatres do not make drama. Neither, on the other hand, do actors. A play has been defined as a script performed on a stage by actors before an audience. Each of these elements must be present, in spite of those who refer to almost anything which is exciting as "theatrical" or "dramatic." It is hoped that this brief study of playhouses will make the influence and contribution of the physical stage clearer and more relevant to the life of the theatre as we understand it.

University of Guelph
1969

Acknowledgements

I wish to express my appreciation to the following publishers, libraries, museums, and scholars, for making material available for this work:

Ernest Benn, Ltd., for figures from *The Globe Restored* by C. Walter Hodges; New York University Press for figures from *Shakespeare's Blackfriars Playhouse* by Irwin Smith; Theatre Arts Books for figures from *Architecture for the New Theatre* by Edith Isaacs; Drottningholm Teatermuseum for plates from *Court Theatres of Drottningholm and Gripsholm*: the editors of *Educational Theatre Journal, Theatre Design and Technology, Theatre Notebook*, and *Theatre Survey* for permission to use materials from articles by me: the Archief Bibliotheek, Amsterdam; the Toneelmuseum, Amsterdam; Bibliothèque Nationale, Paris; the Guildhall Library, London; the Folger Library; Harvard College Library; Boston Public Library; Harvard Theatre Collection for gracious permission to reproduce numerous engravings; Harvard University Press for permission to quote at length from *Vitruvius: the Ten Books on Architecture*, translated by Morris Hicky Morgan; Goethe Nationalmuseum for illustrations and reconstructions of Goethe's theatre at Weimar; New York Historical Society; Professor Edward A. Langhans for gracious permission to reproduce plates of his models; Bruce A. Koenig.

I am also indebted to the College of St. Benedict and particularly to the University of Guelph for research grants which aided in the preparation of the manuscript and in the accumulation of illustrations. Special thanks are also due to Michael Booth for suggestions on the manuscript.

Contents

List of Illustrations

xiv

Introduction

With this volume a modest attempt is made to repair a serious deficiency: at present, there is no work in English which examines the development of Western theatre architecture. There are studies from the eighteenth century which give a brief glimpse of playhouses of previous eras, but these deal almost exclusively with theatres of the ancient world in order to provide a basis for comparison with the playhouses of the time of publication. There are more recent surveys available in Italian, German, and Russian, but most of these are either out of print or difficult to obtain. Theatre history volumes generally are our only source of illustration and comment; some of these present in detail theatres of past eras, but none includes sufficient illustrations to make possible intelligent comparison of architectural styles. Necessarily, such books have been restricted to discussions of theatres connected with historical events of interest to the authors, but not to architectural innovation as such. The majority of information on the history of the physical theatre is contained in studies of selected periods, of individual theatres, and in scholarly articles—sources which are unavailable to the general reader and unsuitable for the beginning student.

Since it is difficult to visualize the development of theatre without a clear notion of the methods used by producers and designers in mounting productions, scenic design and prompt-book notation have become important studies. Only passing references are made to the theatres in which those designs and productions were mounted, however, so it is still difficult to recreate a past performance. The production of a play involves more than an actor, a backdrop, or prompter's remarks; greenroom gossip may be revealing, old scripts may disclose a wealth of traditional business, but none of these items alone can tell us what attendance at a performance may have meant, because they fall short of recreating the entire picture. A study of playhouses, added to the other elements, will contribute to an understanding of the whole.

Architectural styles are seldom derived from the needs of the practical theatre technician, or even from the demands of playwrights, but are dictated by the trend of fashion and mode of an entire generation. A playhouse is a living organism, inseparable from the plays produced within it. One affects the other in every way imaginable. Just as the perfect house must be designed particularly for the persons who will live in it, the perfect theatre must be designed specifically for a producing group with a live tradition (at best), or to accommodate a definite theory of production (at the least). There are theatre designs which dictate the performance style of the actors and the design method of the scenic artist long after the fashion in architecture has changed, but if the production theories and elements are integrated with the playhouse as an organic architectural unit, the viability of the producing organization is seldom endangered. Only when the two are in direct conflict is trouble certain to arise. Architecture is a self-conscious and time-consuming art, one which matures only after many years of thought and practice. The same usually is true of effective production methods. Changes are slow to occur in both because of the vast expense involved, and—in architecture particularly—because of the general inertia of governmental or public agencies. Frequently, changes in playhouse form are not innovative at all, but merely alterations in trim and dressing; the same may be said of production methods within the theatres. In other instances, the form of a playhouse may seem to resemble a former style very closely when it is, in reality, a genuine and influential departure in outlook and method. The parallels between production techniques and playhouse architecture are numerous, and the lessons learned from one may be applied to the other. The inseparability of the two is confirmed by every major theorist who has written about the art of the theatre.

A considerable effort has been directed upon the theatre of the ancients, and with the help of many published illustrations and reconstructions of Greek and Roman theatres we are better able to visualize the plays produced in them. We also recognize the direct relationship among the playhouses, the production style, and the playwriting of Shakespeare's time. But even though we are aware, in a vague way, of the outline of the theatre of box, pit, and gallery, our awareness still is not sufficiently developed for us fully to comprehend plays from the seventeenth through nineteenth centuries as anything but quaint, or to see the playhouses of that time as anything but curious collections of posts and upholstered boxes.

Did the architects of previous generations really not understand theatre? Or did they understand and translate their comprehension into terms suitable to the time, place, and the materials at hand? Our visualization of the theatre of the past is muddled by ignorance of fashion and conventions of building practice. Perhaps we must understand more clearly the views of previous generations and the playhouses that they built to conform to them. As a matter of course, each generation reviles the accomplishments of the one that preceded it. Even as our fathers derided theatre design of the early 1900's, so we in turn laugh at theatres of the last generation. It was not long ago that theatre architectural planning required all patrons to be squeezed into a long, narrow house in which every seat had perfect sightlines so that all the expensive and elaborate realistic settings could be seen by everyone. Only recently have we reversed our view to require a plan which imitates that of the ancient theatre, the so-called thrust stage. We in turn, one suspects, will be laughed at by architects of a generation hence, when yet another form will be fashionable and therefore proper. In reality, most of the design possibilities have been exploited time and again, and old staging methods and techniques still have useful applications, as any producer of opera or ballet will be happy to relate.

An understanding of the actor-audience relationships of period architectural concepts may help to create meaningful theatres for modern audiences. The term "may" is used advisedly, because architects occasionally make mistakes in design approach. A theatre's shape may not be allowed to develop according to the needs of the medium, but may be forced into a form more consistent with current ideas about what is real and true, or what is respectable and therefore worth emulating. The typical errors are noted below, although some particularly striking and even awe-inspiring new buildings are conglomerations of all these.

Error I: *Theatre as Archeology*; designing a theatre to conform to a stylistic revival. Several major theatres of this type were built in the Renaissance, as one may expect, but later playhouses also suffered from such culture-consciousness. Few nineteenth century ladies' seminaries were complete without a Greek amphitheatre in which students tiptoed their way through eurhythmic dances, trailing scarves and looking classic. More recent contributions to education include Greek (or, more accurately, Greco-Roman) amphitheatres, and the current fashion in thrust stage design places the audience in semicircular arcs simulating those of the ancient theatre without either that theatre's production dynamic or spirit. On paper, the arrangement seems to be a suitable one in which to bring large numbers of spectators reasonably close to a playing space, but in practice, the Greco-Roman form is unsuitable for contemporary production; not that it does not work, but that it does not work as well as the forms in which the plays were originally visualized. The geometric arcs in which these amphitheatres are laid out are stiff and formal, precisely the reverse of the mood required for the majority of contemporary drama.

Error II: *Theatre as a Rational Science*; designing a theatre according to a principle to which everything must be accommodated. The eighteenth century brought into the theatre the logical and ordered approach of science. Vitruvius mentioned that Greek and Roman theatres were based upon geometric patterns; later architects seized upon this as an excuse to lay down theatre plans based upon circles, ellipses, squares, oblongs, and combinations of all of these. House plans have been inscribed within semicircles, squares, cubes, double cubes, and more recently into trapezoids. While it is possible that a theatre designed for a specific function may fall into one of these shapes, to begin with the shape betrays a peculiar line of thought. Architects who design according to formulae naively expect a theatre designed according to a fixed principle to be right—providing that the proper principle can be found. The more extreme examples of such drawing-board architecture are almost unusable. Lesser examples are merely irritating.

Error III: *Theatre as Classroom*; designing a theatre according to social desires which are irrelevant to dramatic production. One of the more charming misconceptions of the reformers of the nineteenth century was a belief in cultural osmosis. The era of elevating lectures for the improvement of the minds of the working classes ("cultural enrichment" is the current euphemism) also exploited theatre for propagandistic purposes. Vast pageants on enormous stages were designed to instruct the worker in his proper heritage. "Mass Theatre" is a typical expression used by late nineteenth century middle class intellectuals who thought of proper theatre production as a kind of stimulating rally. The concept flowered briefly and died in the West, but was kept alive and stimulated by the need for mass indoctrination in Socialist countries. The Classroom Theatre, typically, was provided with thousands of seats facing a vast stage designed to show instructive, simplistic tableaux with sloganeering enacted by enormous casts. Contemporary variants of this approach are usually referred to as Epic Theatre.

Error IV: *The Mechanical Playhouse*; designing a theatre as a production machine. The elaboration of scenic materials that developed in the last quarter of the nineteenth century demanded equally elaborate methods of scene shifting. The advent of realism encouraged the erection of mountains of scenery which proved to be almost unmovable. All the resources of science were called to the aid of the scene technician. The Germans led, constructing new and reconstructing old theatres as models of efficiency and stage flexibility. Their vast stage houses, with production area quadruple the size of the auditorium, were the ultimate extension of stagecraft. Multiple merry-go-rounds of revolving stages, ballets of complex elevators, and astounding spreads of canvas or plaster cycloramas and sky-domes were the result of the pursuit of mechanical perfection and enabled staggering productions to be mounted, all perfectly realistic. Scenery proliferated until architects of the 1920s envisioned mechanical stages in rings completely surrounding the audience, upon which a cinematic progression of scenes could be shown *ad infinitum* until audiences were stupefied. More recently, electro-mechanics have been called to the aid of the stage planner. The technician who once was satisfied to be an expert at rigging now discovers that he must be an hydraulic and electrical engineer as well. He is provided with vast, organ-like consoles of buttons which will, he is assured, solve all of his problems.

Error V: *Theatre as Sculpture*. There are some who are not architects in the true sense at all, but sculptors of monuments, men who design buildings only incidentally to be used by human beings. Some frankly admit that they do not care what their buildings are used for as long as they are built. The sculptural building is detected easily, since it is meant to be viewed from the outside or from a particular point on the inside. No clue is given to its size or function, for the human figure is unrelated to its design and purpose. Interiors are treated and textured with no relation to their planned occupancy by human beings and to the theatre production on the stage except in the most general terms. Internal shapes are determined by external form. The modeling has little to do with the requirements of the theatres encapsuled within; indeed, it may even be inhibiting.

Error VI: *Theatre as a Scaffold*; designing a theatre according to the requirements of a fashionable construction method. Upon the introduction of cast iron, it became mandatory that the material be exploited to its greatest advantage, regardless of the outcome. Great balconies were flung over the heads of audiences below, confining them under low ceilings that prevented anyone from hearing very much. Steel construction encouraged profusions of deep, cantilevered tiers, from which audiences could see nothing but the stage floor and were given no sense of enclosure or of themselves as a corporate body. The simple geometries of steel framing spelled the death of gracefully formed auditoria, and covered steel boxes resulted. With the advent of poured and reinforced concrete, freedom of form once more is possible, but the freedom frequently leads not to an appropriate auditorium design but merely to an expression of architectural malaise. With joyful abandon the concrete theatre designer will form his structure into bulbous excrescences, medieval redoubts, canted walls—all hung with bits and pieces in the latest style used by window-decorators. The opposite extreme may also be followed for reasons of economy, that of using the simple plywood sheet as a concrete form. This leads to a series of foursquare modules of bewildering dullness.

Although the above errors are easy to commit, they are also simple to avoid. As it is true that there are few painters and musicians of the first rank, so also is it true that architects frequently handle their materials with less than the greatest skill. It is possible to use the elements of style in a manner that will make the result pleasing and appropriate, something which has been done in the theatre for centuries. As long as the client knows what he is looking for and as long as the architect is gifted, the result cannot be other than satisfactory. When both are insensitive the result can be a parody, a monstrosity, or a joke.

As this book is written there are several experiments being made in theatrical production which have a bearing on theatre architecture. The large, formal, playhouse designed to house an audience affluent enough to pay high prices is paralleled by the development in large scale of the cellar or loft theatres. In these low-rent halls the more adventuresome playwrights, producers, and actors can offer their wares to audiences more concerned with content and method than with comfort and dressing. "Free" theatres have always started with such minimal requirements, but have usually ended becoming imitations of their commercial opponents in prices, production methods, and in the plays chosen. Contemporary variants, however, seem to be pursuing experiment farther than has been common in the past. The happening, a brief flowering of anarchic theatre-like artistic experience, has been followed by such things as the guerilla theatre, a production style that abandons the formal theatre structure entirely, relying on the emotional impact of the content rather than upon any organized surroundings, dialogue, or individualized characterizations. Thus, theatre (in this manifestation) has come full circle: from the primitive dancing-circle, to the formal theatre, to the city street.

I
Rome Revisited

Theatre flourished in the ancient world. Permanent theatre buildings of great pretension were erected from Britain to Syria, and from the Rhine to Libya. At the opening of the early Renaissance, however, hardly a vestige remained. The political, economic, and military collapse of the Roman Empire had destroyed the cultural base upon which civic theatre rested. With the collapse—engendered by the fall of Rome—of the slave labor market everyone was forced to struggle to survive, and the pleasant habit of spending the afternoon at the theatre vanished. The theatre buildings were abandoned. They were too elaborate to maintain, too vast for shrunken populations, and the way of life they were built to reflect had died. Some crumbled into ruin as the cities in which they were built became depopulated. Most, however, were stripped for building material, leaving only the concrete cores behind. Columns went into churches, marble was burned for lime to make mortar, and stone blocks went into walls, peasant huts, and forts, or sank into the earth.

The few Roman theatres that remained relatively intact were regarded with awe. Those theatres from which the seats had not been carted away were used occasionally for meetings, religious purposes, or even for theatrical performances on a reduced scale that must have seemed pitiful indeed. The revival of theatre in the Middle Ages sprang from other inspirations than those of ancient Rome, and the Roman theatres served only as curiosities, except in isolated instances.

The revival of learning brought with it an interest in classical literature, including drama. Drama required theatres, but as there were no theatres to be found, they had to be built. But how and from what plans? A few plans, or at least discussions of plans, were available to those who looked for them.

It is seldom in history that we are able to blame or to credit one man for anything. Complex and difficult-to-attribute forces move us, willy-nilly. Occasionally, however, a single man or a single work may influence events so profoundly that blame or credit may be attached with some justice. Certainly many factors contributed to the shape of the playhouse as it evolved in the Renaissance, but the major single source for information, inspiration, and method was an obscure treatise left by a second-rate Roman architect.

Marcus Vitruvius Pollio wrote *De Architectura Libri Decem* sometime in the second decade of the first century A.D., during the principate of Augustus Caesar. This work is the only ancient architectural treatise that was available to Renaissance scholars, consequently it had an extraordinary influence on Renaissance architecture. Vitruvius included in his *Ten Books* a study of theatres as a form of civic architecture, making observations on playhouse acoustics, auditorium planning, stage house design, and scenery.

The manuscript was copied many times after

5

its publication, and those copies, in turn, were copied during the Middle Ages. The original, with its numerous illustrations "at the end of this book," did not survive, nor did the illustrations that may have been appended to later copies. Without the drawings upon which the author depended for clarification of his descriptions, many references are obscure. Despite this, it is difficult to imagine what direction Renaissance architecture might have taken had Vitruvius's work not been available. The Roman's authority was cited nearly as frequently in architecture as was that of Aristotle in philosophy, and all subsequent architectural treatises were indebted to his manuscript.

The descriptive terms Vitruvius used were common during his lifetime, and therefore were clear to his contemporaries. We have discovered the meanings of some of these terms through our research into the period, but other words still elude accurate definition. For this reason, editions and translations of the Roman work differ slightly from one to another as each translator or editor makes his own interpretations of the author's meanings. Early architects misinterpreted Vitruvius's use of some terms whose meanings the Romans took for granted; therefore, structures erected previous to independent Renaissance studies of Roman ruins showed similarities to ancient buildings, but in most cases, similarities only. Before we are tempted to treat early misinterpretations with scorn, we should examine the portions of the *Ten Books* which refer to theatre construction. We may then appreciate the ease with which certain elements are understood, and the difficulty of piecing others together. In the Fifth Chapter of the Fifth Book, Vitruvius discussed acoustical reinforcement in the following manner:*

Sounding Vessels in the Theatre

1. In accordance with the foregoing mathematical principles, let bronze vessels be made, proportionate to the size of the theatre, and let them be so fashioned that, when touched, they may produce with one another the notes of the fourth, the fifth, and so on up to the double octave. Then, having constructed niches in between the seats of the theatre, let the vessels be arranged in them, in accordance with musical laws, in such a way that they nowhere touch the wall, but have a clear

* as translated by Morris Hicky Morgan

6

space all around them and room over their tops. They should be set upside down and should be supported on the side facing the stage by wedges not less than half a foot high. Opposite each niche, apertures should be left in the surface of the seat next below, two feet long and half a foot deep.

2. The arrangement of these vessels, with reference to the situations in which they should be placed, may be described as follows. If the theatre be of no great size, mark out a horizontal range halfway up, and in it construct thirteen arched niches with twelve equal spaces between them, so that of the above mentioned "echea" those which give the note nete hyperbolaeon may be placed first on each side, in the niches which are at the extreme ends; next to the ends and a fourth below in pitch, the note nete diezeugmenon; third, paramese, a fourth below; fourth, nete synhemmenon; fifth, mese, a fourth below; sixth, hypate meson, a fourth below; and in the middle and another fourth below, one vessel giving the note hypate hypaton.

3. On this principle of arrangement, the voice uttered from the stage as from a center, and spreading and striking against the cavities of the different vessels, as it comes in contact with them, will be increased in clearness of sound, and will wake an harmonious note in unison with itself.

But if the theatre be rather large, let its height be divided into four parts, so that three horizontal ranges of niches may be marked out and constructed: one for the enharmonic, another for the chromatic, and the third for the diatonic system. Beginning with the bottom range, let the arrangement be as described above in the case of the smaller theatre, but on the enharmonic system.

We may see from this advice that one unfamiliar with the exact meanings of the words, and without illustrations graphically representing the plan as described, cannot duplicate this system of acoustical reinforcement. Although Vitruvius admitted that there were no theatres rigged in such a fashion in Italy, he insisted that some provincial theatres (with clay instead of bronze vessels) and theatres in Greece were so constructed. If we, with our more complete knowledge of the original forms of the theatres of the ancient world, cannot fully understand the architect's descriptions, it is not surprising that translators and editors of the first printed editions had difficulty. While the resonating chambers described by Vitruvius were not employed by Renaissance architects, chambers of a different nature performed a similar function in some eighteenth century theatres.

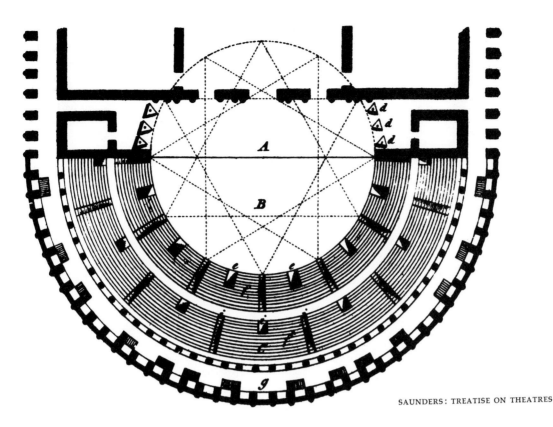

Fig. 1. Plan of a Roman theatre, according to Vitruvius.

Vitruvius's arrangement of the components of the theatre building was clear enough to enable later scholars and architects to draw reasonably accurate conclusions and from these to develop workable plans. The Roman master made it plain that he described no particular theatre but only a general design that would prove helpful to local contractors; he fully expected local conditions to require modifications.

The Plan of the Theatre

1. The plan of the theatre itself is to be constructed as follows. Having fixed upon the principal center, draw a line of circumference equivalent to what is to be the perimeter at the bottom, and in it inscribe four equilateral triangles, at equal distances apart and touching the boundry line of the circle, as the astrologers do in a figure of the twelve signs of the zodiac, when they are making computations from the musical harmony of the stars. Taking that one of these triangles whose side is nearest to the scaena, let the front of the scaena be determined by the line where that side cuts off a segment of the circle (A–B), and draw, through the center, a parallel line (C–D) set off from that position, to separate the platform of the stage from the space of the orchestra.

2. The platform has to be made deeper than that of the Greeks, because all our artists perform on the stage, while the orchestra contains the places reserved for the seats of the senators. The height of this platform must not be more than five feet, in order that those who sit in the orchestra may be able to see the performances of all the actors. The sections (cunei) for spectators in the theatre should be so divided, that the angles of the triangles which run about the circumference of the circle may give the direction for the flights of steps between the sections, as far as up to the first curved cross-aisle. Above this, the upper sections are to be laid out, midway between (the lower sections), with alternating passage-ways.

3. The angles at the bottom, which give the directions for the flights of steps, will be seven in number (C, E, F, G, H, I, D); the other five angles will determine the arrangement of the scene: thus, the angle in the middle ought to have the "royal door" (K) opposite to it; the angles to the left and right (L, M) will designate the position of the doors for guest chambers; and the two outermost angles (A, B) will point to the passages in the wings. The steps for the spectators' places, where the seats are arranged, should be not less than a foot and a palm in height, nor more than a foot and six fingers; their depth should be fixed

7

at not more than two and a half feet, nor less than two feet.

4. The roof of the colonnade to be built at the top of the rows of seats, should lie level with the top of the scaena, for the reason that the voice will then rise with equal power until it reaches the highest rows of seats and the roof. If the roof is not so high, in proportion as it is lower, it will check the voice at the point which the sound first reaches.

5. Take one sixth of the diameter of the orchestra between the lowest steps, and let the lower seats at the ends on both sides be cut away to a height of that dimension so as to leave entrances (O, P). At the point where this cutting away occurs, fix the soffits of the passages. Thus their vaulting will be sufficiently high.

6. The length of the scaena ought to be double the diameter of the orchestra. The height of the podium, starting from the level of the stage, is, including the corona and cymatium, one twelfth of the diameter of the orchestra. Above the podium, the columns, including their capitals and bases, should have a height of one quarter of the same diameter, and the architraves and ornaments of the columns should be one fifth of their height. The parapet, above, including its cyma and corona, is one half the height of the parapet below. Let the columns above this parapet be one fourth less in height than the columns below, and the architraves and ornaments of these columns one fifth of their height. If the scaena is to have three stories, let the uppermost parapet be half the height of the intermediate one, the columns at the top one fourth less high than the intermediate, and the architraves and coronae of these columns one fifth of their height as before.

. . . .

8. The scaena itself displays the following scheme. In the center are double doors decorated like those of a royal palace. At the right and left are the doors of the guest chambers. Beyond are spaces provided for decoration. . . in these places are triangular pieces of machinery which revolve, each having three decorated faces. When the play is to be changed, or when gods enter to the accompaniment of sudden claps of thunder, these may be revolved and present a face differently decorated. Beyond these places are the projecting wings which afford entrances to the stage, one from the forum, the other from abroad.

9. There are three kinds of scenes, one called tragic, second, the comic, third, the satyric. Their decorations are different and unlike each other in scheme. Tragic scenes are delineated with columns, pediments, statues, and other objects suited to kings; comic scenes exhibit private dwellings, with balconies and views representing rows of windows, after the manner of ordinary dwellings; satyric scenes are decorated with trees, caverns, mountains, and other rustic objects delineated in landscape style.

The layout of the triangles and their associated reference points is simple; an approximation of a Roman theatre may be drawn with little trouble. A similar description is given by Vitruvius for the plan of a Greek theatre (that type which we would call Greco-Roman), except that this plan is based upon a square instead of a triangle. Not until paragraphs 8 and 9, which refer to the scaena and the decorations, does confusion occur. Pictures of Roman ruins and of reconstructions based upon them render the scaena immediately understandable. Without such clues, however, the words of Vitruvius are almost meaningless. "Three stories;" three stories of what? The three doors may be located by means of the triangle apexes, but how large were they? What, if anything, was revealed behind them when they were opened? If periaktoi (the revolving prisms) were in common use, exactly where were they located? How large were they? How much decorated and painted surface was there in comparison to the unchanging scaena? Were the three scenes represented on the periaktoi, or were they different, additional, decoration? Were the periaktoi placed individually and separately, as isolated illustrative backgrounds, or were they placed together, providing on either side the equivalent of a large scenic drop? These questions cannot be answered even from our own studies of Roman ruins, so we can imagine the confusion they caused to Renaissance architects. The Vitruvian references to scenery, as the ones to acoustical reinforcement, remain mysteries. The wonder is not that Renaissance architects misinterpreted some passages, but that they managed to make interpretations at all.

Long before the printing of the Vitruvian manuscript, temporary theatres with Roman characteristics were erected, usually for revivals of classic farces. These were numerous enough that it is clear that classical influences were strong at an early date—if indeed they had ever completely disappeared. These theatres were not copies of the vast amphitheatres of Rome, how-

Fig. 2. Scene from a 1518 edition
of Plautus, Venice.

ever, but were designed on a more restrictive formula. The amphitheatrical form was adopted only for a few rows of benches. The *scaena frons* was not understood, either in form or in function, and usually no attempt was made to imitate it. Vitruvius had made it plain that there were five entrances; these were occasionally provided in something resembling classical architecture. Late medieval and early Renaissance artists rarely provided representational backgrounds, for the nature of such items was not understood. The scenery and decoration was derived from the iconographic pieces long in use in medieval religious drama. More frequently than not, simple pavilion enclosures, provided with curtained openings, were used.

Early productions of Terentian farces occasionally inspired attempts to construct Roman stages. A strikingly sophisticated version of a classical stage may be seen in the print of a Roman comedy performance on what we assume to be a medieval stage. Actors wearing thirteenth century dress are shown on a stage backed by three arched openings. At one side, an additional large structure houses a door below and a window above; this is presumably duplicated on the opposite side. A painted illustration of open country may be seen behind the triple arches in the background. Were it not for the costumes of the actors, this print might be assigned to the sixteenth century. Apparently, however, the producers of this early entertainment were more determined than many of their contemporaries to present a performance in the classical style.

More typical of early Renaissance classic revivals is the theatre indicated in the print cap-

tioned "Coliseus sivi Theatrum," from the Venice Terence of 1499. Shown is an outdoor amphitheatre of only a few rows, arranged in a semicircular form and backed by a row of square columns. Curiously enough, the columns support

Fig. 3. A renaissance *theatrum*.

9

a large dome with a practical walkway around it. The amphitheatre may have been classically inspired, but the stage bears no resemblance to that described by Vitruvius. It is on the same level with and indistinguishable from the semi-circular orchestra, and there is no evidence of any background except simple mansion-style pavilions with curtained openings. While the dome may be fanciful, the arrangement of the seating was clearly meant to echo that of the Roman theatre. Vitruvius may have been the influence (one suspects not), or perhaps the ruins of ancient theatres as they stood then. In any event the intent is clear.

Similar to this print is the theatre illustrated by Dürer in the Ulm edition of Terence published *circa* 1496. This amphitheatre is drawn with a few more rows of benches and no columns in the rear. It is an indoor theatre rather than an outdoor one, and apparently no supporting columns were

Fig. 5. A *theatrum* by Johannes Trechsel.

thought to be necessary. Again, the orchestra and the stage are one and the same, and there seems to be no attempt at a Roman *scaena*. The additional woodcuts of the series are representations of Terentian characters within local settings, but which do not seem to be set on stages or in a theatrical *milieu*.

Only in Johannes Trechsel's illustrations for the Lyons Terence of 1493 do we have a view of an entire playhouse. While the theatre seems peculiar to us because of its stylized rendering, it clearly is derived from Roman examples. An amphitheatre is shown within an octagonal building. The lower storey, labeled *Fornices*, or vaults, is precisely that, a series of connected arched supports for the upper storey. The *Theatrum* proper is located above, with graduated rows of seating. The area for spectators is surrounded by great pillars. These support the frame for a large canopy which stretches over the entire structure in imitation of the Roman *velarium*, or awning.

Fig. 4. An auditorium designed by Albrecht Dürer.

Fig. 6. The stage of Trechsel's *theatrum*.

In addition to seating for general patrons, a separate box is provided, labeled *aediles*, in which two figures may be seen. Roman *aediles* were public officers in charge of the peace at (among other places) the public games. Seating locations for these functionaries was not mentioned by Vitruvius, so obviously the inspiration for the *Theatrum* came from other sources as well.

The stage of this theatre, unlike the ones pictured in other editions of Terence, is separated from and raised above the orchestra. Trechsel's other prints from the same edition show us actors upon the stage. The *scaena* consists of a series of curtained openings in a large structure that has no stylistic relationship to the Roman theatre. Instead, decorated interiors are revealed behind the curtains when they are pulled back. Since the number of openings does not follow Vitruvius's dictate, but is determined by the number of locations required by the play, the *scaena* is clearly medieval in character, bearing little resemblance to the antique.

The influences upon this remarkable design are difficult to determine. Certainly it was a serious attempt at a reconstruction of a classic amphitheatre, but one that became garbled in translation, so to speak. The stage and its appurtenances derived directly from medieval mansion pavilions, but is as satisfactory a solution as those developed by later Renaissance theorists. The form of the classical stage was lacking, but not the spirit, for the Lyons *Theatrum* offered what the classic theatre had provided, a platform for actors located before a relatively neutral background facing audience accommodation in graduated tiers.

The official date for the rediscovery of Vitruvius's manuscript is given as 1416, although dozens of manuscript copies were well known at an earlier date. The first printed version of *De Architectura*, containing the author's original comments on theatres, was edited by Leone-Baptista Alberti, whose critical edition, *De Re Aedificatoria*, was published in Florence in 1485. Alberti has been credited with the design of a *Theatrum* for Pope Nicholas V at the Vatican in 1452, but no information about this structure remains. Alberti's Eighth Book contained a summary of Vitruvius's observations on the Greek and Roman theatre, but offered no illustrations.

The first edition in which an attempt was made to clarify the Roman architect's meanings was that of Antonio San Gallo, Fra Giocondo (Jocundus), published in Venice in 1511. Unfortunately the woodcuts by the famous architect-author are coarse and thus fail to present satisfactory explanations of what Vitruvius meant. Instead of clarifying the issue, Jocundus's illustrations served as a new element of controversy. In spite of this, however, the edition was reprinted six

11

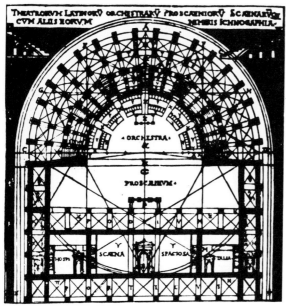

CESARIANO: ARCHITETTURA

Fig. 7. Plan of a Roman theatre after
Vitruvius, 1521.

CESARIANO: ARCHITETTURA

Fig. 8. Exterior of Cesariano's Roman theatre.

times between 1513 and 1535, and was the standard reference work on classical architecture during that time.

In 1521 a superior edition of Vitruvius, prepared by Caesar Caesariano, was printed in Milan. The illustrations appended to the text are far superior to those of Fra Giocondo. Caesariano presented an exquisitely drawn plan that recognizably resembles a Roman theatre. Being able only to guess at some of Vitruvius's meanings, the author illustrated the Roman theatre with a narrow podium stage with an arcaded front. Although he did show elevations of three doorways and made reference to two others, the elevation does not presume to reconstruct the *scaena frons*. The doors are not indicated on the plan; the solid lines of unbroken walls carry completely around the stage, with no visible access to the offstage spaces. While he indicated the parts called for in the Vitruvian text, Caesariano sidestepped the problems where he could not solve them.

Caesariano's plan is accompanied by drawings of the interior and exterior of his concept of a Roman theatre. While the groundplan may suggest that Caesariano was familiar with antique theatres, his perspective drawing of the facade makes us realize that he was ignorant of Roman ruins and the evidence they presented. His exterior looks like nothing so much as a modified

version of the Lyons Terence theatre. The interior view shows only the amphitheatre and nothing of the stage, because he had no suggestions about the *scaena frons*. The partial view of the amphitheatre indicates five tiers of seating arranged in a semicircle surrounded above by two arcaded galleries, one above the other. In the exterior view the theatre is topped by a vast dome crowned by a lantern, even though the interior shows an awning spread over the seating. While the section of the interior may bear some resemblance to Roman models, the exterior suggests nothing of the kind, being a *tempietto* of Renaissance inspiration. For thirty years this edition of Vitruvius circulated throughout Europe, although the author despaired because it did not bring him immediate fame. It was not supplanted until the edition of Danielo Barbaro in 1556.

Fig. 9. Half-section of Cesariano's Roman theatre.

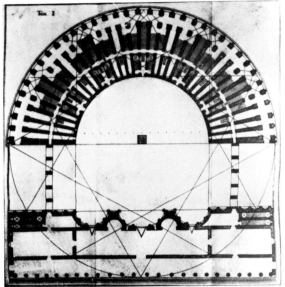

Fig. 10. (above) Plan of a Roman theatre, according to Vitruvius, 1556.

Fig. 11. (below) View of the Theatre of Marcellus, Rome, in 1830.

Until 1556, then, the sole authority for the revival of Roman theatre architecture was Vitruvius unalloyed by archaeology. Barbaro, in collaboration with Andrea Palladio, offered more accurate architectural plans, based upon actual observation of Roman ruins, instead of solely on the Vitruvian text. In 1561, in his *Second Livre d'Architecture*, Jacques Ducerceau presented conjectural restorations of half a dozen Roman theatres based upon observations of their ruins.

Barbaro, however, had not ventured so far afield in his study of the Roman theatre. His observation of ruins was restricted to what he was able to discover about the old theatre of Marcellus in Rome, so his plan was basically derived from Vitruvius. Unfortunately the Marcellus had been stripped of its interior when it was converted into a villa-fortress by the Pierleone in the eleventh century. Most of the appointments and much of the brick and stone of the interior were used in the villa construction, so Barbaro and Palladio were able to study little more than the great vaults and the facade. For this reason, the plan they offered is based on fact for the support-

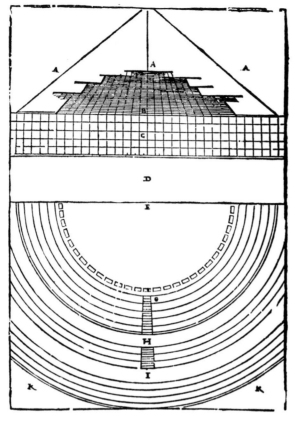

Fig. 12. Plan of a theatre by Serlio, presumably the Teatro alla Palazzo Porto, Vicenza, ca. 1530.

ing structure of the Roman theatre, but upon fancy in the reconstruction of the *scaena frons*. Unlike Caesariano, they made a specific attempt to approximate the *scaena frons*. Within an architectonic facade is a royal door of monumental proportions, apparently modeled after the extant arch of Titus, which it closely resembles. This was to have repercussions when Palladio designed his own Teatro Olimpico a generation later, for the triumphal royal door is so large that it necessarily requires something within it or behind it. The two doors to *hospitalia* were also included in the 1556 plan.

Vitruvius's remarks on the use of scenery in the ancient theatre obviously puzzled Barbaro and Palladio as they had others before them, but they attempted to locate the revolving machines, something former architects had not dared to do. Unfortunately the only places they found in which to put the *periaktoi* were the entrance openings, a solution of highly suspect practicability.

While some architects were trying to imitate the Roman theatre in both its form and its function, others were attempting to work within the medieval tradition, modifying it to suit contemporary tastes. Festival stages for special court entertainments were designed by numerous architect-artists, including Girolamo Genga for the Duke of Urbino in 1513, Baldasarre Peruzzi for Pope Leo X in 1514, Sebastiano (Aristotile da San Gallo) for the Medici in the 1530's, and many others. Each of these was similar to the medieval style, in which decorated mansions or pavilions would be placed about the "stage" as required. The Renaissance architects changed the individuality and artistic isolation of these iconographic pieces, imposing upon them a unity of style in Roman fashion, thus the former mansion-filled stage became a city street or Forum, the structures having an ensemble effect that made the stage picture both novel and imposing. As Vitruvian translations became available these static architectural vistae (laid down in the marvelous new perspective) were rearranged to conform with the Roman's description of the three scenes. Later designers merely enclosed this medieval outgrowth within a unifying decorative frame and the scenic proscenium theatre was born.

A description of one of these early stages, one erected for the production of *Poenulus* in Rome in 1513, is given by George Kernodle in his *From Art to Theatre*. "The stage was almost a hundred feet wide, twenty four feet deep, and about eight feet high . . . At the back of the stage was a highly

Fig. 13. Section of Serlio's theatre.

14

decorated arcade screen divided into five sections by columns with gilded bases and capitals, each section framing a doorway covered with curtains of gold cloth. Above was a frieze of beautiful paintings and a gilded cornice. At the ends of the screen were two great towers with doors, one marked 'Via ad Forum.' " Here we have the five doors plus entrances to either side—clearly a misreading of Vitruvius—arranged with curtains in the old pavilion style.

A blending of the Vitruvian theatre and the medieval decoration described above was achieved by Sebastiano Serlio in the 1530s. He constructed a stage and auditorium within the courtyard of the Palazzo Porto in Vicenza. This temporary wooden theatre had amphitheatrical seating in a semicircle, the ends of the curved sections truncated to fit within the rectangular courtyard, and a wide and shallow podium style stage was placed in front of an open semicircular orchestra. Behind the acting platform there was no *scaena frons* in the Roman style, but a built-up architectural vista in sharply forced perspective, a static arrangement of mansions taken one step further. The stage was no longer filled with an ensemble of practical pavilions in contemporary style but was almost completely pictorial. Only the extreme downstage units could be used by the actors without destroying the perspective effect. This theatre plan and Serlio's own transcription of Vitruvius's three scenes were published in 1545, in his *Regole generali di architettura*, with elaborate explanations not only of the style but also of the means whereby the most realistic effects could be achieved. The architect included within his work elevations and plans of the Marcellus and Pola theatres.

Some architects experimented with forms of scenery that bore little direct relation to Vitruvius's teachings. One such was Baldessare Lanci, who was responsible for the design of

Fig. 14. (top) "Tragic Scene" by Serlio.
SERLIO: ARCHITETTURA

Fig. 15. (center) "Comic Scene" by Serlio.
SERLIO: ARCHITETTURA

Fig. 16. (bottom) "Satyr Scene" by Serlio.
SERLIO: ARCHITETTURA

scenes and machines for a great festival at the Teatro Mediceo in 1589. For this spectacular event he developed a system of changing scenes which included the use of five *periaktoi*, two small ones at either side of the stage and an extremely large one at the rear. The *periaktoi* and the possibilities of scenic change fascinated architects for generations to follow; in particular the prisms were exploited to their fullest by Sabbatini, Furttenbach, and, later, Inigo Jones.

Architects of the fifteenth and sixteenth centuries, then, were faced with a specific problem: the revival of classical styles in the theatre. The principal guide in this revival was Vitruvius, with archeological studies coming into prominence only in the last half of the sixteenth century. The solution manifested itself in two approaches: first was that of the Vitruvian amphitheatre adapted to a structure otherwise medieval in form; second was that of the Vitruvian amphitheatre built to face not a series of practical pavilions but a pictorial view of architectural splendor. The Vitruvian-medieval combination was a natural attempt to unite the best elements of the Roman stage, as it was then understood, with the familiar and workable forms of contemporary popular theatre, where the emphasis was upon the performing artist. Of the two, the pictorial stage, regardless of Vitruvian trimmings, was the more logical development from trends noticeable in medieval production, in which the spectacle was of at least equal importance with the actor. The pictorial stage was destined to win out, in spite of isolated and essentially reactionary constructions modeled on the antique.

II Classicism Compromised

By the middle of the sixteenth century there were four general styles of theatre architecture. The first was the public theatre style originated in the middle Ages; the second came more or less directly from early Renaissance preoccupation with Terentian and Plautean revivals; the third was designed for revivals and reconstructions of antique tragedies and their imitations; and the fourth was the festival theatre designed for mounting spectacles upon the occasion of a royal alliance or of a civic entry. Each production method engendered a theatre design to suit its purpose. Productions of revived Roman plays stimulated an interest in the physical theatre of the Ancients, as we have seen from Chapter One, but they had little direct bearing upon later theatre construction.

An example of the medieval-style public theatre is the Hôtel de Bourgogne, a playhouse opened in Paris in 1548 and known by the name of the villa that formerly had occupied the site. This was the first permanent public theatre that had been built since the time of the Romans. Almost nothing is directly known about the Bourgogne, but there is related material which gives us an understanding of the structure. Apparently it was a small building, oblong in shape; it is believed to have been a little more than three times as long as it was wide, a proportion common to the tennis court (upon which the later Théâtre de Marais was based).

An engraving of a scene from the interior of a Paris theatre in the seventeenth century may depict the Bourgogne—there is no way of being certain—but even if it is not, it gives us a view which corresponds with the descriptions we find in contemporary accounts: shallow galleries, a narrow house, a small high stage—all located in a makeshift structure. Scholars have reached a measure of agreement about the form of the Bourgogne, based upon bits of evidence from various sources. The theatre is almost certain to have had two galleries, each with nineteen boxes, although exactly how they were arranged is still a disputed question. Scene designs by Mahelot, for productions given at the Bourgogne a century after it was built, show a proscenium opening of proportions appropriate to a low-ceilinged, narrow house, although we cannot be certain that this was indeed the case. It is clear that the French public theatre employed simultaneous settings of a medieval nature rather than a unified architectural setting of the Italian variety. The Bourgogne was a building with no classical antecedents, and was practically unrelated to the development of theatre architecture elsewhere.

In Italy, the academic societies established specifically to produce plays from the ancients pursued a different course. While the design of the popular theatre followed an amalgam of ancient and medieval practices, the theatres of the

Fig. 17. Interior of a seventeenth century Paris playhouse which may be the Bourgogne.

academies were an attempt at historical reconstruction, either with scholarly exactitude or in compromise with the contemporary love of spectacle. The archeological reconstruction phase was short lived, but it produced an important theatre for the Accademia Olimpico in Vicenza, built by the antiquarian and architect Andrea Palladio. The Accademia Olimpico, founded in 1455, produced plays from the ancients in temporary theatres built as the occasion demanded. In 1575 the Academy decided to construct a permanent building to house its theatricals, and selected one of its members, Palladio, to be the architect, evidently impressed by his research and by his illustrations of Roman theatres in the 1556 edition of Barbaro's *Architettura*. The plans for the building were complete in 1580. Palladio based his design loosely upon that of a Roman theatre, making several significant exceptions to the classic plan: the theatre was under a roof rather than in the open air; the audience amphitheatre was widened from a semicircle to a semiellipse, apparently to allow better sightlines and a wider stage for the size of the house; and an arrangement was made for the five doors mentioned by Vitruvius. The roof was not so much a concession to physical comfort in such a benign climate as it was to dramatic necessity. By the time the Olimpico was built, there was a sophis-

ticated understanding of the uses of light for dramatic effect on the stage, mainly through experiments made in that other branch of theatrical activity, the court festival. The Olimpico was fitted with specially shaped glass jars with metal wick-caps, which were designed to hold oil. These were fitted into holders placed so that the stage could be lighted as required.

Palladio's exact plans for the use of the five doors are not known, for the architect died before the building was completed. The remainder of the supervision and planning was left to his son, and then to his former pupil, Vincenzo Scamozzi. It was Scamozzi who designed the vistae in vanishing perspective which were erected behind each of the five doors—vistae which partially fulfilled Vitruvius's requirements for scenery. These vistae were derived directly from Renaissance studies in the art of perspective, particularly from Baldesarre Peruzzi, and must have lent the new theatre a "modern" tone not quite compatible with its antique form.

It is difficult to evaluate the Teatro Olimpico from plans and photographs, for they do not reveal scale. Without the presence of human figures, the theatre seems small and intimate in nature, a "jewel-box" of a playhouse. Not until one realizes that the opening night audience numbered about 3,000 can one understand that Palladio's theatre was of modern opera house dimensions, with a stage 82 feet wide. It would be difficult to exaggerate the effect of the theatre on Palladio's contemporaries. The elaborate *scaena*

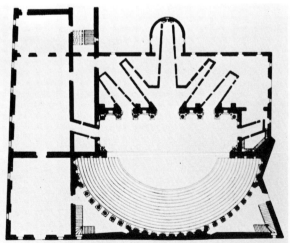

Fig. 18. Plan of the Teatro Olimpico, 1585, by Palladio.

Fig. 19. Interior of the Teatro Olimpico.

frons, the elegantly proportioned and detailed gallery surrounding the top of the amphitheatre, and the beautiful statuary all made a tremendous impression on those who viewed them. The first production, *Edipo Tiranno*, was a modernized version of Sophocles's play, magnificently costumed, and produced (accurately, as the Accademia thought) as an opera, with singing chorus, orchestra in the large pit, and recitatives for the principals.

By the time the Teatro Olimpico was completed, however, it was already an anachronism. Palladio's research into Roman theatre construction had led him from his Teatro alla Basilica of 1561, and Teatro della Compagnia della Calza of 1565, directly to the Olimpico, without outside influences altering his point of view. The studies of Peruzzi, Sebastiano Serlio, and others, had developed theatre production techniques in a different direction, away from the two-dimensional *scaena frons* and toward a large pictorial repre-

sentation of place in three dimensions and one-point perspective. Serlio developed a plan, published in his *Architettura* of 1545, which is believed to be an illustration of a festival courtyard theatre designed by him in 1539. Once this type of scenic spectacular had been seen by the public it was inevitable that the antiquarian theatre would not gain popular acceptance. So the Teatro Olimpico was successful as a specialized academic playhouse, but its stage form was not imitated in Italy. Serlio's stage, on the other hand, was imitated habitually until the introduction of the wing and shutter settings in the next century.

Whether Scamozzi was entirely sympathetic to Palladio's designs is open to doubt. His addition of scenic vistae to the Teatro Olimpico was an attempt to bring it into the then current mode of scenic representation and away from simple antiquarianism. Scamozzi wrote of his passion for

19

Fig. 20. Amphitheatre of the Teatro di Sabbioneta.

Roman architecture mainly in terms of those elements appropriate for monumental display. When given an opportunity to design a theatre according to his own wishes, he did adopt some of the features of Palladio's playhouse, as can be seen from his original designs; but as constructed, the Teatro di Sabbioneta resembles the Olimpico only superficially. Built for the court of Vespasian Gonzaga in 1590, it reflected Roman influences in trim and decoration but not in plan. The amphitheatre resembles that of no other contemporary playhouse, but does reflect the contemporary practice of open-floored auditoria in the festival theatres. A direct break with Palladian practice was the widening of the proscenium to dimensions appropriate for a Serlian style of scenic display; this was more in keeping with trends of the time.

The Teatro di Sabbioneta frequently is cited as an example of the slow evolvement of the Italian stage toward the modern proscenium, but festival productions had long displayed large proscenia with elaborate scenic vistae, and the Teatro di Sabbioneta was actually several decades behind the practice in other court theatres. One has only to glance at designs for festival productions given in Turin, Siena, Florence, and elsewhere to realize that Scamozzi's proscenium was barely usable for the type of scenic spectacular popular with the Italian princes. Of course, the restricted size of the hall contributed to this; had the building been larger there can be little doubt

that Scamozzi's playhouse would have been similar to those at other courts.

Typical of the great halls converted into theatres for court entertainments and festivals was the one in the Uffizi Palace in Florence, the Teatro Mediceo. This hall was adapted for spectacle in 1586 by Buontalenti. While we would not consider it a theatre by modern standards, it was an accepted mode of theatre architecture of the period, one whose form persisted as long as masque entertainment remained in vogue. The vast hall was approximately 172 feet long, 67 feet wide, and 46 feet high. Five rows of benches in a U-shaped amphitheatre were arrayed against three of the sides, with the chair of state at the center front. The auditorium floor was raked downward toward the stage so the standing audience could see over the heads of those in front, and the seating was raised so that part of the audience could see over the heads of the standees. The stage was raised to provide room beneath for the machines, and the floor was trapped so that mountains, castles, and other constructions could rise from below. Buontalenti's scenes were

Fig. 21. Interior of the Teatro Mediceo in 1617.

Fig. 22a.
Scene 3 from *Il Solimano*,
given at Florence, 1620.

enormous in size, but in keeping with the Serlian tradition they were comparatively shallow. The stage was 38 feet deep, a mere apron when compared to that of the later Teatro Farnese. Steps were provided so that actors within the scene could descend to the auditorium floor. To help illuminate the stage, footlights were installed, one of the first recorded instances of their use. *Periaktoi* served for scenic change, and great cloud machines which covered the entire stage were suspended from the grid to be used as required, particularly to mask scene changes that took place behind them. The only illustration we have

of the entire interior of the Uffizi theatre is one drawn by Callot, some years after its conversion, of a production of *La Liberazione di Tirreno* given in 1617. From this we may judge the magnificence of display which such a large hall required.

Festival performances were given often and with lavishness by most of the larger Italian courts. Much energy was spent on the spectacular element of production, on settings, costumes, and especially on mechanical effects. Characteristic of the festival production was the open-floored auditorium with banks of seats on three sides. The stage served as a box of mechanical marvels,

Fig. 22b.
Scene 5 from *Il Solimano*

Fig. 23b. Scene 3, *Le Nozze Degli Dei.*

Fig. 23a. Opening scene of *Le Nozze Degli Dei*, presented in the courtyard of the Pitti Palace, Florence, showing hemispheres turning in the void.

masked by proscenia elaborately and fancifully decorated for the production given. The players spilled out into the auditorium by means of ramps or stairs, for the spectacle was not confined to the stage alone.

We think of the tournament as a strictly medieval preoccupation, but while the knightly joust was originally a means of exercise or of settling disputes, the tournament became more a social and theatrical event as the centuries wore on. Whereas the festival stage was rigged to entertain a favored few, the tournament remained a public spectacle performed in the open air. Special playhouses were built to accommodate this style of entertainment. It became a fifth branch of theatre architecture with special requirements of its own, but which influenced indoor theatre development in many ways. Tournament exercises were sometimes part of marriage festival entertainments, but they were also staged regularly in more formal surroundings. One well illustrated example of the tournament theatre is sufficient to present us with the style of event and with the structure appropriate to it, but several are of interest. The earliest example is the Teatro del Torneo, Bologna, first erected in 1598 in a temporary form. This special outdoor playhouse was designed for spectacles involving mounted men engaged in combat, and for large-cast displays of equestrian skill, frequently with a dramatic spine of an allegorical nature. While no illustration of the 1598 version remains, a permanent theatre was built in 1628 and from this we may see the basic form of the structure. A large open area of ground was arranged with sections of seating on three sides. The seats were raised and separated from the arena by high barrier walls, both to protect the patrons and to allow them to view the event from the same height as the mounted horsemen. There were usually three entrances into the open center, each sufficiently high and wide to accommodate a pair of mounted men with lances at rest. One end of the enclosed area was assigned to scenic representation, from which the tournament spectacle took its theme. An analogue to the Teatro del Torneo was the temporary arrangement installed by the Medici in the courtyard of the Pitti Palace for festival entertainments of a similar nature. While the tournament theatre may seem to be a specialized item, we shall see that it influenced other branches of theatre architecture in many ways.

Except for the Teatro Olimpico in Vicenza, perhaps the most frequently illustrated Italian theatre of this period is the Teatro Farnese in Par-

Fig. 23c. Scene 4, *Le Nozze Degli Dei*.

Fig. 23d. Scene 5, *Le Nozze Degli Dei*

ma. Constructed in 1618 by the architect Giambattista Aleotti, this court theatre usually is shown without comment as an example of late Renaissance playhouse design. This raises innumerable questions about the plan of the seating in relation to the stage, an arrangement patently poor for the viewing of dramatic entertainments.

The Teatro Farnese was not built for standard dramatic entertainment, but as a combination festival and tournament theatre. A glance at the familiar illustrations will confirm this. A barrier wall separated the seating from the open floor; large entrances (since walled up) were provided for mounted men and wagons; the great open floor was left free for combats and displays. Aleotti's original plan, completed in 1618, called for a semicircular bank of seats in the Roman fashion, but was amended the same year to the present U shape. The contemporary accounts of performances in the theatre make the festival and tournament nature of it clear. When the Duke of Parma commissioned Aleotti to erect a theatre in the Great Hall of Arms, it was not to displace the events for which the hall had been built, but to bring them closer to the semidramatic festival productions offered elsewhere, particularly in Florence. The hall eclipses the Uffizi in size, being approximately 285 feet in length, 105 feet in width, and 87 feet in height. A stage 133 feet deep was fitted within this area, together with an elaborate architectonic proscenium with an opening of 40 feet. The design was particularly fortunate in being acoustically perfect, a virtue attributed by later architects to the wooden interior and to the vertical laying of the boards.

Aleotti's first venture into theatre architecture was not the Farnese but the Teatro d'Accademia degli Intrepidi, Ferrara, built in 1606. It is widely supposed that the architect began his experiments with movable scenery in this earlier theatre. One of the principal differences between the Farnese and other contemporary structures was the use of wings moving in grooves on the stage floor instead of fixed Serlian vistae or *periaktoi*. The Serlian system was a scene built of angled pieces placed on a raked stage in sharply forced perspective. The pieces frequently were built with three-dimensional trims, and the vista ended in a back piece painted as the scene required. The system became more flexible when the backscene was designed to split in the middle and move off to the sides, exposing a second painted view. This simple arrangement provided a generalized foreground, which served for an entire production, together with a simple backscene change that provided specific place reference. The large and cumbersome angled pieces moved with difficulty, if at all, and change of the entire stage scene was

Fig. 24. Interior of the Teatro del Torneo, Bologna, 1628, by Coriolano.

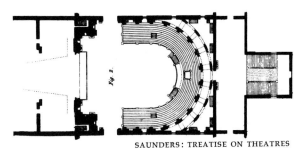

Fig. 25. Plan of the Teatro Farnese, Parma, 1618, by Aleotti.

neither expected nor used. Later artists, like Sabbattini, developed methods to change the angled wings, but by that time they had been displaced by *periaktoi* and the new flat wing. The *periaktoi* allowed three changes of scene without moving any units on or off the stage. *Periaktoi* were used in the great festivals of the Medici, and changes were masked by the lowering of full-stage cloud machines.

Aleotti wished to change the entire scene, not merely the backshutter, and to offer more than the three changes possible with *periaktoi*. He achieved this by abandoning both the angle wing and the prism, using instead pairs of flat wings which were painted to resemble pieces in perspective. The flat wings were placed in groups and maneuvered on and off stage in grooves made by fixing strips to the stage floor and on a special scaffold above. In this system the first wing could be withdrawn, revealing the second wing behind. When wings from each group were withdrawn simultaneously the entire stage setting changed. This striking innovation was to sweep Serlian wings and *periaktoi* from the stage, because it allowed a multiplicity of changes instead of the few cumbersome ones previously possible. With scenic vistae painted on two-dimensional surfaces instead of constructed in three, stage depth had to be increased to make the two-dimensional illusion as effective as the built-up one. With the increase in stage depth, the stage and scenic units no longer needed to be abruptly raked, which allowed the human figure to operate deeper within the scene. This progression of changes altered the presentational style, opening up possibilities that could not have been exploited previously, as a comparison of scene designs from before and after the introduction of the flat wing makes clear. Thus, although the Farnese has been referred to rather casually as the first true proscenium playhouse, the real influence of the struc-

ture lay not with its proscenium—a feature already in use for over half a century—but with what went on behind it. Completed in 1618, the Farnese did not open its doors until 1628, so the novelty of the great stage and its complex machines was not fully appreciated.

The largest festival theatre in Italy was the Teatro Ducale of Mantua, built in 1608 by Antonio Maria Vianini. With a capacity of over 4,000, this playhouse overshadowed the Uffizi's 3,000 and the Farnese's 3,500. The theatre was noted particularly for its vertical-rising counterweighted curtain in contrast to the falling curtain in the antique style used at Florence. Because the Teatro Ducale used angle-wings and *periaktoi*, the opening production required the services of 300 stagehands.

An elaborate and magnificent tournament theatre was built in Modena in 1660. It contained a vast oval amphitheatre, two large galleries divided into boxes, an open top gallery, and several ornate pavilions, all of which encircled an area large enough for troupes of riders to maneuver in easily.

In 1628 the original tournament theatre of Bologna was replaced by a permanent structure, the Teatro del Torneo, designed by Giovanni Coriolano. The large open center was retained, and three-tiered galleries were raised on two of the sides with an open gallery on each roof. The rear of the "house" was a great semicircular amphitheatre with four main divisions in rising levels. The fourth side was given to a vast arched proscenium. The semiformal tournament stage was completely formalized into a great open air theatre. Prints depicting spectacles given in the Teatro del Torneo show enormous floats, great processions of mounted men, and the spectacular costumes and appointments we associate with the grand entries of monarchs into the capitals of

Fig. 26. View of the amphitheatre, Teatro Farnese.

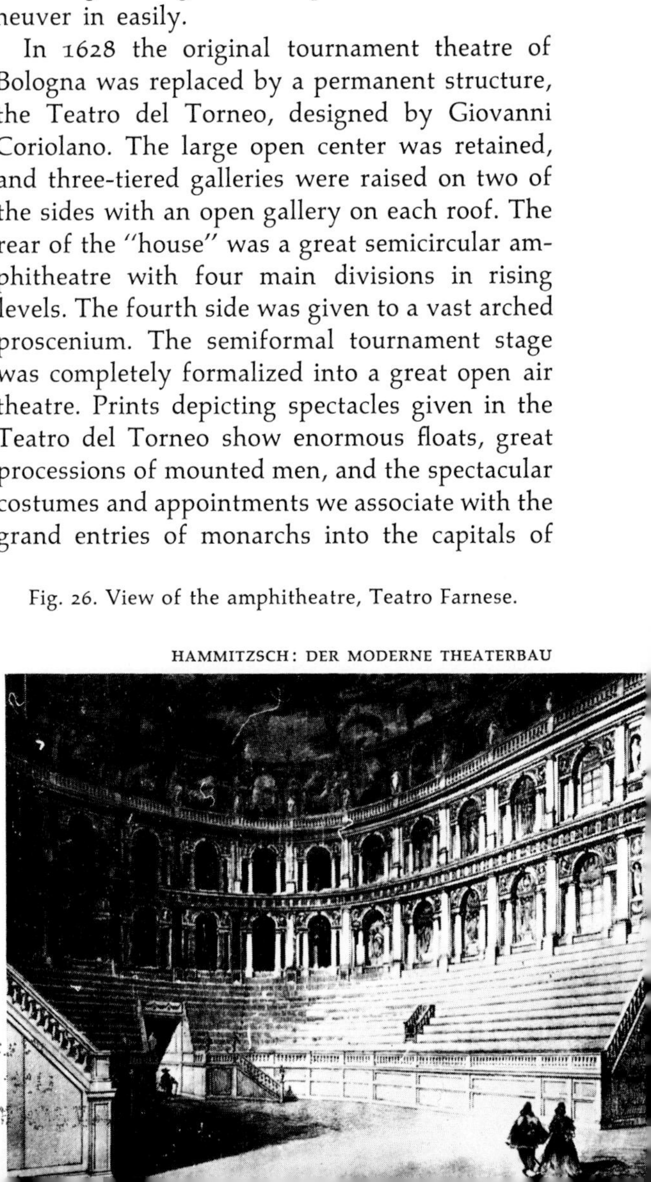

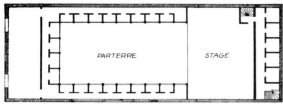

Fig. 27. Reconstructed ground plan of the Théâtre de Marais, Paris, 1629, after the original by S. Wilma Dierkauf-Holsboer.

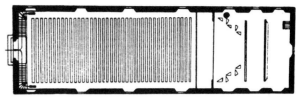

Fig. 28. Plan of the Ulm Stadttheater, 1641, by Furttenbach.

their fiefs. Clearly, the arrangement of the tournament theatre suited elaboration and display on a scale that even a great festival playhouse could not match.

Little record has been left us of the forms of the early public theatres of France. From materials relating to the stage we can reconstruct the playhouses with what we hope is some degree of success. The mystery surrounding the original form of the Bourgogne is echoed in a lesser degree in the Théâtre Marais. This, the second public playhouse in Paris, was constructed in 1621 in a former tennis court in the Marais district. We have sufficiently detailed information of contemporary tennis courts to enable us to judge that the Marais must have been long and narrow, with a gallery along at least one side; and it is generally agreed that the stage was a simple platform at one end and that the audience stood on an open pit floor without benches. While there is little data on the first Marais, the architect's plans for the reconstruction of the theatre after a fire have been unearthed. The new theatre of 1644 was somewhat larger than the old but it is almost certain that it was only an improvement upon the form of the old structure and not a change from it. The new Marais was 114 feet long, 39 feet wide, and 53 feet high, with a stage that has been estimated to have been a little over 31 feet deep. It is clear that the Marais, like the Bourgogne, was hardly calculated either for the comfort of the audience or for the appropriate display of theatrical entertainments in the Italian fashion. How the French public theatre remained so little influenced by Italian examples remains a mystery, as does the fact that no reasonable and appropriate native form developed into a comfortable theatre structure, as did the theatres of England and the Netherlands.

A truly original building that owed little to any previous theatre construction was the Stadt-

theater at Ulm. Designed by Joseph Furttenbach in 1641, the Stadttheater was constructed according to principles set forth by the architect in his earlier treatise on civil architecture. Furttenbach was interested in a type of scenic change made possible by the use of *periaktoi*, and his study and development of the possible refinements of this system paralleled that of Nicola Sabbattini. In Furttenbach's designs, the *periaktoi* were used in multiple pairs, along with a backshutter for each change. For the appropriate display of scenes thus mounted, the architect designed a theatre of approximately 800 capacity, containing 40 benches on a sloping platform. The stage was approximately 45 feet wide and 20 feet deep with additional space behind the last backshutter, and the proscenium opening was 30 feet wide. There were no boxes along the side walls of the auditorium; every seat was designed to provide the best possible view of the perspective scene. For

Fig. 29. A stage setting by Furttenbach.

25

this reason the house was long and narrow, so all patrons were guaranteed a better illusion of the display on the stage than in any other contemporary playhouse, or, for that matter, than in any theatre constructed until modern times. The *periaktoi* had been generally abandoned in Italy long before their advocacy by Furttenbach, because their built-in limitations precluded the easy mounting of multiscened productions. By the time the German architect and the Italian, Sabbattoni, had developed their preference to the greatest possible flexibility, they were badly out of date. A detailed explanation of the *periaktoi*

Fig. 30. Plan of the Teatro El Buen Retiro, by Lotti, 1632.

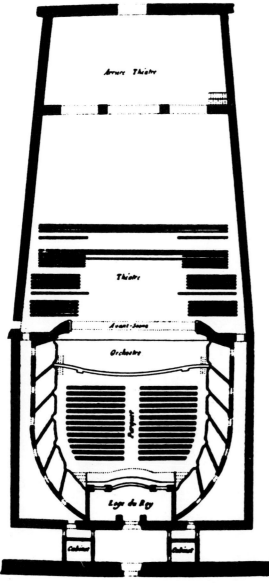

and the ways in which they were used may be found in the appendix.

Outside of Italy the theatre of the court of Philip IV of Spain was of considerable interest. It was built in the summer palace of El Buen Retiro by the Italian architect Cosimo Lotti in 1632. In this theatre, a bare four years after the opening of the Farnese, the wing-in-groove system was fully developed, although the stage was a modest one. Five sets of wings were used, plus two sets of multiple backshutters. Lotti anticipated many of the features found in later Venetian playhouses, although those theatres are generally thought to be the first of their kind. Lotti's theatre had a sophisticated auditorium plan, some elements of which did not find their way into general practice for another century. The divisions between the boxes were angled toward the stage, assuring reasonable sightlines and supporting the trend away from court spectacle in the middle of an open floor and toward dramatic production restricted to a raised proscenium stage. The box fronts protruded slightly from the forward edge of the gallery, again for the improvement of sightlines, a feature that was not found in the French theatre until a century later. The pit was not only provided with benches parallel to the front of the stage, but was given a central aisle for easy access. In all, El Buen Retiro, although its form was common in later generations, was an architectural leap of some imagination in 1632.

Several important court theatres were constructed elsewhere during the same period. For these we have accounts of productions and personalities but no concrete evidence of architectural form. The theatre in the Hofburg, built in 1626 in the Imperial palace at Vienna, was the first of a long line of Viennese opera houses, and was most likely an arrangement of seating within the ballroom, based on Italian examples. The Barbarini Theatre, in Rome, opened in 1634 with a production whose settings were designed by Bernini, but of the architect and form we are uncertain.

One of the principal court theatres about which we do have information was the Petit Bourbon in Paris, constructed in the great hall of that palace in 1635. The room was long and narrow, with dimensions of approximately 221 feet by 45 feet, and a contemporary account states that the ceiling seemed as high as the church of St. Eustache. The installation of particularly elaborate ma-

Fig. 31. The great hall, Petit Bourbon,
set for the ballet Circe, 1581.

chinery by Giacomo Torelli a decade later made the theatre a match for the Italian playhouses. No illustration of the hall after its conversion is extant, but an engraving of an entertainment held in 1581 has been left to us, and it is from this that we suppose the final form to have been similar to the theatre of the Palais Cardinal, described later in this chapter.

The advanced design of Lotti's Spanish court theatre seems the more remarkable when compared with another major European playhouse of the same decade, the Schouwburg in Amsterdam. Erected by the city in 1638 as a municipal theatre, the Schouwburg owed much of the inspiration for its design to native festival stages. It reminds us at first glance of an Elizabethan theatre, as it had a large apron stage and a decoration based on native forms instead of classical designs. The central tower at the back of the stage was topped by a second level used for the raising and lowering of deities. The lower part of the tower held a dais for a throne, in back of which—when the throne was removed—was a large door. Other entrances with practical galleries above were located to the sides. It hardly seems possible that the architect, Jacob van Campen, studied in Italy and was an admirer of the work of Palladio and Scamozzi.

At a second glance, however, we notice that there was a definite Vitruvian plan to the theatre.

Fig. 32.
Exterior of
the first
Schouwburg,
Amsterdam,
1638.

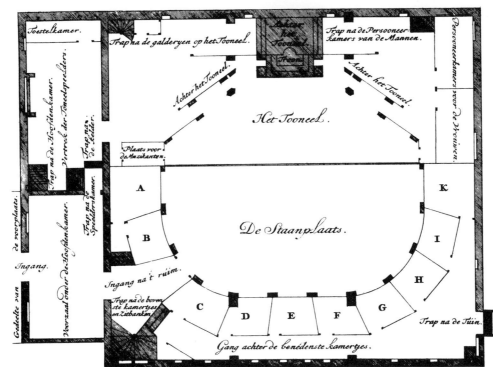

Fig. 33. Plan of the first Schouwburg.

ARCHIEF BIBLIOTHEEK, AMSTERDAM

To either side of the central door were two other entrances, bringing the total to the classic five. These smaller entrances were each backed by a panel upon which appeared a scene representative of the place of dramatic action, and these panels could be changed as required. Although the interior trim and decoration of the theatre were arranged in the native manner, they were of Roman inspiration. Because it was a public playhouse, the normal Vitruvian single-class amphitheatre was replaced by the contemporary Italian semicircular tiers of galleries, and the pit was reserved for standees in the French and Elizabethan fashion. The Schouwburg was a compromise, as we suspect the Elizabethan theatres to have been, with as much classicism incorporated in it as local audiences would accept.

In 1637 the first of the great opera houses, the San Cassiano, was built in Venice by Benedetto Ferrari. It is in this theatre that the first division of galleries into boxes is thought to have been made. The San Cassiano must have been impressive, for it inspired Sir William Davenant to consider building a like playhouse in London in 1639, as his original patent implies.

The only seventeenth century Venetian playhouse for which we have the plans is SS. Giovanni e Paolo, first erected in wood in 1638 and reconstructed in stone in 1654. The extant plan is thought to be of the reconstruction, not of the original, although it is likely that many of the characteristics of the older theatre were carried over to the new. The pattern here established spread throughout Europe, and remained the

Fig. 34. Interior of the first Schouwburg.

Fig. 35. Stage of the first Schouwburg.

ARCHIEF BIBLIOTHEEK, AMSTERDAM

FROM THE AUTHOR'S COLLECTION

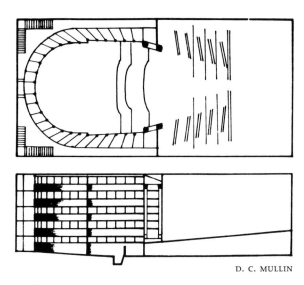

D. C. MULLIN

Fig. 36. Plan and section of the Teatro
SS. Giovanni e Paolo, Venice, after reconstruction
in 1654.

basic form for large public theatres for three hundred years. Whether the U-shaped auditorium and the separate boxes were introduced in the San Cassiano, or whether they developed from the influence of the tournament theatres is an unsolved puzzle. In any event, the form of the public playhouse developed differently from that of the theatres of the academies and courts. The single-class semi-circular amphitheatre was inappropriate for the public theatre; the division of social orders—and in Venice the sexes—required a separation of accommodation. The number of boxes indicated in the Giovanni e Paolo plan shows the scale of the house at a glance, because we know that the boxes held about six persons. The size of the stage, together with the angled box divisions, shows an emphasis in the attention of the audience on the space for scenes and machines. The number of tiers of boxes was echoed in most theatres of this type, as well as the degree of curvature to the rear of the house.

The reason for the installation and continued use of boxes in the traditional theatre seems obscure to the casual student, but the choice was a deliberate one. In spite of the difficulty of seeing around posts, the raised tiers of boxes allowed the cubic space of the hall to accommodate many more patrons than would otherwise have been possible. True, the hall could have been given a larger floorplan, but this would have placed a strain on available land—a major consideration in urban areas—and enormous trusses

would have been required to support such an unencumbered space, which in turn would have required heavier load-bearing walls. It was simpler, more efficient, and less expensive to keep the hall to a smaller dimension and to mount galleries up the sides and rear; this was the best means of utilizing the space available with the building materials at hand.

The SS. Giovanni e Paolo was designed to accommodate a fundamental alteration in the mounting of theatrical productions and in the organization of architectural spaces. A permanent orchestra pit was included to replace the simpler barrier between orchestra and audience common to the festival stages. No steps connected the pit and the stage; the spectacle was to be confined to the stage and to rely primarily upon scenic decoration instead of upon the combination of costume and fancy properties that were the stock-in-trade of the festival theatres.

The SS. Giovanni e Paolo and the San Cassiano were followed by many other Venetian playhouses of much the same style, including the San Moise in 1639, the Novissimo in 1641 (with scenes and machines by Giacomo Torelli), San Samuel in 1655, San Salvatore in 1661, San Angelo in 1676, and San Giovanni Crisostomo in 1667. An identified illustration of the last survives, and since the pattern of Venetian opera house construction seems not to have altered substantially over the years, we assume that this is also an acceptable view of the seven other theatres of the same century. There were five tiers of thirty-one boxes each; the stage was approximately 85 feet deep and 63 feet wide; the proscenium was as high as the top row of boxes, and in its thickness additional boxes were located, making the arch—in effect—a surround for the

Fig. 37. Interior of the Teatro San Samuel,
Venice, 1655.

forepart of the stage. The most remarkable feature of the hall was the lighting provided for the auditorium: a chandelier was let down from a well above the ceiling when needed, and withdrawn when the play was in progress, leaving the audience in semi-darkness. Subsequently, this manner of dimming the house was occasionally used elsewhere, but the majority of theatres preferred to keep the audience chamber illuminated throughout the production. Darkening the house, of course, was done primarily to make the stage lighting sufficiently bright by contrast (almost a necessity in theatres whose productions were mounted within the scenes), not to add to the realism of the stage illusion.

The Bolognese Teatro del Torneo of 1628 was followed in 1639 by the Teatro della Sala. This was also a tournament theatre, but one influenced strongly by the Venetian opera house with its multiple tiers of boxes. The Teatro della Sala had five tiers plus an open gallery on top. A high barrier wall was included; large entrances were provided at either side of the proscenium; and a large ramp from the open pit to the stage enabled mounted men to participate in the action within the scene. A vast stage flanked by enormous engaged corinthian columns reflected the interior treatment of the Farnese.

Fig. 38. Interior of the Teatro della Sala, Bologna, 1639.

HAMMITZSCH: DER MODERNE THEATERBAU

Also of consequence in the first half of the seventeenth century was the Teatro del Sol, built in 1636 by Nicola Sabbattini at Pesaro. We know little of this theatre but that the architect used it for experiments in the development of the *periaktoi* as a scenic device. He refined the system to an amazing degree, much as did Furttenbach, but in spite of the refinements the prisms could never have the flexibility of the other methods already in common use. Another theatre of which we know little was the Teatro Formigliari in Bologna, constructed in 1640 by Andrea Sighizzi, which was noted for an attempt to improve sightlines from the side boxes. The individual boxes in each tier were mounted *en escalier*, or stepped down from one another as they approached the proscenium, much as seats would be set on succeeding levels on the pit floor. This innovation was not adopted by other architects until the following century.

In France, Richelieu caused a playhouse to be built in 1641 within the great hall of his Palais Cardinal which had considerable influence. The plan developed differently from what was then fashionable in Italy; it was not laid down on the modern Venetian model, but was an imitation of the Italian festival stage. There were no boxes, only shallow galleries along the walls—much like those in the Petit Bourbon—and the pit floor was free of benches. The proscenium, the first permanent one in France, was connected to the pit floor by stairs, which indicates the dual purpose of the theatre design. The proscenium opening was unlike that of any other contemporary playhouse: it had considerable depth to the arch (without boxes being located within it), and the thickness was decorated with statues in niches; it was a triumphal arch reminiscent of the *scaena frons*. Engravings illustrating the first production given in the new theatre (*Mirame*) unfortunately suggest the proscenium was monumental in size. The plate illustrating the interior, however, shows us a probably more realistic scale.

The structure of the theatre altered radically during this 150 year period. The sixteenth century was an era of experimentation primarily in the development of scenic stage. The initial struggles with static Serlian scenes gave way to more flexible arrangements using combinations of *periaktoi* and shutters, which in turn lost favor when the movable two-dimensional wing was introduced in the seventeenth century.

Fig. 39.
Proscenium of
the theatre in
the Palais Cardinal.

The several types of theatres developed from the needs of the several varieties of entertainment given, and they found their ultimate expressions as this period came to a close. Several types of production languished and later were abandoned, their theatre forms dying with them, leaving the architects to worry less about compromises and more about an ideal form for dramatic production. The changes in the stage and scenery were reflected in the arrangement of the auditorium. As scenic production became intricate and flexible enough for the stage to simulate reality, instead of being an iconograph, the focus of audience attention changed and with it the seating. By the middle of the seventeenth century, the pattern to be followed by all later theatre construction had been firmly established. Pleasant but anachronistic reconstructions and cumbersome scenic methods had been left by the wayside. The *scaena frons* had been abandoned, as had the wide but shallow Serlian stage, the limited *periaktoi*, and the pageantry on the pit floor. After 150 years, theatre architecture had found its course, one that was not to be abandoned except in isolated instances until the present century. It was the changes and developments in the use of scenic spectacle, as well as the rise of the public theatre, that influenced alterations in auditorium planning. By 1650 the basic problems of playhouse form had been settled.

Fig. 40.
Interior of the
Petit Bourbon
in 1635.

III The Triumph of Albion

Perhaps the most fortuitous bit of bureaucratic imperiousness in history was the harrassment that drove the majority of players from the City of London. Were it not for this attempt to remove sinful temptation from the populace, the companies might have been content to continue performing on makeshift stages set up in available halls, and the development of the English stage might have been delayed for another century. As it was, the Lord Mayor's zeal drove James Burbage to build a new playhouse (called by the fancy French name, The Theatre) near Finsbury Fields in 1576. Richard Farrant opened the first Blackfriars playhouse the same year, locating in the former religious enclave that was then a Liberty outside the jurisdiction of the City; and The Curtain was constructed not far from The Theatre in the following year. We know nothing about Burbage's playhouse except that its timbers were used to construct the later Globe, so the two must have had some form in common. We suspect The Curtain to have been modeled after The Theatre; several views of the former survive on contemporary maps and panoramas of the City. We will probably never know what prompted the initial design of these first public playhouses, but certainly considerable thought was given to form before construction. It is at least certain that the stage proper derived from the simple trestle platforms used all over Europe for years, consisting of a floor raised high enough for those standing around it to see, and backed by a decorated curtain through which the actors came and went. This type of temporary "stand" had been used for centuries—some believe by players in ancient Roman Atellan farces—and continued to be used by itinerant players almost to modern times.

There were a number of playhouses built during and shortly after the reign of Elizabeth I. The Theatre and The Curtain were followed by Newington Butts, of uncertain date, and by The Rose in 1592. The latter was built on the Bankside, as was The Swan in 1594 and The Globe in 1598, which last was erected by James Burbage when the lease was not renewed for the ground upon which The Theatre stood. The Red Bull was built in 1599, the first Fortune in 1600, and a new Globe in 1614 to replace the original which had been destroyed by fire. The Hope, a copy of The Swan, was raised the same year. Each design seems to have been influenced by the preceding ones until the second decade of the seventeenth century, when the first covered public playhouses were built. The Cockpit (later the Phoenix) was constructed in 1617, and Salisbury Court in 1629. Thus, by 1630, there were ten large-capacity public playhouses near the city of London, not to mention the private theatres and those at court, while Paris was served at that same time by only two cramped halls, the old Bourgogne and the newer Marais. The English playhouses were not all devoted entirely to drama, however, as the names Red Bull, Bear Garden, and Cockpit imply.

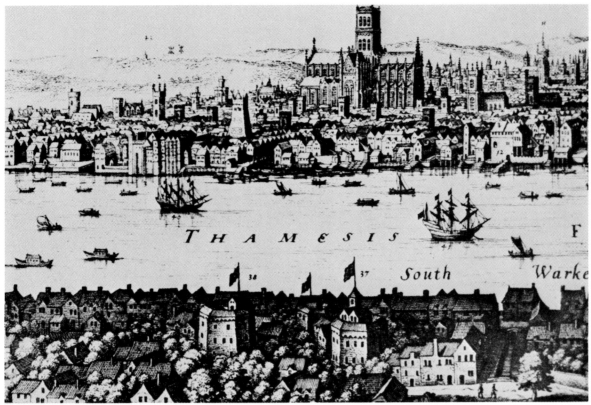

Fig. 41. The bankside, London, 1638, from the Merian View.

There have been almost as many books written about the form of Shakespeare's stage as there have been about Shakespeare, and with as little information to support them. The concrete evidence that remains to us about Elizabethan theatres is meager at best; it includes a few tiny illustrations from contemporary panoramic maps, a sketch drawn after the description of a foreign visitor, and a contract for the building of the Fortune. Other pieces of evidence are secondary in nature, including references to physical items in the plays, records of transactions, diaries, comments in miscellaneous writings, and the like. While the sum of these bits may be construed to point in one direction, they may just as logically be made to point in another. We know the materials from which some of the theatres were made, who built them, how they differed from one another, what plays were performed within them, who acted on their stages, what the weather was, what the gate receipts were, but not what the playhouses looked like on the inside.

Contemporary maps and panoramas show us Elizabethan public theatre buildings with round or polygonal exteriors, their roofs partially open to the sky. There is evidence that the majority of the public theatres in the late sixteenth century were round inside, not polygonal as their exteriors might suggest. The sketch after a description by the visiting Hollander, Johannes de Witt, shows the interior of The Swan to be round, with an acting platform and tiring house to one side of a space open to the sky. Certain of the theatres

Fig. 42. The Globe and Bear Baiting ring, from Hollar's Long View of London, 1647. The titles on the theatres are reversed.

LUKOMSKII: LES THÉÂTRES, ANCIENS ET MODERNES

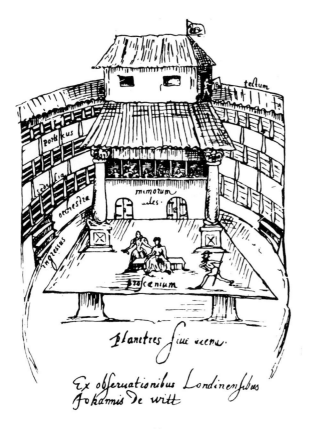

Fig. 43. Interior of The Swan, after a sketch by Johannes de Witt.

served double-duty, being not only playhouses but also entertainment centers offering animal-baiting, jousts, cockfights, and whatever else the public would pay to see. This leads us to suppose that the stage and the tiring house in such multi-purpose theatres were of a temporary nature, capable of being dismantled when the need arose, and contemporary records bear this out.

Opinions have changed about the possible form of the Elizabethan public playhouse as new pieces of evidence have come to light. Since the views of modern scholars generally have not filtered down to undergraduate colleges or to the general public, it might be pertinent to reiterate some of the arguments and conclusions of the last ten years. Various older studies have presented conjectural restorations of The Globe and other Elizabethan theatres, their authors choosing a variety of plans and decorative forms. All are equally possible, equally unprovable. In spite of overwhelming evidence that the playhouses were round inside, popular knowledge still believes these outdoor theatres to have been octagons with half-timber construction, practical leaded glass windows, and the other paraphernalia of a romantic vision of Merrie Olde England. In the past, widely published reconstructions of the typical Elizabethan theatre have listed:

1. a tiring house included within the frame of the building;
2. a platform stage with a balcony in the rear;
3. a second, inner, stage beneath this balcony (the "inner below");
4. a third stage behind the balcony (the "inner above");
5. practical leaded glass windows above each entrance door (and in at least one instance these are conjectured to be large bay windows).

Script references to windows have more recently been understood to mean that upper acting positions were intended to represent them, and not that actual windows were involved. The de Witt sketch shows no windows, bay or otherwise, no half-timbering, and no elaborate trims.

The evidence we have "proves" that the Elizabethan playhouse (if such a term may even be used for so generalized a concept) was a circular, wood-frame building, with three stories of galleries which were roofed, and which faced an unroofed center. The open pit contained

Fig. 44. A reconstruction of The Hope, 1614, by C. Walter Hodges, from *The Globe Restored.*

ERNEST BENN, LTD.

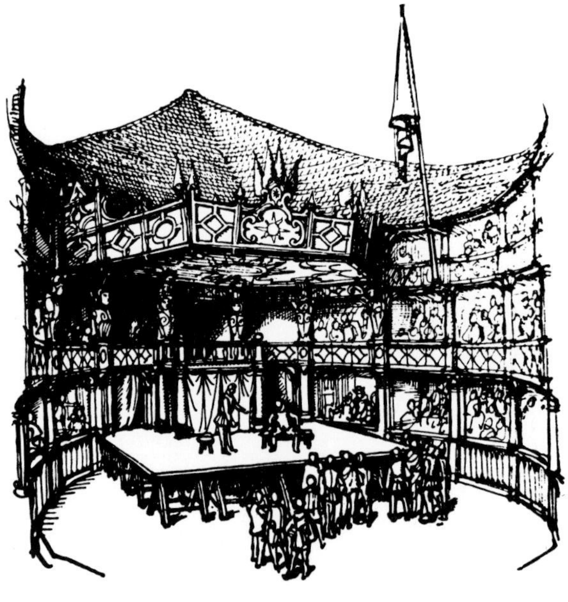

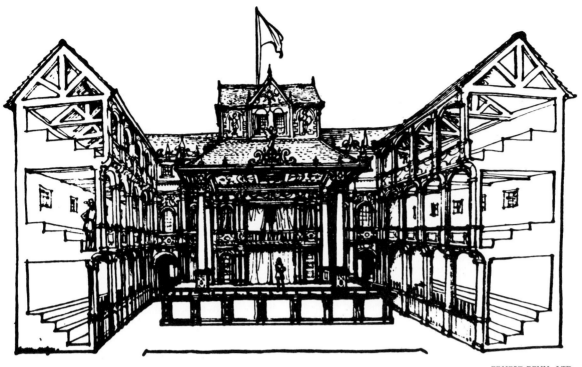

Fig. 45. A reconstruction of The Fortune by C. Walter Hodges, from *The Globe Restored*.

either a permanent or temporary trestle stage (depending upon the theatre). This was backed by a tiring house that was, in at least two instances, separate from the main structure; its face contained at least two large doors and a shallow gallery; and traditionally it was draped with an arras, or figured curtain. A projecting roof was located above some of the stages dedicated more to drama than to other diversions. This was supported in some instances by posts, but in at least one instance it was cantilevered out from the main structure. Above this roof may have been an additional level for the music room, although more recent conjectures suppose the musicians were contained in gallery spaces. Some theatres seem to have provided space for a machine for the raising and lowering of deities, although how this was rigged and precisely where it was located is not known.

The Fortune Contract gives us some data on the form of that theatre, but even this is precious little. Unlike other playhouses of its time, the building was square: 80 feet "every way square without" and 55 feet "square every way" within. There were three stories, the first 12 feet high, the second 11 feet, and the third 9 feet, and each

of these was 12 feet wide; the two upper stories included a "juttey forwards" of 10 inches over the first; a "stage and tiring house to be made . . . with a shadow or cover over the said stage . . ." was an important part of the structure; and the stage was to be made 43 feet wide and to extend to the middle of the pit. The stage and the tiring house were to be set up "within said frame," and the builder was to provide "convenient windows and lights glazed to the said tiring house." Although there was to be a shadow, or roof, over the stage, there was no mention of posts for that purpose. Other specifications were to be "like the Globe," except that the posts holding up the frame and the stage were to be square "palasters" instead of turned columns.

Although the contract is clear about the stage *and* the tiring house being "within" (inside the enclosure of) the frame of the building, restorations without exception have placed the stage against the frame and have made the frame itself into the tiring house. The de Witt sketch of The Swan indicates clearly that the tiring house (in rather crude perspective, one must admit) was enclosed by the circle of the playhouse and not incorporated within it. The depth of the Elizabethan stage, as suggested by the figures in the Fortune contract, is given from the middle of the open yard to the face of the main structure. If the tiring house indeed was separate from the main building, as indicated in the de Witt sketch, we would be left (at least in the case of the Fortune) with a stage considerably shallower than any in the conjectural restorations. If this is so, we must reexamine many accepted thoughts about staging methods in Shakespeare's time, because all the elaborately worked out conjectures on movement, blocking, timing, and emphasis must be abandoned.

One of the reasons practical leaded glass windows have been included in numerous restorations is the reference to "windows and lights" in the Fortune contract, wording which obviously denotes carpentry and glazing. The de Witt sketch shows us two windows in the room above the stage roof; others were doubtless included in the sides so that the interior of the tiring house could be illuminated by daylight through open-

Fig. 46. A reconstruction of the interior of Blackfriars, by Irwin Smith, from *Shakespeare's Blackfriar's Playhouse.*

NEW YORK UNIVERSITY PRESS

ings which could be secured against the weather.

The origin of the form of Shakespeare's theatre has been credited to such influences as medieval inn yards, pageant wagons, and late Gothic circle-mound arenas. Both the playhouses and the baiting rings were referred to as being Roman in style; one may wonder what was then meant by "Roman," when published observations of ruins of ancient theatres had not yet become readily available. Since the de Witt sketch shows multiple galleries supported upon orders of columns, and since translations of Vitruvius had been both illustrated and widely circulated since the earlier part of the Century, it is perhaps reasonable to believe that the theatres were English Renaissance versions of Roman combat arenas.

Although copies of Elizabethan plays were usually broken into the five acts considered *de rigeur* by imitators of Seneca, there is every indication that originally the performances were presented without breaks. If one thinks of Elizabethan production in terms of more modern methods—using scenery and decorative properties—it is difficult to imagine continuous performance except by use of multiple inner stages, where large, realistically oriented scenes could be represented, with the more presentational scenes restricted to the forestage. Since this reconstruction conflicts with the primary evidence, it has been abandoned by recent scholarship. There is evidence that some scenes were prepared for discovery, but no evidence that this took place to the rear of the platform within an enclosed area, nor that it involved the use of scenery. Perhaps the most logical analysis of the problem to date can be found in C. Walter Hodges: *The Globe Restored*, in which the author attempts to divest himself of preconceptions influenced by later staging techniques. Professor Richard Hosley, also, has reached interesting conclusions based almost entirely on primary sources.

The term "private theatre" denotes those playhouses which appealed to a more restricted clientele than did the public theatres. Prices were considerably higher, and the selection of plays reflected a greater interest in classical models than those offered to the general public. Lest this be construed to suggest a different staging technique —and thus a different theatre architecture—we must recall that players from the public houses gave performances within the private theatres during the winter months, and that there was an

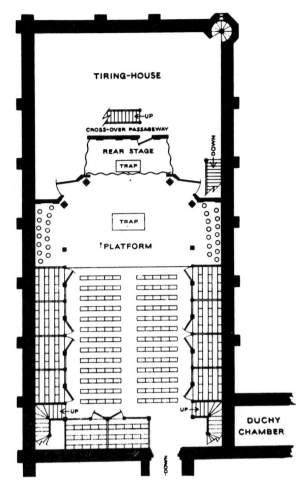

Fig. 47. A reconstructed plan of Blackfriars by Irwin Smith.

adult company at the Second Blackfriars in later years whose members received the majority of their training and techniques in the public play-houses. Thus, there are likely to have been no ma-jor structural differences between the two types of theatres. For this reason, also, the general style that has been previously accepted for the Globe has also been accepted for Blackfriars; platform stage, inner-below, inner-above, leaded glass windows, and lavish Tudor trim.

Almost all of the indoor playing spaces used during the late sixteenth century were still in use during the first half of the seventeenth cen-tury, and many of the plays of Elizabeth's time were revived regularly during the Jacobean era. While there is no specifically identified descrip-tion or illustration of a playhouse of the later period, there are two drawings of indoor stages

which served as frontispieces to published edi-tions of the plays *Roxana* (1630) and *Messalina* (1640). Since the illustrations obviously were meant to suggest the type of stage on which the plays were performed, we assume that the draw-ings are acceptable representations of private playhouses of the Jacobean era, and that they are similar to, if not identical with, those of Shake-speare's time. The two prints show trapezoidal stages with none of the elaborations attributed to them in the usual reconstruction. The acting areas are bounded by railings and backed by the usual arras (through which entrances and exits were made and behind which concealments were effected). The *Roxana* print shows a stage rigged directly against a gallery, with patrons watch-

Fig. 48. Frontispiece to *Roxana*, 1630.

ing the action from the position normally attributed to the "above." The *Messalina* print illustrates a brick or stone tiring house structure, a window incorporated within it, and a stage thrust out before it. It is unlikely that players trained on a complex "Merrie England stage" could transfer their productions to a *Roxana* stage intact. If, however, we accept the evidence of the de Witt sketch, it was indeed possible to transfer productions from public to private stages without difficulty. Speculations about the multiple stage playhouse—while now considered highly suspect—are persuasive, and lead even the best of scholars into unnecessary apologia. C. Walter Hodges, for example, excuses the presence of figures on the balcony in the de Witt sketch by suggesting that they represent actors watching a rehearsal, not paying patrons at a performance. This may well be so, but we need not hesitate to assume that they were patrons; in the Theatre Royal, Drury Lane, as much as a century later, actors reached their playing positions for a balcony scene only by elbowing their way through spectators seated in the boxes over the stage doors.

An appropriate restoration of the Elizabethan stage is so complicated (and such an intriguing puzzle) that perhaps we should examine a typical series of conjectures about the multiple stage. The accoutrements usually are carefully worked out, and are based upon evidence drawn from interpolations and inferences inspired by plays of the period. While such reconstructions are no longer taken seriously by many scholars, the books illustrating them are on every library shelf and continue to serve as references for students.

For those familiar with the multistage concept it might be of value to note each of the items usually included in it and to compare them with modern evaluations of probable production techniques. Discussion of these matters rests upon our understanding that the Elizabethan stage conventions have been traced directly to medieval practice, and that the theatre of the Middle Ages was iconographic, not illusionistic, in character.

First is the matter of the inner-below. Proponents of the multiple stage conclude that a curtain was drawn aside in the rear of the platform stage to reveal a second acting area within which practical properties were preset. We now give weight to notations in many scripts that such properties were "thrust out," not discovered. They conclude, further, that the back wall of the inner-below contained a door and a window; this they justify by citing plays in which references to such items occur subsequent to the opening of the discovery curtain. We have come to suspect, however, that once actors were discovered they made use of the platform stage and did not remain within the area supposedly below the balcony. The doors and windows referred to are likely to have been the doors and gallery divisions of the playhouse proper, not specially introduced items in a separate location. Place usually was indicated either by textual reference or by sign-board, and we suspect that illusion was neither intended nor attempted. Exactly where the curtain was located, and what it concealed or revealed, cannot be determined with accuracy. We now accept it as one of the parts of a playhouse compatible with primary evidence. The use of a discovery curtain admits of several possibilities (none of them certain): that in some theatres there was a third door located upstage center behind the arras; that a temporary construction of a "mansion" or pavilion was erected on the stage forward for those plays which demanded one; or that one of the large entrance doors was covered temporarily with an arras for the same purpose.

Window references—particularly in the Fortune contract—have led to the introduction of practical lights set within casement alcoves in most reconstructions. Modern theory accepts the practice, common at Drury Lane, of using a simple gallery box as a window, as probably descended from Elizabethan practice. The stage illustrated in *The Wits* shows us exactly how such a window might be rigged; it was no more than a gallery division masked by a curtain. The *Messalina* print—with its construction resembling a tiring house facade—has a simple curtain above.

Postulation of the inner-above is based upon references in certain plays to curtains drawn in the gallery, by characters already in that location, in order to discover additional characters or scenes. This has been presumed to suggest two separate spaces, a forward balcony and a rear enclosed area, giving in effect a duplication of the double area suggested for the lower stage. An examination of the Swan drawing discloses a balcony whose overhead lintle is supported by turned posts; we now suspect that curtains were draped between these posts as required—as in the *Messalina* print—and that an actor within one of the divisions could discover actors within another division simply by pulling the curtain to one side. Thus scenes could be played directly to the front of the balcony rather than within an inner stage.

Some reconstructions include large bay windows placed above the doors at either side of the stage; these are derived from directions in scripts for actors to "stand close" (or to remain out of sight from those above by stepping back beneath some overhanging projection); but the term may have meant exactly what it said. In order to be hidden from one looking out from a window the actor had only to "stand close" to the door below; he would then be hidden within the door frame and necessarily out of sight from all but the most determined gaper from above. We must all be reminded occasionally of the oldest stage conventions; those which mean "I am invisible" and "I cannot be heard."

Concurrent with productions in public and private theatres of the sixteenth century, a different style of dramatic presentation developed at Court. Entertainments for resident and visiting royalty—as well as special displays for royal progresses—were a part of the theatrical scene from the earliest Renaissance. Pageants, processions, and semidramatic performances were highlights of certain times of the year both in town and at Court. Henry VIII was amused by masked ladies and gentlemen performing simple recitations and dance figures, as was Elizabeth I. While these were not dramatic in the strict sense, they developed rapidly into fullfledged theatrical exercises, the court masques.

Originally simple "momeries" or "disguisings," these entertainments revolved around an allegorical theme, usually of a classical nature, in which laudatory speeches were interwoven with masquerade dances. The performances were held in the great halls, and were set similarly to the Medieval cycle plays—in "mansions" of an iconographic nature which were scattered around the edges of the room. This type of setting may be seen in a print illustrating an early ballet performed at the Petit Bourbon in 1581 (See Fig. 31). A characteristic of the court masque was the participation of the audience; the spectators were

invited to join in the final dance with the masquers. It was this special portion of the program which determined the spectacle and later the form of the hall in which it was to be presented. The masque, including semidramatic recitations, songs, processions, dances—involving more or less elaborate scenic pieces—placed requirements upon the building which housed it and especially upon the great halls that later were constructed to accommodate it. There had to be sufficient space for the display of temples, rocks, prisons, and other stock pieces, as well as free passage for processions and ready access from the playing area to the audience. At first any large hall was deemed sufficient, for initially the large open space was used by both masquers and dancers. In the early seventeenth century, however, the Court entertainments of the type seen by Henry and Elizabeth gave way to more elaborate productions based upon Italian models. In these, the structure of the dramatic portion became more disciplined, and the scenic requirements were greatly expanded.

In earlier years the poet and the costumier were the prime movers of the masque; in later years it became the scenic artist's sphere of influence. The greatest of these, and the real founder of the English court masque as we think of it, was the Surveyor to the King, Inigo Jones. In collaboration with Ben Jonson and others, he produced elaborate spectacles in the great hall of Whitehall Palace for the court of Charles I. Within this space temporary seating and a temporary stage were erected, conforming to the open floor pattern appropriate to the masque alone. In the first quarter of the seventeenth century there were certainly three—and perhaps four—masking places on the grounds of Whitehall. First was the old Great Hall (or Tudor Hall), which was modest in size, being 39½ feet wide and 87 feet long. It was in this hall that *Florimene* was presented in 1635. Second was Inigo Jones's splendid new Banqueting House, a state hall which was the first truly Renaissance building of any size built in England. Completed in 1622, the hall was over 111 feet long, 55 feet wide, and 55 feet high, the double cube beloved of Renaissance architects; it served as a setting for masques of great splendor. The hall was primarily illuminated by torches, however, and it was soon felt that the Rubens paintings on the ceiling were being affected by the smoke, so a new Masking House

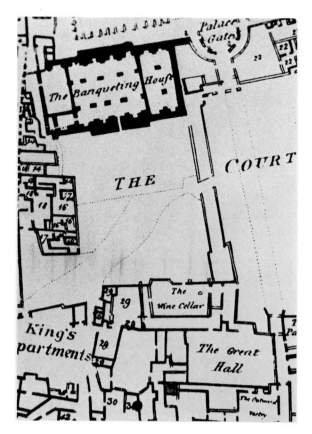

Fig. 49. Map of Whitehall showing the Banqueting House in relation to the old Great Hall.

Fig. 50. View of the Banqueting House from the Thames. A detail from Hollar's Long View. The roof of the Great Hall may be seen to the right of the Banqueting House.

was built close by. Although it was a temporary structure of weatherboarding built up on a brick foundation, this third hall was said to have cost the King 2,500 pounds, a great sum at that time. The Masking Hall is believed to have been slightly larger than the Banqueting House: 120 feet long, 57 feet wide, and 59 feet high. The simplicity of construction and the great sum spent upon it suggests that much of the funds went into more elaborate machinery than could be temporarily rigged in the Banqueting House. A fourth hall was supposed to have been built by Balthazar Gerbier, Surveyor to the Duke of Buckingham, but no information remains relating to it.

When rigged for production, each of these halls was of similar design to those used for court festivals in Italy. A large stage, fitted with considerable machinery and numerous wings and shutters, was set behind an elaborately designed frontispiece designed as a thematic emblem of the production. Steps led from the stage to the flat hall floor, and benches were erected about the sides of the hall *en amphithéâtre* so that the center was left open. The platform containing the King's "state" was located in the center of the open space.

Yet another theatre on the grounds of Whitehall was the Cockpit-in-Court, built by Henry VIII as a cockfighting arena and converted to a theatre at a later date. A contemporary map of Whitehall gives a rough plan of the Cockpit, showing it to be a little less than half the size of

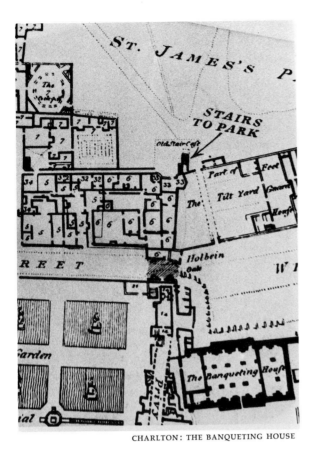

CHARLTON: THE BANQUETING HOUSE

Fig. 51. Map of Whitehall showing the Banqueting House in relation to the Cockpit-in-Court (upper left).

the Banqueting House, with at least one gallery. It had a steeply pitched conical roof topped by a lantern, and the building seems to have been about 50 feet in diameter. Inigo Jones's pupil and friend, John Webb, made a rough plan and an even rougher *scaena* elevation of an installation within the building, and from this we are able to guess its arrangement and proportions. The structure was used regularly for dramatic performances, but probably boasted no more than a simple platform stage because of the severely restricted area that was available to the actors. To our knowledge, Webb's proposed conversion of this hall into a Palladian *scaena frons* —thought to have been drawn ca. 1632—was never carried out. Although the restricted size suggests family entertainments of an intimate nature, Pepys recorded visiting the playhouse for public performances. It is from this structure that we may be able to guess at the form and size of the Cockpit-in-Drury Lane (The Phoenix). The

addition of a gallery seems to have increased the capacity of these converted cockpits.

In the period between *Salmacida Spolia* and the Restoration no playhouses were constructed. Just the reverse. Many of the public theatres that remained from the Elizabethan and Jacobean eras had their interiors pulled down by direct order of the Puritan Parliament. Still, although no theatres were built, there is reference to construction plans made by Sir William Davenant, both before and during the *interregnum*. In 1639 Davenant had been favored by Charles I with a patent which gave him permission to erect a theatre near Fleet Street, which construction was to encompass in total "forty yards square at the most." From the knowledge of both the allowance of 120 front feet for the erection of a theatre, and the interest Davenant had expressed previously in the Italian system of scenes and machines, we suppose that he planned to build a large playhouse in the Italian style, the first of its kind in England. Its model, apparently, was the Teatro San Cassiano in Venice, for the patent states that Davenant was permitted to build a playhouse like that built in Venice two years before. Davenant's plans were frustrated by the unsettled political situation, so England had to wait for its Italian theatre.

The notions among architects of "Italian" theatre construction may be seen from a plan contemporary with Davenant's patent drawn by Inigo Jones. The theatre proposed in this plan (perhaps prepared for Davenant) combined characteristics of the Teatro Olimpico and Serlio's Teatro della Palazzo Porto. Whatever Jones's involvement, Davenant was persistent; in 1655, in company with others, he planned the construction of a playhouse near the Charter House, and even raised funds for its erection. Although work seems to have begun it was never completed.

Davenant did finally succeed in producing plays in the Italian style, but not in a new theatre designed for them. He was forced to rig a temporary stage within the hall of his own home, Rutland House, where he produced *The Siege of Rhodes*, a drama-cum-opera with an acceptably high moral—if not intellectual—tone. It was the first attempt at scenery in the Italian manner for the English public, however, and therefore is considered to be of seminal importance. The space available for the scenes of *The Siege of Rhodes* was small; the frontispiece was only 22 feet wide

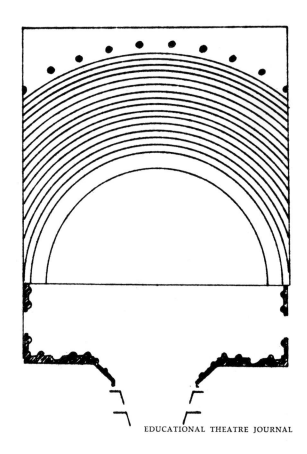

Fig. 52. Inigo Jones's plan for a Serlian playhouse, drawn by D. C. Mullin.

EDUCATIONAL THEATRE JOURNAL

and 15 feet high; the backshutter of the modest setting was 9 feet wide. The whole was strictly iconographic and only the backshutter changed, thus the magnificent spectacles of the Italian festival theatres were reduced to their least common denominator, one that was to serve the English stage in the years after the Restoration.

IV
Deux ex Machina

Once the various types of Italian theatre architecture were joined into a single design appropriate for general dramatic entertainment, the style spread throughout Europe, first challenging, then supplanting native forms (although, as is the case with all fashion, a remote area might, still construct a *démodé* theatre). The experimentation and innovation of the second half of the seventeenth century resulted in overlapping influences upon theatre design outside Italy, but by the early eighteenth century a more specific channel of development had been established. The designers of the Venetian houses of the forties and fifties abandoned the elaborate pilastered proscenium of the frontispiece style (which itself was a remnant of the *scaena frons* of the Vitruvian theatre).

In spite of this, the Munich opera of 1657 was built with an architectonic stage front, similar to those frontispieces popular for Italian court festival productions a century before, having an extravagance of classically inspired decoration. The elaborate proscenium served a decorative and thematic function, suitable as long as the scenes behind it were relatively static. This kind of proscenium was particularly favored for stages equipped with Serlian angle wings. As scenic change came into regular use, however, the elaborate *scaena frons* proscenium became more distracting and irrelevant. There is a direct relation between the proscenium decoration and the stage spectacle, and from the design of the former we

can judge the amount of movables offered within the latter.

Italian architects of the 1640's were less concerned with the arrangement of the auditorium—a matter which was essentially resolved—and more concerned with the elaboration and expansion of the use of stage machinery. The *ne plus ultra* of seventeenth century scenic spectacle was developed for the Venetian theatres by Giacomo Torelli da Fano, whose settings and machines were considered diabolically clever by his contemporaries. His designs for the opera *La Finta Pazza*, which opened the new Teatro Novissimo in 1641, were especially remarked upon. The designer-architect was summoned to France to install modern scenic devices in the Petit Bourbon, and it was there that *La Finta Pazza* was revived for presentation before the King. The French court was stunned. Previously, scenery had been used to represent general locale, and scenic changes were restricted in number. Special and elaborate flying rigs had long been available for ascents and descents, but their use was limited because efficient methods of handling them had not yet been devised. As the use of machinery increased, it became more and more difficult to handle, and the manpower requirements were enormous. The changes became more time consuming and irregular until further elaboration of scenic spectacle seemed impossible unless the dramatic portion was suspended entirely. Torelli

Fig. 53. Setting from Torelli's *La Finta Pazza*, Paris, 1645.

and his followers overcame this hurdle by mechanizing the entire operation. Mechanization enabled the designer to present in the public theatre what had previously been restricted to the court theatre: scenes which opened, shut, rose, sank, changed shape, and which were large in scale. The areas below and above the stage became

Fig. 54a. Frontispiece to Corneille's *Andromède*, with scenes and machines by Torelli, presented at the Petit Bourbon.

nests of wheels, levers, ropes, pulleys, and counterweights, sophisticated to a degree which enabled scenic movement and changes to occur as scenes were played. Animal power was introduced, and this—plus mechanical advantage—made changes both more rapid and less laborious. Playwrights were encouraged to make use of the new effects. For example, Corneille (with a little prodding) wrote *Andromède* to exploit the new mechanicals to their greatest advantage.

Torelli abandoned changes made with the use of manpower on each unit, and introduced mass changes accomplished with large winches attached by ropes to many pieces at once. The movement of these was aided both by animal power and by the release of counterweights. The wing sliding in a groove on the stage floor was replaced by a wing rigged to a special mounting called a chariot. This was a vertical frame that moved in a slot in the stage floor; the part below the stage was composed of a wheeled truck which could be attached to a windlass as was required; wings could be attached to the upper part in the order needed (see Appendix 5). The machinery and stagehands remained completely out of sight of the audience, so the scenes seemed to move mysteriously by themselves.

Mechanization made the movement of scenic units not just simultaneous but almost instantaneous as well. No longer required were the drum rolls or trumpet blasts from the rear of the auditorium formerly used to distract the audience from the mob of workmen changing units on the

Fig. 54b. Scene 1, *Andromède*.

44

stage. The structural changes in the architecture of the stage house engendered by this system were considerable; other theatre architects adopted the practices only as large sums of money became available. The effect of the technical revolution upon spectacle was so great, however, that no architect could afford to ignore it. Eventually all but the smallest provincial public theatres incorporated elements of Torelli's system. England was the only exception; the wing-in-groove system remained in use there until modern times.

After designing the machines in the Petit Bourbon, Torelli became the architect for two playhouses in his native Fano, the Teatro da Fano of 1661 and the Teatro della Fortuna of 1662. These were more modest structures than the Petit Bourbon, but they were rigged with the Torelli system of scenic change.

Torelli's place at the French court was taken by Gaspare Vigarani, who also had labored to perfect the Venetian theatres, and who had been architect of the Teatro di Modena of 1659. Vigarani was invited to install a theatre within the *grande salle* of the Tuileries. His auditorium plan was a modified horseshoe—as dictated by the design of the hall—with the majority of the seats located on the parterre. A few rows of benches were placed along the side walls, and an additional few in the gallery to the rear. Vigarani's inventiveness was not expressed in the auditorium design, but upon the stage. While the proscenium opening was a modest one, the stage had a working depth of 132 feet, the largest in Europe.

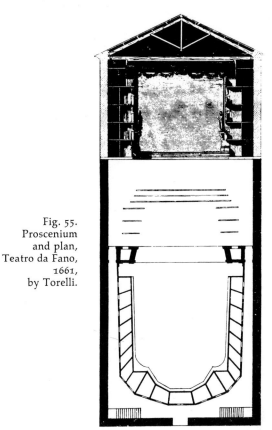

Fig. 55.
Proscenium
and plan,
Teatro da Fano,
1661,
by Torelli.

Within this great space the designer included scenic machinery of the type developed by Torelli, but increased in size and complexity. Because it was designed for spectacular effects, and constructed to make them possible, the theatre was called the Salle des Machines.

Fig. 54c. Scene 2, *Andromède.*

Fig. 54d. Scene 5, *Andromède.*

45

Fig. 56. Plan of the Salle des Machines, 1659, by Vigarani.

Fig. 57. Scenes from *Ercole in Tebe*, presented at Florence, 1661.

Scene 3

Scene 1

Scene 2

Scene 4

Scene 5

The impact of scenic extravaganzas upon the courts of Europe was tremendous. The monarchs who were tempted to build imitations of Versailles were also determined to erect opera houses.

While the Salle des Machines remained unrivaled, its existence changed opera from popular musical drama into a display of wealth and power, much as the festival entertainments had done in the

Scene 6

Scene 9

Scene 7

Scene 10

Scene 8

Scene 11

Italian courts. The Venetians initiated the practice of presenting in their public theatres the type of scenic spectacle traditionally reserved for the courts. This secularization of opera and spectacle did not take root as a popular art form elsewhere in Europe, but was exploited for political ends (which colors our attitude toward opera to this day).

Fig. 58. Proscenium of the Teatro Farnese and curtain for *L'Eta del'Oro*, presented in 1690.

The Teatro de la Pergola was constructed in Florence in 1657, apparently similar in design to the festival theatres. It was reconstructed in 1688 to resemble the Venetian opera houses. The auditorium, however, was cast in a definite horseshoe instead of the open U form, and the stage boasted considerable depth to allow for the necessary scenic spectacle. The plan for this theatre is one of the earliest illustrations of the use of scenery in the latest style of that time.

Fig. 59. Plan of the first Teatro di Tor di Nona, Rome, 1660.

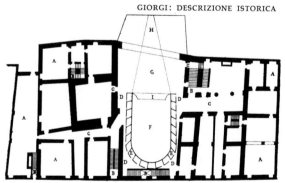

One of the better documented examples of the changing fashion in playhouse design is the Teatro di Tor di Nona in Rome. First erected in 1660, the plan followed SS. Giovanni e Paolo's U-shaped auditorium. No provision was made for an elaborate proscenium, but scenic spectacle was considered so important that the rear wall of the stage was knocked out and an addition built on to accommodate an extra depth of scene. When the theatre was reconstructed in 1671 by Carlo Fontana, the auditoruim was given the shape of an egg. The egg design was to become the pattern for much future opera house construction; its purpose will be discussed later. In the case of the Tor di Nona, the additional space required by the enlarged style was not contained within an expansion of the original building; a second theatre was constructed crossways within much of the same space occupied by the original. The wall which had been knocked out was patched up and became the side wall of the new theatre. Succeeding reconstructions (and there were many) kept this new orientation.

If wings running in grooves or placed on chariots are mounted parallel to the proscenium, they must be either very wide to mask the backstage area or present in great numbers. In order to reduce the area needed for the wings and to reduce their numbers, wing placement was reorganized so they could be mounted at an angle to the proscenium. This freed more offstage space, necessitated fewer wings, and reduced the amount of equipment needed for shifting scenes. Mechanically this seemed to be the answer to the problem of proliferation, but the architect-designers soon found that while perspective rendering on flat surfaces required skill, rendering the same scenes on angle wings required genius.

Fig. 60. Plan of the second Teatro di Tor di Nona, 1671.

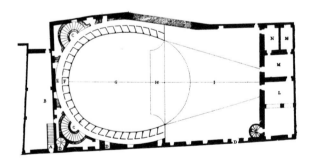

Also, the degree to which the wings could be angled was limited. The extant mechanical devices could be adapted to shift scenery at a slight angle by passing the connecting lines over an extra set of blocks. An increase in angle, however, required a multiplication of equipment, not a reduction. The problem of moving a wing on a chariot, mounted at an angle on a raked stage, was almost insurmountable. The law of diminishing returns eventually caused the system to be abandoned.

Northern Europe reacted slowly to the Italian influences. Entertainments were given in the palace at Darmstadt as early as 1607, in a small theatre built for the occasion, but the form of the temporary playhouse is not known. Since it was fitted within the Great Hall, it probably did not differ much in style from the simple bleachers used by Inigo Jones at Whitehall. Somewhat more elaborate and permanent arrangements were common after the middle of the century. In 1652, Giovanni Burnacini constructed a stage for opera in Vienna and a theatre in Regensburg. Munich's first opera house was a palace hall, converted in 1654, and rigged with scenes by Francesco Santurini. A more permanent Ducal theatre was built in Darmstadt in 1665.

In 1667, Lodovico Burnacini completed the new Vienna Opera, a rectangular hall with three tiers of raised galleries, a ceiling with an enormous vista of deity-filled architectural splendor, and a proscenium flanked by a veritable forest of columns. Provision was not made for a royal box (for this was an innovation introduced at a later date); the sovereign still sat in state upon a dais on the main floor, surrounded by his courtiers. The galleries were not divided into boxes, but contained simple amphitheatrical seating, and there were no boxes or seats on the stage. The orchestra pit was located almost directly beneath the grand valence, and the edge of the stage coincided with the line of the main curtain; there was, in other words, no apron. The entire display was restricted to the scenic area, although the pro-

Fig. 61. Scenes from Burnacini's *La Zenobia* on the stage of the Hoftheater, Vienna, 1662. From the top: Scene 1, Scene 4, Scene 5, Scene 9.

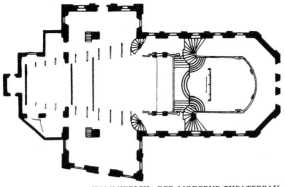

Fig. 62. Plan of the Komödienhaus, 1667, Dresden.

dienhaus, was designed by Wolf Kaspar von Klengel in 1667 and completed in 1678 by Alessandro Mauro. As first built, the theatre had four tiers, a spectacular columned and broken-pedimented proscenium arch, and a bewildering series of staircases sweeping up from the pit to the first gallery level. This baroque confection seated some 2,000 persons, all at some distance from the scene because of the elaborate proscenium arch and its approaches. The stage was mounted with ten sets of wings and had a depth equal to that of the house.

scenium elaboration and the ceiling painting made the division irrelevant. The building was destroyed in 1683. A temporary opera house was finally devised in 1697, and a large, permanent house, of the size and style of the Salle des Machines, was completed in 1707, when an elaborate hall was made from the Redoutensaal.

In 1657, Francesco Santurini built a large permanent theatre in Munich, the San Salvator, which was to be for the Bavarian capital what Burnacini's opera was for Vienna. While no plan survives of the San Salvator, engravings of the interior show us a semicircular amphitheatre on the main floor, with three levels of galleries above. An elaborate baroque proscenium contained four sets of wings and a backcloth.

The first opera house in Dresden, the Komö-

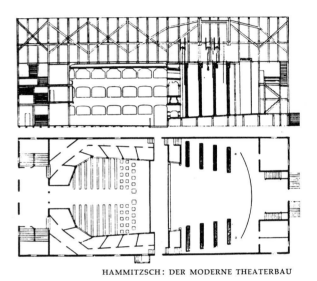

Fig. 64. Section and plan of the Kleine Komödienhaus, Dresden, 1697.

In 1697, the more modest and simple Kleine Komödienhaus was built to house plays. The wooden building contained three tiers of boxes, a raked auditorium floor fitted with benches, and armchair seating for royalty; the capacity was approximately 900. The small stage boasted only four sets of wings plus an unusual curved backcloth. In the same year, another small court playhouse was built in the Wilhelmsburg in Weimar. This tiny house was equipped with no boxes; there was a canopy over the location reserved for the State; a shallow gallery in a U shape surrounded a raked auditorium floor; the small proscenium had a large balconied box fitted to either side; and the stage held five sets of wings, and another large curved backcloth.

Fig. 63. Forestage of the Dresden Komödienhaus of 1667.

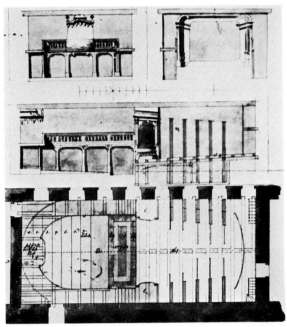

Fig. 65. Plan of the Wilhelmsburg Schlosstheater, Weimar, 1697.

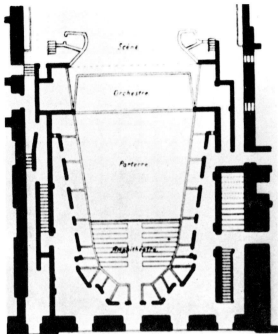

Fig. 66. Theatre in the Palais Royal, 1660, by Lemercier.

In France, Molière was faced with a dilemma when he returned to Paris: there was no theatre for him to use. Paris had only two playhouses for the public, the Bourgogne and the Marais. Molière's troupe of French comedians was invited to use the theatre in the Palais Royal, and although this was unsuited for anything but the spectacles for which it was designed, the troupe moved in after some alterations had been made, and used it for several years. The arrangement within the hall was one that was later to be copied numerous times, both in France and in Germany. There were three tiers of boxes with an open gallery above, and the tiers were narrowed as they receded from the proscenium, making a flattened V shape that allowed better sightlines from all the side boxes. The result was an improvement over the Italian system of parallel sides, for those in the boxes, but the narrowing of the house infringed upon the space in the parterre. The Palais Royal had a stepped amphitheatre which began directly beneath the first tier of boxes (a system to be referred to later as "English") and which descended to a level well below that of the stage. Because of the low overhead of the hall, the tiers were cramped, the proscenium low, and the total effect considerably different from that of con-

temporary German opera houses which were designed by Italians. After Molière's troupe left the Palais, the hall was referred to as the Académie Royale de Musique, and the theatre proved to be more suitable for Lully than it had for the French comedians.

Molière's troupe was encouraged to move into a house of its own, but no theatre was available except the Théâtre de Guénégaud, built for opera

Fig. 67. Portion of the stage of what may be the Théâtre de Guénégaud, Paris.

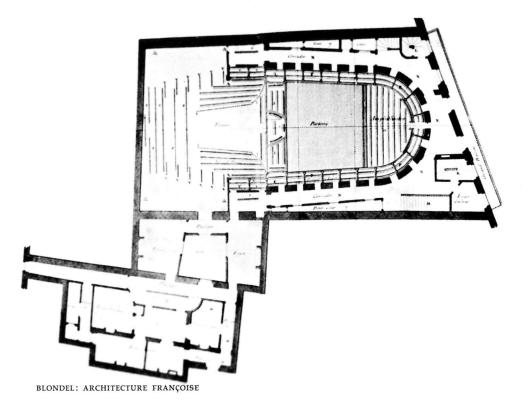

Fig. 68.
Plan of the
Comédie
Français,
by d'Orbay,
1689.

BLONDEL: ARCHITECTURE FRANÇOISE

in 1673. This remained the home of the troupe for many years, and while there are numerous illustrations of scenes performed on its stage, there are none of the house proper, inside or out. A print from later in the century illustrates what might be the Guénégaud, but the connection is tenuous at best. The hall illustrated is modest in size, with two tiers of boxes, a standing pit, and benches at either side of the stage apron.

One of the most completely illustrated late seventeenth century theatres we have is Francois D'Orbay's Comédie Française. This was constructed in 1689 to replace the Guénégaud and to provide a permanent home for the troupe of

Fig. 69.
Section
of the
Comédie
Français.

DUMONT: RECUEIL DES PLANCHES

52

Molière. The characteristics peculiar to the French theatre that were introduced at the Palais Royal were imitated in this design also, with some alterations to accommodate its function as a public playhouse. Unlike the Italian theatre architects, D'Orbay did not make the usual provision for a royal box. Normally, the perspective scene would be designed to give the best illusion from the seat of the sovereign. In the French public theatre the tradition of iconography was too strong, and the fashion of sitting upon the stage too well imbedded. Private boxes were provided for the infrequent visits of royalty, but these were located at either side of the stage and faced the apron. Because the Comédie was a public house, and management was dependent upon receipts and the good will of the patrons, additional seating was allowed on the stage proper. Thus, while a full set of scenes was supplied—plus the apparatus to move them—the effect of scenic representation was spoiled by the view, as the curtain rose, of more patrons. The acting area allowed by the architect was modest enough, but this space was further reduced by the introduction of semi-permanent bench seats, arranged in tiers, upon the stage. Other audience accommodations were no greater nor more comfortable than bare necessity required. Boxes were small and cramped, and their partitions faced the center of the house, rather than being angled toward the stage—a distinct peculiarity in a house built as late as this. Seven rows of benches were placed in an elevated portion of the pit, and the remainder of the parterre was used for standing room.

This playhouse reflects the intense conservatism of the popular theatre. We can see from the plan that in the Palais Royal, seating was arranged for comfortable viewing by pit patrons. The French public had always stood in the pit, however, and the new Comédie was built to cater to their taste. The arrangement of the auditorium showed little concern for the innovations of the Italians in the preceding half century. The only concession toward modernity was the provision for scenes and machines, instead of the simultaneous settings derived from medieval mansion stages.

Parisian designs, however conservative, were influential upon other theatres built during the same period. The later theatres of Montpellier and Metz were copies of the same general plan, with one significant exception: they were dis-

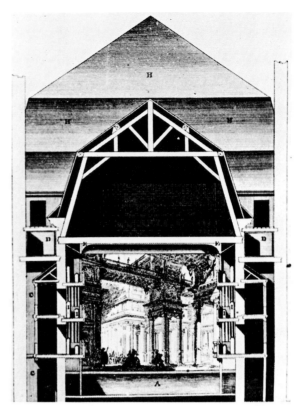

DUMONT: RECUEIL DES PLANCHES

Fig. 70. Section to the stage of the Comédie Français.

Fig. 71. Section to the house of the Comédie Français.

BLONDEL: ARCHITECTURE FRANÇOISE

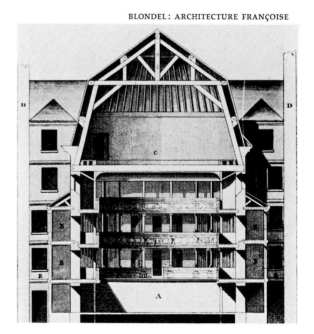

53

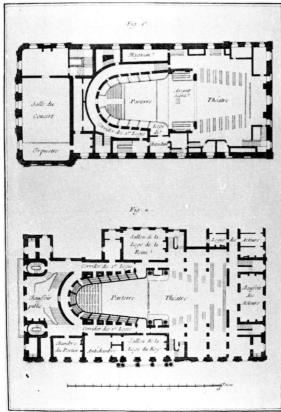

Fig. 72. Plans of the Théâtre de Metz and the Théâtre de Montpellier.

tinguished by their construction as independent buildings. They thus were better able to provide for audience accommodation than was the Comédie. These buildings were among the first in which the theatre was regarded as a municipal monument and worthy of extended space and elaborate architectural treatment. This view of the playhouse as civic center was to permeate Europe.

The new Dresden Opera of 1719, again designed by Alessandro Mauro, was a departure from the plans in vogue elsewhere at the time. The stage was rigged for machines in the Italian fashion—this time with parallel wings—and was twice as large as the auditorium. The open parterre was remarkably small in comparison to the total house volume, which made it unique. Posts held up not a beehive of boxes, but large amphitheatrical galleries mounted in a shallow U, with curious "knees" near the proscenium, at which points the galleries widened to a dimension equal to the stage opening. The open parterre portion

was so narrow that patrons seated at the sides of the U gallery had difficulty in seeing more than a fraction of the stage, unless they straddled their gallery benches. While this arrangement may have given intimacy to what otherwise would have been a cavernous hall, it was not well suited for the viewing of dramatic performances. The attending royalty had little trouble, for their chairs of state were located in the front row, reached by an aisle from a triumphal arch in the center back of the house. There was no provision for boxes—an arrangement peculiar to the German court theatres—and as a consequence, the house plan seems strikingly similar to the one developed by Ledoux much later in the century. The Dresden Opera was rebuilt in 1738 by Andrea Zucchi in a more usual form. The deep galleries were replaced by tiers of boxes in a widened house, and the enlarged parterre was fitted with benches *en amphithéâtre* at the sides, in the manner of the festival theatres.

An example of the U shaped auditorium which still stands is the Manoel Theatre, Valletta, Malta. Built in 1732, the house is a modest one in comparison to some of the elaborate Italian examples, but it is nonetheless effective and beautiful in design. None of the spaces is particularly large or grand; the vestibule and salons are adequate but small; and the boxes are intimate and shallow. The proscenium hardly exists, for the opening is—as is usual with this style—as wide as the theatre interior. The forward edge of the stage is well back within the proscenium opening, limiting the actors to positions within the standing scenes. Open galleries were provided only at the sides of the third tier. The whole may be taken as an example of the Italian style in miniature.

By the 1740's, theatre architectural practice reflected two distinct changes from the previous century. The concept of an evening at the theatre as a social function had generally replaced the idea of going to see a play for its own sake. The opera house—with its political associations and social grandeur—demanded not only a greater scale of magnificence but also many large function rooms. It was not considered enough to enter from a carriage directly into a small foyer and from thence into the performance hall. Foyers were expanded, salons were provided, narrow stairways to the tiers were replaced by triumphal

54

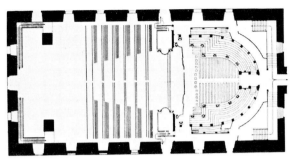

Fig. 73. Plan of the Dresden opera, 1718, by Mauro.

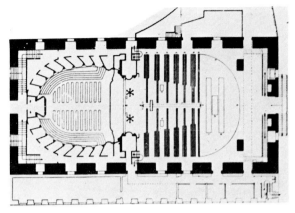

Fig. 74. Plan of the Dresden opera as rebuilt by Zucchi, 1738.

escaliers, and ceilings were raised above the upper gallery level in order to provide the necessary aesthetic volume. The artistic principles of baroque design found expression in the theatre as well as in the palace, for the opera house had become, in many respects, an extension of the royal residence, even when not constructed as a direct part of it. It had been only a few years since the U pattern had been settled, but new ideas were introduced which caused the old plan to be abandoned.

The new auditorium plan was thought out in terms connected with the actor instead of with the perspective scene. Visual and acoustical separation of the actor from the scene was the only way to enable the patron to follow what was going on upon the stage. Sightlines to the stage from the boxes was one item to be considered, and proper reflection and projection of voice and

music was another. The problem was approached first by an evaluation of the auditorium space as a geometric volume. One solution to the question of appropriate configuration was presented in the Comédie Française, where the side walls of the auditorium raked inward at the rear of the house. Another solution—one successful enough to be copied to this day—was to mount the boxes *en escalier*, or in graduated levels or steps down from the back of the house to the stage. Patrons seated in boxes so designed were better able to see over the heads of those in front. This system was inaugurated by Andrea Sighezzi in his Teatro Formigliari of 1640. Although no plan or illustration of this theatre remains, the system was ap-

Fig. 75. Section of the Teatro Reggio, 1736, showing the boxes mounted *en escalier*.

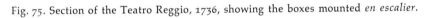

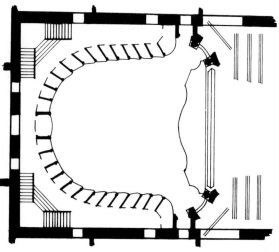

HAMMITZSCH: DER MODERNE THEATERBAU

Fig. 76. Plan of the Teatro Filarmonico, by
F. Galli-Bibiena.

plied in the Teatro Reggio, the Teatro da Mantua
(1735) and the Teatro Filarmonico (1720).

The form selected for the shape of the auditorium altered from the simple U popular in the
seventeenth century to the shape of an egg. In
such plans, the geometry of the auditorium was
related to that of the stage scene. Examples may
be seen in plans of the Teatro di Tor di Nona after
1671, in which the extreme side boxes of the
house are arranged to follow the same line as the
diminishing perspective of the scene. The illusion
of distance was accomplished by having each
succeeding pair of wings placed a little further
onstage, and by having the stage floor raked up
from front to back. In the new eggshaped house
plan, the first several vertical divisions of the
tiers of boxes were laid down on the same line as
the wings of the diminishing scene; the line of
the tiers was then brought slowly closer to the
perpendicular; then raked sharply into a curve

Fig. 77. Plan of the Teatro da Mantua, 1735, by
F. Galli-Bibiena.

HAMMITZSCH: DER MODERNE THEATERBAU

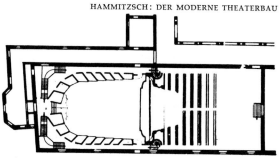

56

at the back. Thus, those seated in the rear portion
of the auditorium had the perspective illusion of
the scene reinforced by the false perspective arrangement of the house. In addition, the interior
stage designs mounted behind the proscenium
frequently echoed the design of the auditorium,
which made the stage setting and the house seem
to be one large room. Another element of the egg
plan was the special arrangement of the forestage. The forward part of the auditorium enclosed the forestage with a proscenium splay
decorated in the older triumphal arch manner, but
which was a part of the auditorium ceiling. This
enabled the actors—and particularly the singers
—to give voice within the acoustical enclosure of
the auditorium and not within the stage house. It
also allowed a separation of presentational and
representational performance that may be gained
in no other way, as modern architects are slowly
rediscovering.

For a time, in the first half of the eighteenth
century, a second house plan was in vogue in

Fig. 78. Plan of the Teatro di Torino, 1740, by
S. M. Sarda.

DUMONT: RECUEIL DES PLANCHES

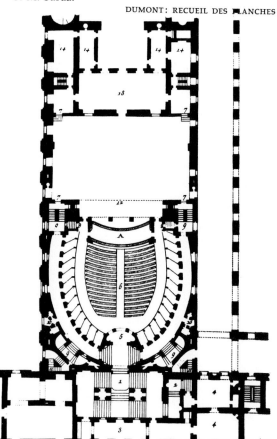

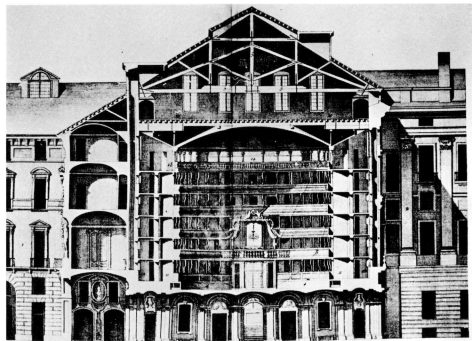

Fig. 79.
Section
to the house,
Teatro di Torino.

DUMONT: RECUEIL DES PLANCHES

Italy, in the shape of a lyre. The pronounced bulge of this shape is a distinct peculiarity and makes sightlines from the side boxes extremely awkward. The aesthetic appeal depended upon the channeling of attention toward the stage by the undulating curve of the house walls. In the extreme examples of this type, such as the Teatro San Benedetto, the auditorium was based upon a circle, connected to the rectangle of the stage house by a narrow neck. While the arrangement aided the voice it almost certainly reinforced the tendency of the actor to play down center for everything except entrances and exits.

Important Italian designs of the first half of the eighteenth century were at Turin (1740), by S. M. Sarda, and at Rome (1732), by Girolamo Teodoli. While the basic plans of the Teatro di Torino and the Teatro d'Argentina differed little from others of the same period, the approaches of the architects to acoustical problems are of continuing interest. In his plan for the Teatro di Torino, Sarda employed an orchestra pit in front of the stage. Unlike those pits which were simple divisions between the house and stage, however, Sarda's accommodation was designed with the new studies in acoustics in mind; it helped to overcome the lack of balance between a large chorus and a small string orchestra. His pit had the usual wooden floor, but below that was a hard-surfaced semi-cylindrical excavation: a sound-reflecting

"dish." This redirected the sound upward, amplifying and resonating the music. In addition, the excavation, or "dish," had openings beneath the stage which made the substage area into a sound

Fig. 80. Plan of the house, Teatro di Torino, showing the geometric forms upon which the auditorium boxes were designed.

DUMONT: RECUEIL DES PLANCHES

57

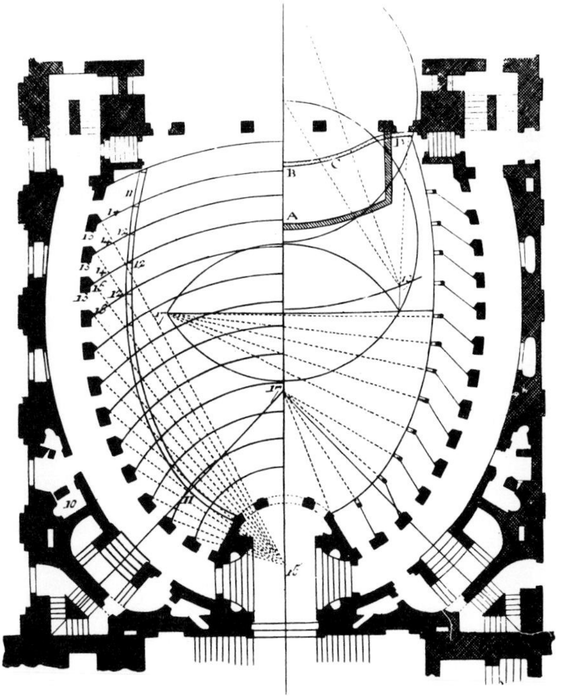

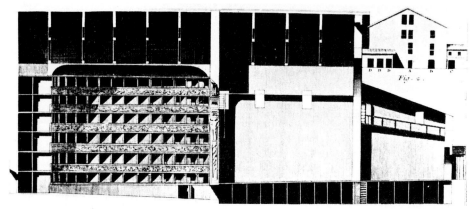

DUMONT: RECUEIL DES PLANCHES

Fig. 81.
Section of the
Teatro d'Argentina,
Rome, 1732,
by Teodoli.

Fig. 82. Plan of the Teatro d'Argentina.

DUMONT: RECUEIL DES PLANCHES

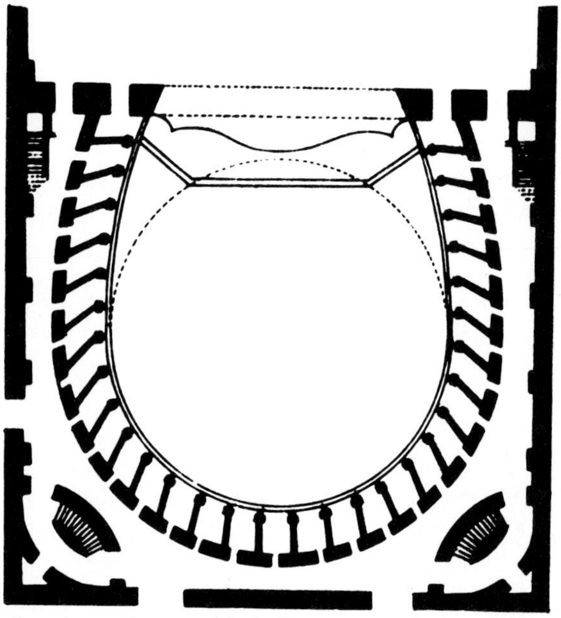

chamber; this enabled the crew and the chorus to hear cues and pitches more clearly. This ingenious development evidently was an effective one, for it was copied throughout the world for more than a century afterward. Experiments in shaped sections of masonry also were made at the Teatro Carlo Felice; an orchestra room was installed behind the stage, the floor of which rested upon a vast semi-cylindrical section of masonry. The Teatro Nuovo, Parma, used an even grander concept. The entire parterre of the theatre rested above an enormous masonry saucer, shallow and elliptical in section, with sound passages entering into it from the orchestra pit. This must have created a sounding board of almost terrifying effectiveness.

58

In the Teatro d'Argentina, Teodoli was faced with a different problem and found a different solution. The Argentina was an extremely large house, with six tiers, built in the latest fashion with no forestage. There it was not the orchestra which needed amplification, but the actors upon the stage. From the back of the house it was difficult to distinguish dialogue. Soon after the theatre was built, a channel was dug under the auditorium floor and filled with water. This highly reflective surface carried sound from the stage and all acoustical problems of the house were eliminated completely.

Italian experiments in house design and with acoustics were in advance of theatre construction principles followed elsewhere. The Burgtheater, Vienna, was constructed in 1741 in an abandoned tennis court, and provided none of the spectacle available in the court theatres and opera houses. It was equipped only with a platform stage of the type long used in Hamburg, Paris, and London.

Fig. 83. Exterior of the Burgtheater, Vienna, 1741.

SCHREYVOGL: DAS BURGTHEATER

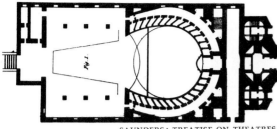

Fig. 84. Plan of the Teatro San Carlo, Naples, 1737.

Considerably different were the theatres in Berlin, Munich, and Bayreuth. A temporary structure had been in use in the palace in Berlin since about 1700, but by 1740 it was decided to build a proper opera house. Freiherr von Knobelsdorf was commissioned to design the building that was intended to be the grandest in Europe. This was begun in 1741, but construction was so slow that the architect was asked to erect a temporary

Fig. 85. Interior of the San Carlo in the nineteenth Century.

Fig. 86. Plan of the Komödiensaal in the Berlin palace, 1742.

house in the palace to serve until the great opera was completed. The temporary Saaltheater was laid down in an ellipse, the wide side facing a modest stage which was fitted with four sets of

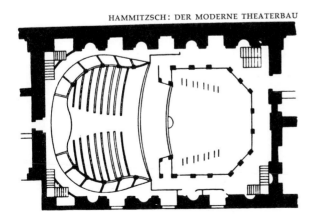

Fig. 87. Plan of the Berlin opera, 1741, by Knobelsdorf.

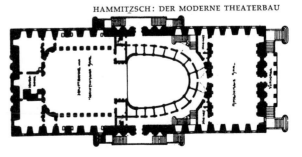

Fig. 88. Exterior of Knobelsdorf's Berlin opera.

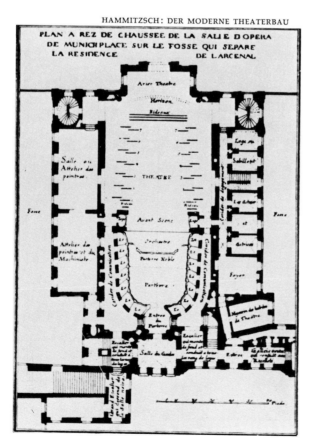

HAMMITZSCH: DER MODERNE THEATERBAU

Fig. 90. Section of the Residenztheater.

wings. When the great opera was completed, it was a grand opera house in every sense of the word. The freestanding building resembled a palace, with monumental stairways leading to pedimented entrance porticos ornamented with engaged columns of a giant order. The auditori-

Fig. 89. Plan of the Residenztheater, Munich, 1752, by Cuvilliés.

HAMMITZSCH: DER MODERNE THEATERBAU

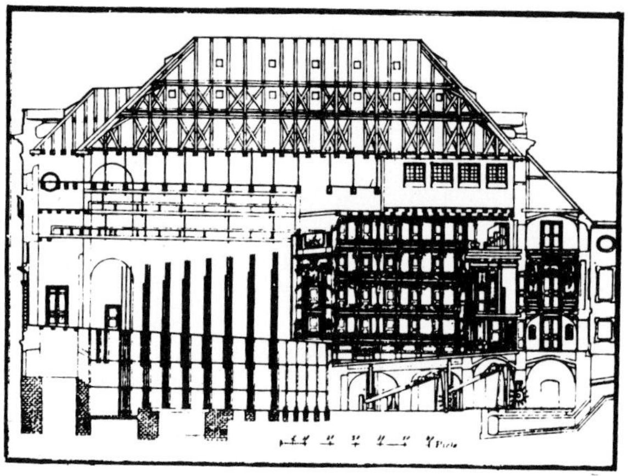

um was laid down in the shape of an egg. The four tiers of large boxes were noted for their commodiousness. The Royal Box opened directly into the Apollo Hall, a reception room as large as the auditorium. The orchestra pit was separated from the house, as usual, but was entered from steps beneath the forestage, an innovation useful to this day. Another modern note was the parking lot for 1000 carriages. The stage was fitted with the usual machines, but in addition, a canal supplied water for two great "water machines," one of which was designed to offer "natural cascades" for special effects.

The Residenztheater in Munich was a court playhouse of limited size but spectacular appointment. It was completed by François de Cuvilliés in 1752. One of its features was a variable-pitch auditorium floor which could be given a rake appropriate for viewing the stage or raised to provide a flat floor for dances or masquerades.

The opera house in Bayreuth, built in 1748 by Joseph St. Pierre and Giuseppi Galli-Bibiena, was a vast structure containing a small auditorium in proportion to its size. The stage was three times as long as the house, and the entire building was covered by a great trussed roof that would do honor to a cathedral.

Although the intimate court theatre, designed to divert the sovereign, would continue to be built, the most ambitious constructions were meant for public audiences. The great court operas of Central Europe were attended not only by the nobility, but also by the rising middle class. In other parts of the continent the public theatres—formerly trestle stages in bare halls—were blossoming into large and elaborate play-

Fig. 91.
Interior of the
Residenztheater.

HAMMITZSCH: DER MODERNE THEATERBAU

houses, fitted with the latest comforts and mechanical devices. The greatest of the civic theatres was yet to come, but by 1750 the future course of theatre architecture was clearly mapped out. The great opera houses, constructed from the purse of the sovereign in Berlin, Bayreuth, Mannheim, Dresden, Naples, Turin, and Paris, were already built for public purposes as well as for entertainment and display. The transition to municipal funding was just one more step.

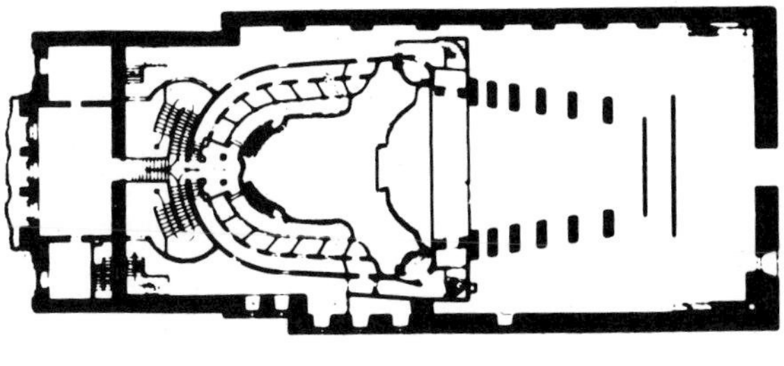

Fig. 93. Interior of the Bayreuth opera.

HAMMITZSCH: DER MODERNE THEATERBAU

Fig. 92. Plan of the Bayreuth opera, 1748, by F. Galli-Bibiena.

HAMMITZSCH: DER MODERNE THEATERBAU

V Second Stage

A common misconception about the early public theatre of box, pit, and gallery is that it was undemocratic in design and purpose. One has visions of the nobility elegantly isolated in plush boxes while the rabble rioted in the pit below. Such a theatre exists only in the minds of historical novelists. The court theatre was attended on a hierarchal basis, but the public theatre was established and operated in order to make money. Places were available at various prices and anyone could sit wherever his purse would allow. The divisions were economic, not social, and while in some instances these may be considered to be one and the same, the reverse was usually the case. The pit, far from being a collection of mere "groundlings," was the meeting place and social hall for bucks of all degrees; certainly it was occasionally riotous, but riots were not distinctly the prerogative of the lower orders. Boxes were for women, groups, families, and for those who did not care to share the crush of the pit. Far from being reserved for the nobility, certain boxes in many an eighteenth century house were the traditional showcases for doxies. Even in the proper Victorian theatre, the marriageable daughter was thrust to the front of the box so that she might be viewed by the opera glasses in the pit. If any portion of the house may be considered to be "lower class" it was the gallery, refuge of footmen, where the cheapness of the seats and the anonymity of the location attracted the less polished patron. From there he had an opportunity to rain down refuse upon the heads of his betters, thus relieving his frustrations and securing the stability of the state.

This style of theatre was developed slowly, over a number of years, and served its patrons well. At almost no other time in the history of the English theatre was the rapport between the stage and the house so complete. The ground plans of theatres from the Restoration to the Regency indicate a change in style which may be puzzling until the context of such designs is reviewed. Productions—as distinct from scripts—became more and more elaborate as this period wore on. With the slow rise in the general level of affluence, and with the increasing urbanization and sophistication of English society, the theatre was required to be both more elaborate and more magnificent. From a simple bare hall, the playhouse grew into a distinct and frequently fanciful construction, expensive to erect and to maintain. The added costs made increased ticket prices mandatory. As prices rose, the populace in general found themselves incapable of affording any but the cheapest seats, and these sold for prices once charged only for the dearest. Since the public theatre was (and is) a business, management had either to provide more cheap seats or to go bankrupt, so the theatres increased in size.

The growth of London made the district which held the Patent houses increasingly hard to reach for those who could not afford coach hire. As the distances grew, and as the Patent houses became larger, more elaborate, and expensive, a need was created which was fulfilled by small, sparely appointed houses which catered to a local clientele of modest income and tastes. The Patent laws forbade these houses the right to produce straight dramatic entertainment, so they were forced to develop a variety program in order to survive. Adaptations from plays became ingenious at those times when the Patent laws were rigidly enforced, and transparent when they were not. At first, plays were performed in pantomime, since spoken drama was the prerogative of the legitimate theatres. In performances at Astley's in the 1790's, the actors carried little scrolls with pertinent exclamations written on them, which they unrolled when pantomime was not sufficient to convey the meaning of the scene. Later (*ca.* 1820), when enforcement of the Patent laws was lax, plays could be performed if songs were included within each act. Thus, the pantomime theatre and the musical-comedy theatre (pretentiously referred to as "English opera") were encouraged to grow by the rigidity of the legal protections afforded the Patent houses.

The theatres of London were closed by order of the Puritan Parliament in 1642, and the edict was enforced until the entry of General Monk into the Capital in 1660, when the theatres were reopened. It was shortly thereafter that the first "new" playhouses that England had seen for two generations were built. The new playhouses were conversions rather than new constructions, however; tennis courts were adapted to become indoor public theatres similar to those the courtiers had seen in Paris. The indefatigable Sir William Davenant—in particular favor with Charles II—was given a renewal of his patent of 1639, and Thomas Killigrew (another courtier) was given a new patent. All other theatres in London were to be closed and their companies suppressed. Protected by royal favor, Davenant and Killigrew moved into their converted tennis courts; Davenant into Lisle's in Lincoln's Inn Fields, and Killigrew into Gibbon's in Vere Street. Lisle's became known as the Theatre of the Duke's Men, or the Duke's Theatre, and Gibbon's became the Theatre of the King's Men, the King's Theatre, later to be referred to as the Theatre Royal.

Davenant introduced a scenic stage into his public theatre, offering a modest imitation of the Italian style, as he had done on the restricted stage of Rutland House for *The Siege of Rhodes*. Killigrew, on the other hand, kept to the native tradition, erecting a simple platform stage of the type familiar to patrons of the former public theatre. Both of the playhouses were extremely small, the Duke's Theatre being approximately 30 by 75 feet in plan, and the King's Theatre only 24 by 64 feet. No identified illustration of the interior of either theatre remains, so speculation on their appearance is dependent upon secondary sources. Conjectural restorations have been at-

WILKENSON: LONDINA ILLUSTRATA

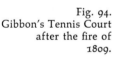

Fig. 94.
Gibbon's Tennis Court
after the fire of
1809.

Fig. 95. Frontispiece to *The Wits*, 1672.

tempted by several theatre historians, and while these are interesting, they must be understood to be only educated guesses. There are several exterior views of the two houses on panoramic maps which show us buildings similar to the French Marais. They were long, narrow, and had high roofs with windows under the eaves.

A print of the interior of a Restoration theatre was introduced as illustration in a 1672 collection of drolls, or comic vignettes, entitled *The Wits*. This depicts an indoor platform stage much like those in the *Roxana* and *Messalina* prints. There is a galleried hall, a trestle stage, and an arras through which entrances were made. While we dare not suppose that this illustration is of Killigrew's King's Theatre, it is an indication that production methods at that time were still similar to those of Shakespeare's day.

Davenant's scenic stage so captured the public taste that Killigrew soon found it necessary to adopt the same methods in order to survive. The Vere Street playhouse was too small for scenes, so he chose to erect a new theatre. Early in 1662 he leased an unused riding yard between Bridges Street and Drury Lane to build upon, and in the spring of the following year the playhouse opened. The identity of the architect of this new theatre remains a mystery, as does its form. From the dimensions of the plot of ground, and from those of the later Drury Lane built on the same

Fig. 96.
Interior of Wren's
Sheldonian Theatre,
Oxford, in 1815.

site, we suspect the building to have been approximately 112 feet long, and because the plot was irregular, the building was 58 feet wide at one end and 59 feet wide at the other. We can only guess at its interior appearance. There is a plan drawn by Sir Christopher Wren of a Serlian-style theatre, but its connection to Killigrew's playhouse is tenuous. More likely than not, it is a rough sketch of projected alterations in the theatre made during the plague season 1665–1666, by which time Wren's interest in architecture was more than academic. The large circular plan of Inigo Jones's old project (left, along with all of Jones's other drawings, in the hands of John Webb) fits well with exterior views found on later panoramic maps, which show a long, narrow hall capped in the center by a large, shallow dome. The possible connections among these bits are interesting to contemplate, but no concrete conclusions can be drawn from them. We do know from secondary sources that Killigrew's stage was fitted with six proscenium doors, and that at least part of the pit was covered by the "cupola" mentioned several times by Pepys. The dome, apparently, was the first erected in England, and it is curious that no mention was made of this intrusion of the Renaissance style into Tudor-style London.

Wren's first recorded attempt at designing an amphitheatre was his Sheldonian Theatre of 1663. This was designed partly as an academic assembly hall and partly as a theatre which could accommodate the annual Oxford "Acts," the frequently riotous mummeries and semitheatricals organized by students. The exterior of the building vaguely suggests a Roman theatre, but the interior view bears a closer resemblance to Continental festival theatres, except without a stage. There were banks of amphitheatrical seating around an open center. The Sheldonian was particularly remarkable for the great span of ceiling without visible support; Wren had no crossbeams large enough to cover the distance between the walls, so he suspended the ceiling from the beams which composed the peak.

Killigrew's new theatre was an instant success, and the Duke's Company was placed under a steady pressure to either equal or surpass it. Land was purchased in Dorset Garden, and a new theatre was built in 1671. This new structure—also attributed to Wren—was built to accommodate more elaborate scenes than even Killigrew's new Bridges Street playhouse could handle. The build-

ing was 57 feet wide and 140 feet long. Only one view of the interior remains to us, and a few descriptions. A French visitor mentioned seven boxes and two galleries, plus a "paradise" above. Illustrations to *The Empress of Morocco* show the scenes of that production as mounted on the stage of the Duke's Theatre. These also show an abbreviated view of the forestage, which may or may not be in accurate scale. The theatre was noted for its gilded elaboration, and the prints show us a highly decorated proscenium, which bears this out. Above the proscenium was a music room, because the English forestage prevented the adoption of the Italian fashion of an orchestra pit.

There are several prints, made at different dates, showing the façade of the Dorset Garden Theatre. The original high tower was later reduced after it was damaged by a storm, and the open, pillared porch was replaced by a series of arches. The four-square construction illustrated in the prints prevents us from drawing conclusions about the interior plan, although it is likely that Davenant was aware of, and influenced by, contemporary Italian practice.

Fig. 97. Scenes from Settle's *Empress of Morocco*, produced at Dorset Garden. Scene 1 (below)

Scene 2 (above)

Scene 4 (above)

Scene 3 (below)

Scene 5 (below)

66

Fig. 98. Facade of the Duke's Theatre, Dorset Garden, 1671.

A fire gutted the Bridges Street Theatre in 1672, and plans were laid at once for the construction of a more modern playhouse. According to tradition, the architect of this building also was Sir Christopher Wren; there remains an architectural section, drawn by Wren, of a theatre which many have accepted as being the Theatre Royal, Drury Lane. While the Bridges Street Theatre had had both a platform and provision for scenes, all accounts indicate that the scene was small and used only for discovery or as a background for the raising and lowering of simple machines. The new plan, which obviously was carefully thought out, proves to be a marriage between the Italian scenic stage and the English platform stage.

Wren's Theatre Royal was not as gaudy as the Duke's Theatre in Dorset Garden, but it seems to have been more felicitously planned. It was to serve as a model for English theatre architects for over a century. Except for the Wren section, the only contemporary view of the interior is a view of the stage given in the frontispiece to *Ariane*, a play produced at the Theatre Royal during the

Fig. 99. Frontispiece to *Ariane*, produced at Drury Lane, 1674.

season of 1674. From available materials and written comments on the appearance of the building, scholars have offered reconstructed ground plans and interior views. While details of these differ, the general form—dictated by the Wren section and the riding yard site plan—is accurate enough to give us for the first time a notion of the interior of an English public theatre. From the plan of the building we may judge both its adaptability to contemporary drama and the relationship of the scenic elements to production. As in the earlier Elizabethan houses, the deep platform stage was thrust far out into the enclosure of the auditorium, placing the actor amid, rather than before, the audience. The scene was a simplified version of what was current in Italy much earlier, and it served either as an illusionistic or iconographic background, as required. Thus, the actors had the benefit of a suggestion of place, and the

Fig. 100. A restored groundplan of Wren's Drury Lane by Bruce A. Koenig.

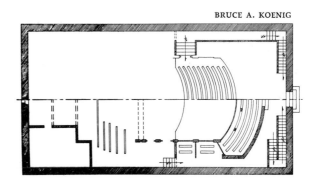

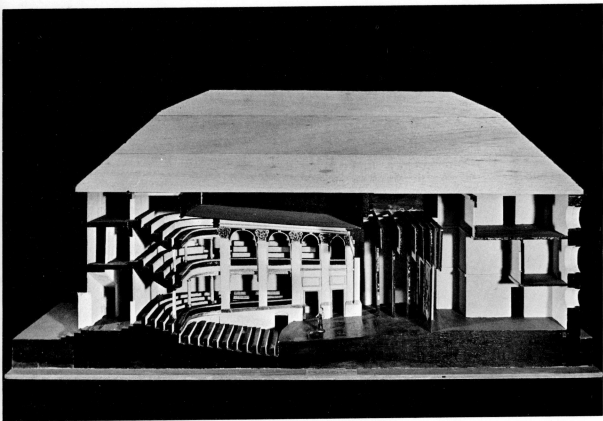

Fig. 101.
Model of the
Theatre
Royal,
Drury Lane,
based upon the
Wren
section,
by Edward A.
Langhans.

EDWARD A. LANGHANS. PHOTO BY STAN RIVERA

freedom of an uncluttered acting platform; and they could also be discovered within the scene, and surrounded by such scenic illusion as was necessary. Unlike the Italian theatres, in which the edge of the stage was placed close to the proscenium, confining the actor within the represented location, the English playhouse allowed a maximum of flexibility and focused attention upon the performer instead of upon his surroundings.

When we consider scenery in this context, we must remember that the painted scene included all that was not actually used by the actors. Furniture was painted on wings and backshutters unless the scene called for practical pieces, which were discovered when the shutters drew open or were simply "thrust out" as had been done in the public theatre since time immemorial. This—coupled with the inevitable laying of the green baize cloth in the act which included a stage death —effectively prevented any consideration of the stage and its furnishings as "real" in the modern sense.

The addition of side boxes to Drury Lane and Dorset Garden might be thought a concession to continental tastes. If one's theatre is constructed on a restricted site, however, an increase in receipts may be obtained only by increasing seating capacity. Side boxes may not be desirable, but their presence insures the maximum use of space for patrons, and fixed prices are not as irritating to the public if less desirable locations are made available at a smaller cost.

The Duke's Theatre in Dorset Garden was a longer building than the Theatre Royal, and apparently some of the additional length was incorporated within the auditorium. This gave, we believe, a distant and tunnel-like impression of the stage. The Duke's platform stage, furthermore, was not enclosed at either side by boxes for patrons, but by architectonic features which echoed the decorated proscenium. The audience, therefore, was seated before a large platform rather than around it, and was remote from the scene. There were two aesthetic separations: the forward edge of the platform with the doors at the sides, and the actual proscenium opening. The closed-in feeling must have been compounded by the great overhanging music room. When the two theatrical companies were united in 1682, it

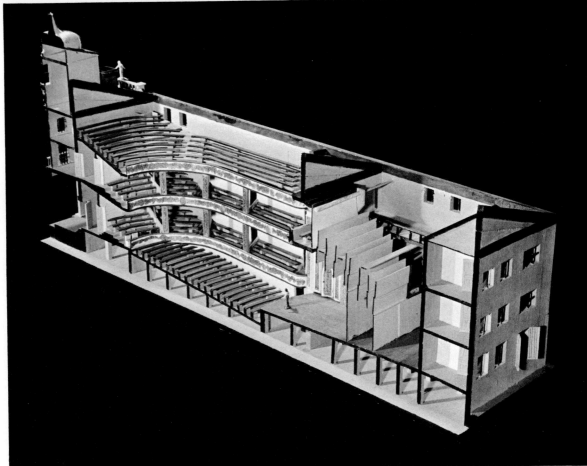

Fig. 102.
Model of a
conjectoral
restoration
of Dorset Garden
by Edward A.
Langhans.

is no wonder that they chose to restrict their play-ing to Drury Lane. It was designed for the best relationship between actor and audience, while Dorset Garden seems to have been an overdressed display piece, formal and remote.

The impact of the design of Drury Lane was great: Dorset Garden was abandoned and later theatres were based upon Wren's new plan. Covent Garden had an almost identical arrange-ment and design, and the company resident in the Queen's Theatre, Haymarket, nearly succeeded in altering Vanbrugh's plan to make it identical with Drury Lane. The Wren plan enabled actors to adapt from older playing techniques instead of abandoning them, yet was flexible enough to encourage the introduction of new styles. We hear little to indicate changes in acting or pro-duction styles before the construction of Drury Lane, but a great deal after. Each modification was thought to be an improvement, and each suc-ceeding generation adapted itself to the newer forms with increasing ease and authority, but as long as Drury Lane stood, the iconographic stage was not entirely abandoned; its traditions, in fact, were kept alive in the English provincial

theatre almost to the present day.

Production demands of Restoration plays dif-fered little from those of Shakespeare's time. Doors were in regular use, representing what-ever the characters referred to them as being; multiple doors and open gallery "windows" seem to have been introduced into the Bridges Street Theatre, allowing a difference in degree of com-plexity if not in kind, since the proscenium of the theatre is thought to have been too small to ac-commodate more than an elaborated discovery.

The only significant architectural development in the English theatre between 1674 and 1732 was the Queen's Theatre, Haymarket, referred to also as Vanbrugh's Opera House. Unlike Sir Christopher Wren, who united continental tra-dition with native practices, Vanbrugh was concerned solely with foreign methods. Disagree-ments with the management of Drury Lane led Thomas Betterton and a group of fellow actors to leave the Theatre Royal in 1695 and reopen the old theatre in Lincoln's Inn Fields. This proved to be unsatisfactory, so Betterton—in conjunction with the dramatist-architect John Vanbrugh—planned a new theatre to be constructed in the

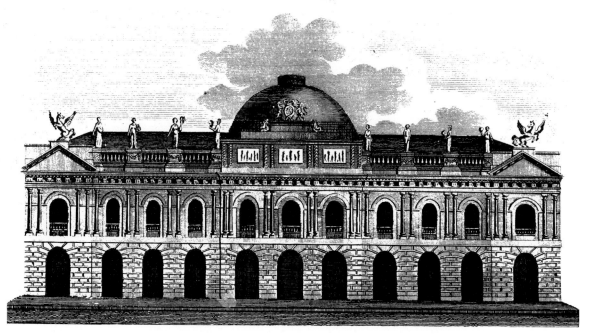

Fig. 103. Facade of the Queen's Theatre, Haymarket, 1705, by Vanbrugh. Presumably this is engraved after the architect's elevation.

Fig. 104. Interior of the Queen's Theatre.

Fig. 105. Portion of the Haymarket view from Kip's *Aerial Views of London*, showing the Queen's Theatre, 1710.

HUGH PHILLIPS: MID-GEORGIAN LONDON

Haymarket. It was to be the largest and most splendidly appointed playhouse in England. The form and value of this building, erected in 1705, was long in doubt, but recent studies have resolved some of the mystery about its design. The structure was unlike that of any previous English theatre, or of any continental one, for that matter. It was designed to be a monument, in the manner of the great court theatres, with a palatial exterior and an awe-inspiring interior. The auditorium was built with the usual (for England) three tiers, but these were subdivided in the Italian fashion rather than being simple open galleries as at Dorset Garden and Drury Lane, and an additional open top gallery was included at the rear of the house. The interior was dominated by a vast Palladian dome. The stage was divided into the usual scenic and forestage areas, but the apron was extremely deep and flanked by three pairs of great corinthian columns which were topped by a vast semielliptical arch. The exterior was intended to have an arcaded and rusticated lower storey plus a pedimented and statue-capped upper one, set off with engaged columns and balustrades. The whole was to be pulled together into a single monumental unit by the dome. While the interior seems to have been completed as designed, a shortage of funds prevented the development of the exterior. As constructed, the roof was high and gabled, not hipped, much

of the elaboration was omitted, and we suspect the dome to have been built within the peak of the roof and not to have been apparent from the exterior.

The Queen's Theatre was designed with special provision for the comfort of the audience, something the other London theatres lacked. Instead of the tiny foyer of Drury Lane, Vanbrugh included a large lobby for box patrons within his house, and soon after 1705 added another large entrance foyer and a great salon. For the first time patrons were not required to go to their seats at once or else to stand out in the weather; they had the opportunity of mingling with other patrons before (and after) performance, in accordance with the emerging continental practice. Fireplaces were provided in the salon so patrons could dry out or get the chill off before going to their seats, an innovation in England which the patrons welcomed. The Queen's Theatre was an early attempt to provide the conveniences we take so much for granted in modern theatre design.

Unfortunately, the reactions of patrons and playgoers were mixed. The magnificence of the interior stunned all who viewed it, but it also tended to overshadow the productions mounted on the stage. The aging actors, and the tacky scenes and costumes they had brought with them from Lincoln's Inn Fields, showed to a decided disadvantage against the architectural pomp, and at least one account complained of the undulations of sound caused by the dome. Within four years, major alterations were carried out in an attempt to make the structure more suitable and to resemble Drury Lane as much a possible. The dome was covered over (or removed if indeed it was an exterior feature), the ceiling lowered, the arch over the forestage flattened and reduced with heavy drapery, and additional boxes were built along the side walls to give the interior a rectangular rather than circular form. The intimacy of the hall was improved, but at the expense of the monumentality of the structure. The Queen's Theatre was meant to be England's first great opera house, but England was not yet ready for such architectural extravagance.

Although architects were called upon to express their expertise in theatre forms, the lowly builder was still on the scene, as he had been since earliest times. In 1720 a builder by the name of Potter, seeking to capitalize upon the scarcity of playing spaces within the city, undertook the construction of a playhouse in the Haymarket. His small theatre was erected off the street, to the rear of a row of shops, on much the same type of site used by Vanbrugh for his adjacent opera house. This new theatre, however, was an extremely modest enterprise, a small rectangular hall with but one gallery and no accommodations for audience other than the seats in the house. This was the first of a type of small, speculative playhouse that was to be constructed in London with increasing frequency as the century wore on. The elaboration of the Patent houses necessitated increased prices, and the new smaller houses provided centers of entertainment for those not wishing—or unable to afford—to pay the tariffs in the Patent theatres. The Little Theatre in the Haymarket, as it came to be called, suffered the trials of a non-Patent house, but in the main was a successful endeavor. It was enlarged in 1766 and rebuilt on a lavish scale in the following century.

The old Lincoln's Inn Fields playhouse was partially reconstructed and entirely refurbished by James Shepherd for Christopher Rich, who had been forced out of Drury Lane. We have little precise information about the variations made in Lincoln's Inn Fields over the years, except that it boasted six proscenium doors in its final arrangement. The original small tennis court was altered by Betterton, as mentioned, but this change is

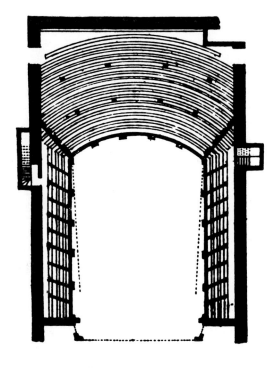

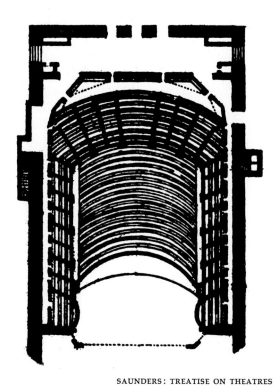

SAUNDERS: TREATISE ON THEATRES

Fig. 106. Floor plan and gallery plan of the Theatre Royal, Covent Garden, 1732, by Shepard.

thought to have included little more than new decorations. Shepherd's third theatre, on the other hand, appears to have been a complete reconstruction. In the nineteenth century, the old theatre was used as a warehouse, and engravings of it show us a large, hip roofed structure considerably different from any shown in the early woodcuts of the tennis court. Whether the additional size means an entirely new building was constructed, or whether it implies only tacked-on ancillary spaces were added, is not clear. In any event, the building was not large enough to provide the income necessary to support a full company of players. Christopher Rich —again with Shepherd—built a new and more elaborate theatre in Covent Garden. While historically this was an important structure, architecturally it was not. The lesson of Vanbrugh's opera house had been well learned. The new Covent Garden Theatre was constructed in imitation of Drury Lane, but with a few "improvements." In the Theatre Royal, increasing expenses had made the seating capacity insufficient to cover the cost of production and to pay a sufficient return on the investments of the patentees. Covent Garden, therefore, was constructed on a larger scale. Its width of 56 feet was almost the same as Drury Lane, but the auditorium measured 86 feet from the proscenium to the back of the house, a considerable difference from Drury Lane's 48 feet. The majority of the additional space was taken up by deep galleries. The second gallery, for example, had sixteen rows of benches, in comparison to Drury Lane's four. The apron stage was sharply reduced, in the continental fashion, in order to allow more benches in the pit. Instead of having stage doors well down toward the edge of the apron—doors with boxes above—Covent Garden had large double boxes at stage level, and stage doors well upstage, set at an angle for better viewing.

The extra depth of the house caused difficulties at once. Those patrons seated at the rear of the deep galleries could barely hear; the galleries at the sides had low ceilings and were cramped; and patrons in the back rows could hear little and see less. The situation was recognized as deplorable but remained uncorrected until 1784. In other respects Covent Garden was superior to Drury Lane. Audience accommodations in the front of the house were better, and included a lobby that, though by no means as commodious as that of the

Fig. 107. The stage of Covent Garden in 1732.

Queen's (now King's) Theatre, was still larger than that afforded by the Theatre Royal. Most important of all was the fact that Covent Garden could pay its way because of its large capacity. The larger stage and greater receipts enabled the management to mount more lavish productions than was possible on the stage of Drury Lane, and the Theatre Royal suffered proportionately until it also was increased in size in 1794.

David Garrick promoted frequent attempts to increase the capacity of the Theatre Royal. Earlier, the deep semicircular apron had been cut back by Christopher Rich in order to expand the pit. Garrick increased the depth of the galleries. The bother of patrons seated directly upon the stage could be eliminated only by the provision of comfortable accommodations within the house. This was achieved by moving the pit benches around. One row was removed and the extra

Fig. 108. The stage of Covent Garden in 1763.

space used to add an extension to the first gallery, within which two rows were fitted. This move was soon followed by an extension added to the second gallery, and in 1775 by a complete re-working of the interior by the brothers Adam. The Wren design which had been modified previously was now changed beyond all recognition. Adam added a new facade which allowed additional space for house purposes. In the interior, the galleries were pushed back to the old exterior wall, a move which doubled the number of rows available. Wren's great pilasters were replaced with narrow pillars, enabling patrons in the side boxes to see more of the stage, and making it possible to place more seats in those locations. The ceiling was raised and a third tier was added to the sides. In spite of the shortening of the apron, the position of the actors was still forward among the patrons.

It is the Adam version of Drury Lane which is so frequently reproduced, because the brothers were so pleased with the results of their work that they had an engraving made of it. Unfortunately, the scale of the engraving was changed in order to make the house seem monumental, a trick architects still use in order to give stature to their work. Other changes of a less important nature were made subsequently—some by William Capon, the theatre's scenic designer—and these were recorded in a sketch by Capon made just previous to the demolition of the building in 1791. It is this drawing which gives us a more realistic view of the interior, and which enables us to judge the feeling of the house.

Fig. 109. Engraving of a sketch by William Capon of the interior of Drury Lane before its demolition in 1791.

Fig. 110. Interior of the Little Theatre in the Haymarket, as remodeled by Foote, 1766.

Potter's "Little Theatre in the Hay" prospered, and was enlarged in 1766 by the actor Foote. The enlargement was accomplished by moving through adjacent walls into neighboring buildings; a house in Little Suffolk Street was incorporated; two shops in Haymarket were gutted to form an entrance lobby, in front of which a portico was constructed to provide protection from the weather for those alighting from carriages; corridors and entrance doors were enlarged; and a second gallery was added. The improvements were dignified by the appellation "Theatre Royal," for Foote had received a Royal Patent which entitled him to produce legitimate drama during the summer. It is the Little Theatre of 1766 that we see illustrated in engravings; it

Fig. 111. Stage of the Little Theatre in the Haymarket in 1795.

74

Fig. 112. Interior of Sadler's Wells in 1815, showing the new water tank used for aquatic spectacle.

was a modest affair, and one may only guess at the humble appearance before the enlargement.

The proliferation of London playhouses began in 1765, when the old wooden "music house" was replaced by a new theatre at Sadler's Wells. The modest structure was a successful speculation, and in 1778 the entire interior was rebuilt. A higher ceiling was made in order to allow a greater elevation to the pit, and later a large tank for spectacular acquatic effects was installed under the fully trapped stage. In 1821 the building again was altered throughout, and the roof was raised so the capacity could be increased to 2,200.

There was also a market for theatricals other than those produced in the legitimate houses, and theatre as a business venture came to be sought by enterprising men. In 1770, James Wyatt designed an elaborate casino-like public gathering place, the Pantheon, to which a theatre was added. This served a short life as a playhouse, and then was fitted up as an opera house in 1788. The Pantheon was dogged by disaster. In 1792 it burned in a spectacular blaze seen by the architect as he drove back to London from the country. It was rebuilt on speculation as an exhibition hall. This failed, and it was rebuilt (once more on wild speculation) as an opera house based on La Scala Milan, with 171 boxes. This arrangement had a stage 56 feet wide and 90 feet deep. The opera house venture collapsed, and the theatre was stripped to the walls to pay accumulated debts.

A somewhat different fate awaited another speculative venture, Astley's Amphitheatre. Originally the enterprise was little more than a sawdust ring in the open air with some covered

Fig. 113.
Interior and stage
of the Pantheon
after its conversion
to an opera house
in 1795.

WILKENSON: LONDINA ILLUSTRATA

benches at one side. As business improved because of the novelty of performing horses and acrobats, the ring was enclosed by a rambling wooden building, tacked together, one suspects, between performances. In 1780, a more formal house of some pretension was built on the basis of the experience gained. This peculiarity was basically an ordinary galleried playhouse, but with a major section of the pit made into a circular riding ring. Since the program of the speculative, "illegitimate" house could not rest on full-length plays, the main show had to be built around other diversions. In order to capitalize upon the novelty of horses (and to avoid prosecu-

tion), Astley's was designed for equestrian and acrobatic acts, as well as for spectacularly staged scenes from plays in which horses could be employed. The first part of the evening was devoted to stage performances of the more pedestrian sort, and tickets for the pit were sold on a half-price basis. When the dramatic portion of the entertainment was concluded, the half-price patrons left, their benches were removed, and the ring was opened for the horse acts. Hippodrama, as the equestrian entertainment was grandly called, was so successful and appealed to such divergent tastes that Astley's later received the appellation Royal Amphitheatre, and received

Fig. 114. Interior and
front of Astley's
Amphitheatre.

the ultimate accolade of being imitated at home and abroad.

The domestic imitation did not fare as well. The Royal Circus was built in 1782 for equestrian and dramatic entertainments, and in 1805 was redesigned by Cabanal on a more elaborate scale. In 1809, however, the horse ring was covered over and added to the regular pit, and the theatre opened under new management as The Surrey.

In 1784 Covent Garden was finally altered by Henry Holland, in an effort to eliminate some of the glaring faults of the original. The deep galleries were cut back, improving sightlines from them, and the additional space was given over to pit seating; the stage apron was built farther into the house in an effort to improve audibility; and the growing affectations of the audience were served by the division of the first gallery into

Fig. 115.
Interior of Astley's
Amphitheatre, 1843,
from the
London Illustrated News.

HARVARD THEATRE COLLECTION

plush boxes. In 1791 a more complete alteration was undertaken, but nothing short of a complete reconstruction could make the house satisfactory. In 1792 the interior was almost entirely rebuilt, again by Holland. The old rectangular hall was altered to a modified lyre; the number of pit benches was increased from 17 to 20; the galleries were reduced in depth, the second gallery from 16 rows to 14; the number of tiers was increased from three to four, and the top gallery was carried around to the sides in divided boxes; an enlarged orchestra pit was provided, with a semicylindrical resonating chamber beneath the floor; the narrow proscenium was widened, and the doors were moved into a straight line upstage of the boxes located on the apron. In 1794 the ceiling was modified and the proscenium made higher to improve sightlines from the upper gallery, whose patrons had expressed displeasure at not being able to see the scenes on the stage. At Covent Garden, as at Drury Lane, the trend was away from sparsely appointed public accommodation toward a new and more comfortable (although more expensive and exclusive) luxury

WILKENSON: LONDINA ILLUSTRATA

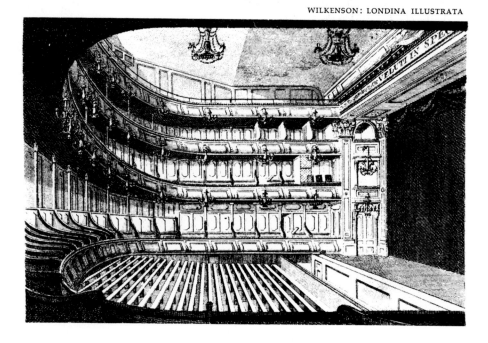

Fig. 117.
Interior of Holland's
Covent Garden in
1807.

Fig. 118. Stage of Holland's Covent Garden in 1804.

Fig. 120. Interior of the Sans Pareil Theatre, London, 1806, showing extended pit benches.

Fig. 119. Interior of the Royalty Theatre.

Fig. 121. Interior of Vanbrugh's Haymarket opera ca. 1780, after alterations by Adam.

house. The pressure of new theatre construction and competition left the Patent theatre managers with little choice.

Other constructions followed in rapid succession. The Royalty Theatre was designed by John Wilmot in 1785, the East London Theatre by Cornelius Dixon in 1787. In 1790 an old concert hall, called the Lyceum, was replaced by the pretentiously titled Theatre Royal English Opera House which was devoted to music, dancing, and variety acts. Even though a new and more elaborate version was designed by Samuel Beazley in 1816, the fortunes of this playhouse fell. Another minor theatre was the Adelphi, erected in 1802 and rebuilt in 1806 as the Sans Pareil, designed

especially for "mechanical and optical entertainments." The Sans Pareil was not fitted with boxes at the pit level; instead, the pit extended from one side of the house to the other in the same manner as the Amsterdam Schouwburg, a fashion that was to be followed subsequently. In this system, for the first time, the old U pattern was abandoned on the main floor, and all patrons faced front.

Vanbrugh's opera house, referred to as the King's Theatre after the accession of George I, remained unchanged after the alterations of 1709 until it, too, was redesigned by the brothers

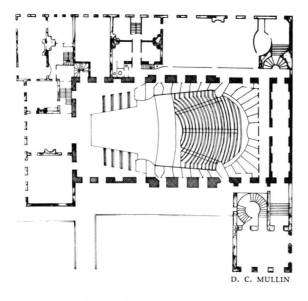

D. C. MULLIN

Fig. 122. Plan of the Haymarket opera *ca.* 1782, after the original in the Soane Museum.

Adam in 1778. Unlike the brothers' successful work at Drury Lane, this was almost universally condemned. Unfortunately, we cannot substantiate the contemporary opinions, because few views remain which can be identified as the Adam reconstruction. A ground plan might resemble that of Covent Garden and Drury Lane, as the house was later described as being altered to make it a circular room. A third reconstruction was made in 1782 by Michael Novosielski, the opera's resident designer. This time the interior was given an Italian treatment, with the auditorium laid down in the horseshoe shape favored abroad. This reconstruction was a happy one and all the critics were content. They were not to remain so for long, however, for the building was completely destroyed by fire in 1789. A newer and more spectacular structure was planned at once, again under the direction of Novosielski.

Fig. 123. Interior of Novosielski's Haymarket opera in 1805.

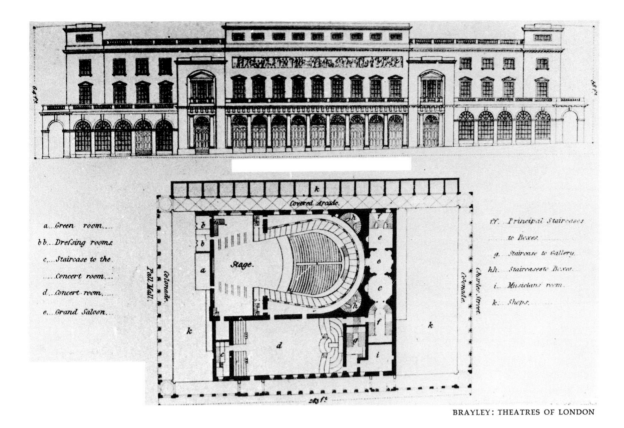

a. Green room.
bb. Drefsing rooms.
c. Staircase to the
   Concert room.
d. Concert room.
e. Grand Saloon.

rr. Principal Staircases
   to Boxes.
g. Staircase to Gallery.
hh. Staircases to Boxes.
i. Musicians room.
k. Shops.

BRAYLEY: THEATRES OF LONDON

Fig. 124. Facade and plan of Novosielski's Haymarket opera.

Fig. 125. Section through auditorium and grand saloon of Novosielski's Haymarket opera.

HARVARD THEATRE COLLECTION

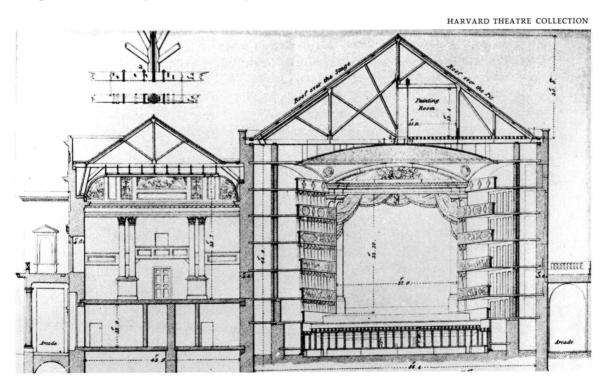

81

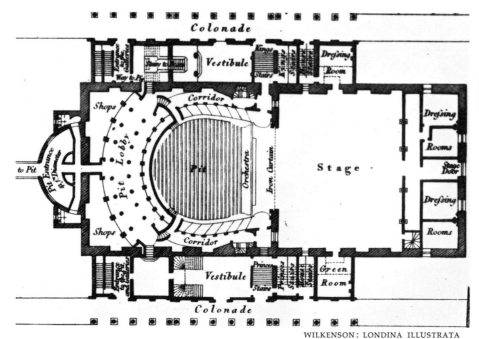

Fig. 126.
Plan of Holland's
Drury Lane, 1794.

This time the entire block within which the house was located was designed as a monumental unit, with those portions not actually a part of the opera house made up into shops and let. This method of giving added dimension and monumentality to the building, as well as increasing revenue, was adopted later by both Smirke and Wyatt. The opera house was altered once more in 1818, and then ran slowly down hill until it burned once more in 1867.

In 1791, Wren's old Drury Lane was considered unfit and condemned. Henry Holland was commissioned to design a new Theatre Royal, which opened in 1794. It was a hastily built structure with a capacity of 3,600, a vast number at the time. The increased size was provided so that receipts could cover the cost of production, as well as provide a comfortable return for the Patentees. The actors were not consulted, however, nor were they prepared for what they found. The hall was much too large for the acting style and stage business that had developed over the previous centuries; acting had to be changed into bellowing, and he who could bellow loudest was most favored. There were bitter complaints but nothing could be done: the house was built and much had been spent on lavish appointments. The structure was of brick, raised on a stone

Fig. 128. Interior of Holland's Drury Lane in 1794.

Fig. 127. Front of Holland's Drury Lane.

Fig. 129.
Interior of Smirke's
Covent Garden in 1810.

foundation, but the entire interior was of wood in order to save money. To prevent the building from flaring up at the first overturned candle, a great cast iron fire curtain was installed, and large tanks filled with water were placed in the attics for emergency use. Naturally, the house burned down, for by 1809 the iron curtain had rusted into uselessness and had been removed, and the water tanks had long since sprung leaks and run dry. It was later commented that if the house had not burned, it would have tumbled down anyway because of the shoddy construction.

The fire in Drury Lane was not the only catastrophe of the season. Five months previously, one of the most spectacular blazes of the century destroyed Covent Garden completely, leaving not a wrack behind. In former years when the Patent houses had been closed for one reason or another, the companies had moved to Lincoln's Inn Fields, temporarily making do under the most primitive conditions until they could return to their refurbished or rebuilt quarters. By 1809, however, the companies could move into any of the numerous speculative houses with barely an interruption. The Covent Garden company, for example, opened in the Haymarket until their house was rebuilt. While the companies were waiting, yet another new playhouse was added to the London scene, the Regency. Originally it had been constructed to be a concert hall in 1792, but was reconstructed into a playhouse of no particular distinction in 1810.

Fig. 130.
Section of Smirke's
Covent Garden.

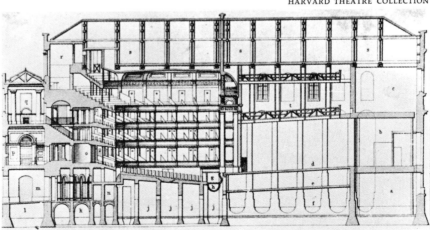

Fig 131. Exterior of Smirke's Covent Garden.

The new Covent Garden was designed by Robert Smirke in the neoclassic style favored by Regency taste. It was considered pretentious by many; certainly it was a vast and magnificent structure, whose cost of 150,000 pounds staggered the contemporary public. Stone vaulting instead of wooden construction helped elevate the cost, but after the fires of the past this expense was thought necessary. The columned portico proscenium echoed the one used a century before by Vanbrugh for his Queen's Theatre. It was 42 feet wide, a triumphal arch within which the actors felt overawed. The new building was de-

signed to provide the commodious and comfortable facilities long requested by the audiences. The distance between seats was increased; the boxes were enlarged; the third tier was given over entirely to luxury boxes which boasted high barriers, chairs, and private retiring rooms; function rooms were both larger and more numerous; and the Grand Saloon was 86 feet long and had coffee rooms at either end. While these were noticeable improvements, the new Covent Garden was compared unfavorably with Drury Lane, for which a more felicitous choice of architect was made in Benjamin Wyatt. Wyatt designed the new The-

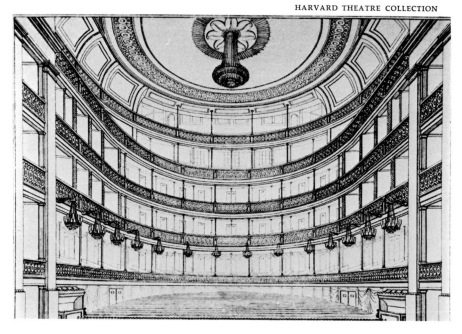

Fig. 132.
View of the house,
Smirke's
Covent Garden.

Fig. 133.
Interior of the
Royal Coburg
(later the Old Vic).

atre Royal in a manner so beautifully proportioned and so elegantly appointed that it charmed
and impressed all who saw it. Holland's cavernous hall was not repeated—the new auditorium
was of a more comfortable dimension, seating
2,600. The proscenium, however, like that of
Covent Garden, was a magnificent triumphal arch
so grand that audiences took exception to it and
actors complained. Wyatt did not include stage
doors, either, and the actors rebelled against this
attempt to thrust them back behind the proscenium. The first of many modifications was the
reinstatement of the honoured proscenium door
and its attendant window above.

Fig. 134.
Front of the Theatre
Royal, Haymarket,
1821, by Nash, showing
the front of the old
Little Theatre
next door.

Fig. 135.
Interior and plan of Nash's
Theatre Royal, Haymarket,
on opening night, 1821.

WILKENSON: LONDINA ILLUSTRATA

With the construction of the new Patent houses the boom in English theatre construction began to slow down. It was not yet ended, however; the Royal Coburg was built in 1818, to be renamed the Royal Victoria in 1833, and it is with us today under the name Old Vic. In 1821 Potter's Little Theatre in the Hay was abandoned in favor of the elegant new playhouse which had been constructed next door. Designed by that most glittering of all Regency architects, John Nash, this house was a considerable improvement over the old Little Theatre. It was not only larger, but also more comfortable and better appointed. Unlike the horseshoe designs of the new Patent houses, however, the new Haymarket retained the old rectangular form.

A remarkable change had come over the English theatre in a relatively short time. Not only was the attitude and philosophy of management altered, but also the playhouses were changed almost beyond recognition. One cannot even compare the playhouses and production techniques of the Restoration with those of the 1820's. Continental ideas and values had been adopted wholesale, although the peculiarly English notion of the precedence of actor over scenery still managed to prevail. What did not change was the belief of the audience that theatres were built for their convenience and pleasure, and that attending a play was a right, not a privilege. Patrons were vocal about plays, productions, and even about prices and policies, as the Old Price riots proved. The time had not yet come when management could afford to cater to a select group and say "Public be damned."

VI Revels and Revolution

The continental picture was considerably different in 1750 from what it had been in 1650. There were now theatres throughout Europe. The majority were either elaborated court theatres or simple trestle stages for public entertainment, but the movement toward commodious public playhouses had begun. Centers like Venice, Paris, and Amsterdam had pretentious public theatres, but patrons in cities outside the charmed circle of national capitals had to be content either with strolling players, working from the backs of wagons, or with temporary installations in rented halls. While theatre had a life among the people from time immemorial, permanent theatre architecture did not. It took the influence of the courts to provide the example of buildings constructed specifically as theatres, and eventually outlying districts found themselves affluent enough to erect local monuments to culture and civic pride. The theatres of Lyon, Metz, and Montpellier were among the first in France to be built free standing, and to be given locations where splendid architectural effects might be exploited. Several other playhouses of the same type were built in the 1750's, and by the end of the eighteenth century hardly a provincial city in Europe did not have its opera house and its "grand" public theatre. Only in large cities with an appropriate financial base were there small, speculative private developments catering to the public taste. The commercial ventures we note in Venice, Paris, Vienna, and Amsterdam, were not emulated elsewhere on the continent to any extent until the nineteenth century.

The design of theatre spaces appropriate for comfortable public accommodation had received short shrift during the first stages of the development of the modern playhouse. The initial problem had been the accommodation of large numbers of people in an arrangement that would allow stage action to be seen and the voice to be heard. This was further complicated, in the court theatres and opera houses, by the requirements of state protocol and ceremonial. After the initial experiments had evolved into a generally accepted pattern, however, improvements were seen to be necessary. New concepts and new methods to implement them abounded. In an era of transportation by horse on wretched roads, the new ideas circulated with startling rapidity. Inspiration in Italian design flourished, but Italian architects no longer travelled over Europe with the abandon of earlier times. Instead, architects from foreign countries came to Italy to study and to learn, and then went home to build variants of what they had seen in Italian cities.

These architects had seen the establishment of a new form. The older style was typified in the interior designs of the Teatro d'Argentina and the Teatro San Carlo which were based upon the circle. At the diameter, the sides were flattened into shallower arcs as they approached the proscenium, giving the familiar horseshoe shape. In the Argentina the circle touched the front of the

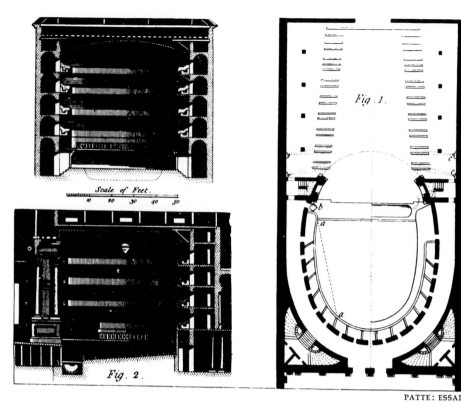

Fig. 136.
Sections and plans
of an ideal theatre
by Pierre Patte,
1782.

PATTE: ESSAI

apron. In the San Carlo it overlapped the apron. In both instances the circle shape fell short of the proscenium opening, as it did in other houses based upon the same figure. In 1740, however, S. M. Sarda took a new approach to interior design which proved to be influential. In the Teatro di Torino, built within the palace, the plan was based on an ellipse—two overlapping circles with the center of the second located on the circumference of the first—whose form protruded well past the apron and into the proscenium. The entire interior was governed by carefully thought out geometrics, including the ceiling height and shape, the angles of the partitions of the boxes, and the shape and height of the proscenium opening. Although the architect's reasoning has not come down to us, the principle was expounded upon in 1782 by Pierre Patte, whose illustrations to his *Essai sur l'Architecture* show us what Sarda and his followers intended. The solid box fronts, the ceiling, and the coves were all intended to reflect sound to the back of the house instead of allowing it to bounce around aimlessly. The principle seemed to operate satisfactorily because it was imitated regularly. The satisfaction was not complete, however, because in spite of the reflection from elliptically formed surfaces, those seated at the rear could not hear as well as those

at the sides. This was inevitable in a house considerably longer than it was wide, but the shape—however worked into geometric figures—was required by the intended capacity. The ellipse continued to be favored for large-capacity opera houses, followed closely by the circle-horseshoe. For smaller theatres other solutions had to be found. Architects more concerned with late baroque fashion than with acoustics—like the Bibienas—designed theatres of glittering grandeur without reference to acoustical studies. Antonio Bibiena, for example, began the Teatro Communale in Bologna in 1756 with a ground-plan almost identical with that of the Cuvillies-theater in Munich, and of stone and brick throughout. While this certainly made the building fire-resistant, and while the seats were nicely arranged for viewing the elaborate scenery favored by the architect, it was a disastrous acoustical misfit. Torino, on the other hand, was so carefully planned that a wooden ceiling was installed, with a resonating chamber above it, in order to achieve acoustical balance. Bibiena was not concerned with such niceties, and patrons of his theatre paid the price.

It is not always easy to deduce influences upon changes in architectural styles. Usually one assumes that innovations became known through

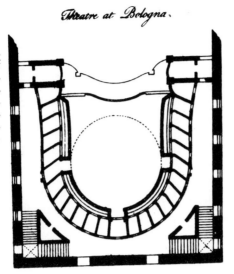

Theatre at Bologna.

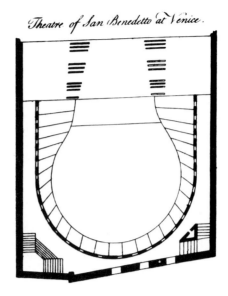

Theatre of San Benedetto at Venice.

Fig. 137.
Comparative plans of
the Teatro Communale,
Bologna,
the San Benedetto,
Venice,
the Teatro d'Imola,
and La Scala, Milan.

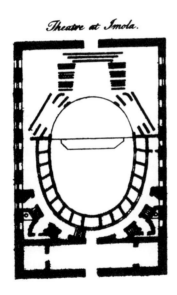

Theatre at Imola.

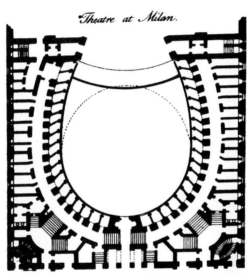

Theatre at Milan.

SAUNDERS: TREATISE ON THEATRES

word-of-mouth, printed treatise, or by actual viewing of the building. Occasionally a new playhouse is built which digresses entirely from previously accepted styles and standards, and which in turn influences architects for generations afterward. What prompts an architect to work in one direction rather than another must remain a mystery. In 1752, fully twenty years before Victor Louis was to shake the theatre world with a revolutionary playhouse design, Luigi Vanvitelli built a court theatre in the enormous palace of the Bourbon kings of Naples at Caserta. This theatre has many of the features normally assumed to have been introduced by the French architect in 1773. For his theatre Vanvitelli chose a

circle barely widened into a horseshoe at the proscenium opening. He banished the pigeonhole system of numerous boxes supported by many small posts, and erected instead an auditorium whose ceiling was supported by ten large columns. Between these, large boxes were fitted. This new form—not quite perfected at Caserta—was to sweep the old system of many posts from the scene in most parts of the Western world.

The French architect Soufflot toured Italy in 1750 with his friend Charles-Nicolas Cochin, *fils*, of whom we shall hear more later. Exactly what Soufflot saw is unrecorded, but when he submitted his design for the Grand Théâtre de Lyon in 1754, it reflected many Italian ideas

89

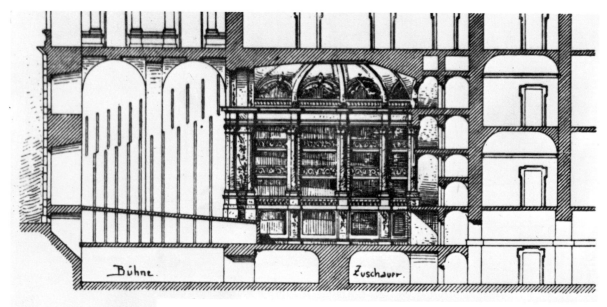

Bühne.   Zuschauer.

HAMMITZSCH: DER MODERNE THEATERBAU

Fig. 138. Section and plan of the court theatre at Caserta, 1752, by Vantivelli.

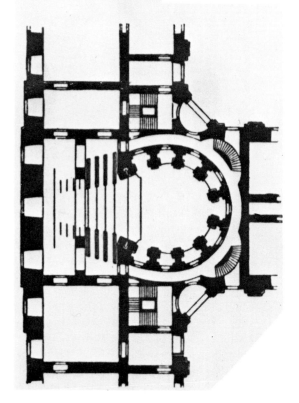

modified to suit French tastes. The theatres of Metz and Montpellier were independent buildings whose interiors were based upon the French V shape. Soufflot imitated the effort of Sarda in Turin and built his theatre in the form of an ellipse. Box divisions were not angled toward the stage in any sort of mathematical system, how-

ever, and the orchestra floor was broken up into the usual French arrangement—*amphithéâtre* to the rear, parterre, or standing room, in the middle, and several rows of benches close to the apron. The building was the first of the "grand theatres," however, and the first freestanding theatre in France. The structure was provided with a monumental entrance, and with all the required ancillary spaces; grand staircases led to the tiers, and salons abounded.

The "grand theatre" served a provincial city in much the same way as royal residences and government buildings served national capitals, as a visible expression of local pride, power, and wealth. Lyons had no monumental civic theatre until manufactories had created enough wealth to support one. With this wealth came the need for display, and grand theatres were the result.

Even as the monumental public playhouse was being born, the monumental opera house and the court theatre continued to flourish. De la Guépierre's design for the reconstruction of the Stuttgart Opera in 1759 was, like the *Salle des Machines*, to have a great mechanical stage, and like the Berlin Opera it was to have grand ancillary spaces. The scale was truly magnificent,

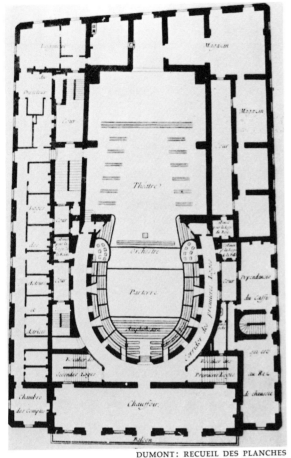

Fig. 139. Plan of Soufflot's Grand Théâtre de Lyon, 1754.

larger and more elaborate than any previous theatre. The baroque setting was translated into stone, providing enormous salons, numerous articulated reception rooms, and corridors of vistae. The foyer was almost as large as the house, and the baroque splendor of the remainder of the house would make even the most pampered modern diva envious. In this house the operatic dream world was realized in stone, stucco, crystal, and gilt.

The court theatres were erected as much to impress as to entertain, a typically baroque concept. The change from feudalism to absolutism required architectural expressions of power. As the ceremonious retirings and triumphal arisings of Louis XIV gave way to the comparative simplicity of the daily life of later monarchs, so the court theatre became more intimate and fanciful. No more exquisite example of the small court theatre still stands than at the Swedish royal summer

Fig. 140. Section of the Grand Théâtre de Lyon.

seat at Drottningholm. In 1754 a small baroque playhouse was built, much like those found at smaller German courts. This playhouse burned in 1762 and Charles Fredrik Adelkrantz was commissioned to design a new theatre. His original

Fig. 141. Section and plan of the Stuttgart opera, by de la Guépierre, 1759.

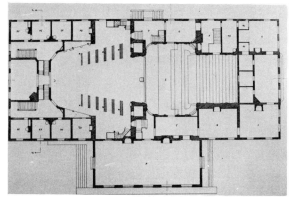

Fig. 142. Plan of the Drottningholm court theatre, 1766.

Fig. 143. Section to the stage, Drottningholm.

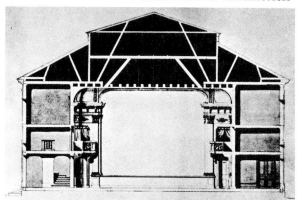

Fig. 145. View from backstage, Drottningholm, showing wings and borders in position.

plans were pretentious, but his later ones—from which the theatre was built—were simple and delightful. The Drottningholm theatre is a free-standing house complete with salons, reception rooms, and the appropriate ancillary spaces. The interior was decorated in the French neoclassic

style which was fashionable at the time. The machines were installed by Donato Stopani in 1766, the year of the opening, and were of the type commonly used in France and Italy since their introduction in the seventeenth century.

The theatre was rebuilt and extended in 1791, but upon the death of Gustavus III, an actor and playwright, it was closed, not to be opened again

Fig. 144. View toward the stage, Drottningholm.

Fig. 146. Salon of the Drottningholm theatre.

Fig. 147. Farmhouse interior set, Drottningholm, showing all furnishings painted on the scenes.

Fig. 149. Street setting, Drottningholm.

Fig. 148. Exterior setting, Drottningholm, showing ascending cloud machine, wave machine, and practical boat.

Fig. 150. Exterior view, Drottningholm.

until 1922. The building still stands and retains much of the original scenery and all of the original machines. Plans and photographs cannot convey the real sense of wonder that actually seeing the operations of an eighteenth century scene change can instill. The effect—with borders, backcloths, and wings all moving simultaneously—may best be compared with the film technique of moving from one picture to the next by lapping images so that one fades imperceptibly into the other. Before one is really aware of it, all the scenery has been changed, and one is moved magically from one place to another. The stage may take on another form and dimension entirely. To modern audiences, familiar with television and film, the effect seems logical and

appropriate, though a little quaint. A close examination of the methods used at Drottningholm makes it clear why the Italian scenic inventions held the stage for two hundred fifty years, and also why the system was abandoned when Realism demanded from it more than it was designed to give.

The old castle at Gripsholm still frowns over the surrounding countryside and its battlements conceal amenities that the grim exterior does not suggest. Within one of the great turrets, a miniature theatre was installed at an early date. In 1781 this was enlarged and refurbished into a more suitably scaled playhouse by the architect Palmstedt. A giant order of corinthian columns rises from the gallery floor to the cornice and supports

DROTTNINGHOLM TEATERMUSEUM

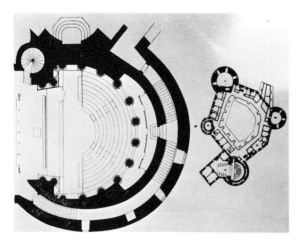

Fig. 151. Plan of the Gripsholm Theatre, 1781, by Palmstedt.

DROTTNINGHOLM TEATERMUSEUM

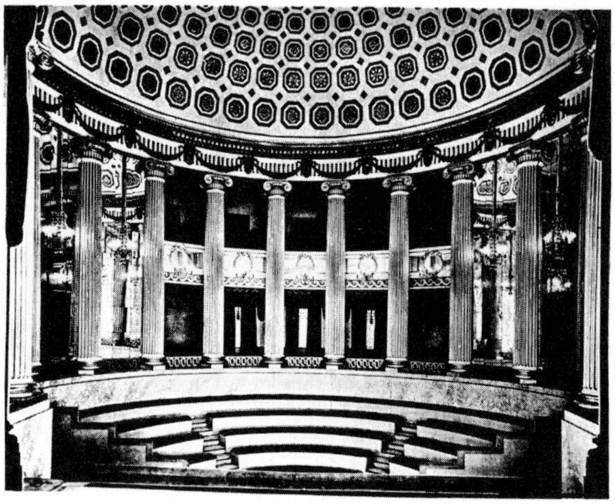

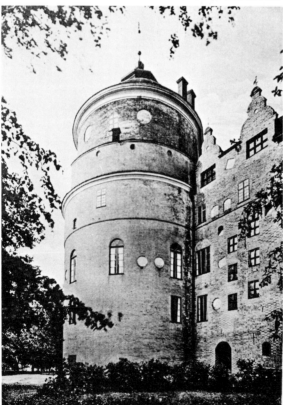

Fig. 153. The amphitheatre, Gripsholm.

a magnificently coffered semidome. An elaborate, pillared proscenium with a triumphal arch opening leads to a modest stage. The decor is French neoclassic but in a different style from that of Drottningholm; it echoes instead the form and style popular in France just before the Revolution. The semi-circular auditorium and magnificent columns are reminiscent of an Imperial Roman excedra rather than a theatre, and the scale of the treatment belies the tiny space within which it was erected.

Fig. 152. Exterior, Gripsholm Theatre. The playhouse is constructed within the tower.

DROTTNINGHOLM TEATERMUSEUM

When Louis XIV commanded entertainments at Versailles, they were given in halls fitted up temporarily as theatres, or in the gardens before thousands of spectators. Vast areas were covered with scenery for the garden festivities, and the whole was lighted by a million candles (each lighted by a banknote, as later reformers alleged). Versailles divertissements offered by Louis XV, however, were presented in the new Théâtre de Versailles, an opera-playhouse constructed by

Fig. 154. Section through the auditorium, Gripsholm.

DROTTNINGHOLM TEATERMUSEUM

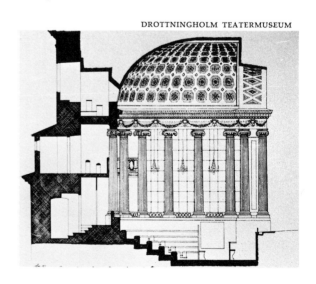

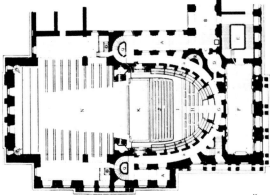

Fig. 155. Plan of the Théâtre de Versailles, 1770, by Gabriel.

Jacques Ange Gabriel in 1770. Two galleries surrounded a large, elliptical auditorium, the ellipse truncated more abruptly than was usual to bring the audience closer to the scene. The auditorium was divided in the manner of the court theatre and not of the public playhouse: the parterre was open and unencumbered so that the view of the royal patrons would not be obstructed; seats for royalty and favored guests were provided in a shallow U on this level; and following the curve of the ellipse was a shallow amphitheatre of two rows, divided into boxes. The columns which supported the coved ceiling were placed against the back wall of the boxes so all patrons had an unobstructed view of the stage. A large orchestra pit was placed over a semicylindrical reverberation chamber, twelve sets of wings and back-shutters were mounted on chariots in the raked floor, and four substage levels were provided for machines and effects. At a later period an alter-

Fig. 156.
View of the
Théâtre de Versailles.

Fig. 157.
Interior of the
Théâtre de Versailles.

95

ation to the parterre added bench seats in the railinged forward portion, and provided sofas and armchairs in rows at the rear. These were luxurious accommodations in the eighteenth century, but were to become commonplace in the century following.

French opera patrons had to be content with the old house in the Palais Royal until 1764. Finally, a new grand opera house, designed by Moreau in the Italian fashion, was constructed in the Rue St. Honoré. The new house was arranged according to mathematical principles after those developed by Sarda at Turin. The curve of the ellipse ended well within the proscenium, although not so far as the versailles opera of six years later. Moreau's house had fourteen shallow boxes in the first tier, two large boxes with benches *en amphithéâtre* on the apron, and two loges within the proscenium for royalty. The amphitheatrical benches at the apron were a sop

Fig. 158. Plan of Moreau's Paris opera, 1764.

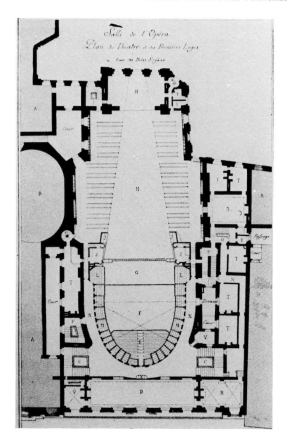

to those who were never content unless they could sit upon the stage. The stage spectators had been banned at the Comédie Française in 1759, but the inclination lingered and was provided for by Moreau. The typically French parterre, with amphitheatre at the rear, was included. The new house was larger than the old one, and provided the public with salons that were by now both expected and required. It was altogether a more commodious and comfortable theatre, though still by no means as large or elaborate as some found in Italy or Germany. Strangely enough—in spite of all previous Italian and German practice—the new opera still had box divisions facing directly forward, instead of angled toward the stage, an arrangement which made it awkward to see from the back of the boxes.

In spite of the backwardness of auditorium accommodation, the opera was provided with the most up-to-date machines and scenic arrangements, and an elaborate system of wells was built within the stage walls for iron counterweights, a system illustrated in Appendix V. While the opera design could not compete with some foreign houses, it was a decided advance over previous Parisian practice, at least admitting the vitality of new ideas from abroad. When the opera was refurbished before the Revolution, in order to provide increased capacity, the ellipse was abandoned and the house widened into a U. This was a retrogression in design, but it provided an additional two boxes in each tier, and this time the box divisions were angled toward the stage.

The German states responded rapidly to ideas from other parts of Europe, and in some instances the German architects were well in advance of

Fig. 159. Plan of the Hannover opera, 1746, by Penther.

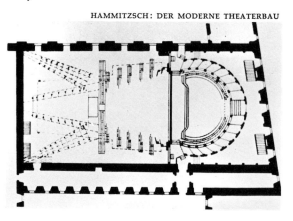

those elsewhere. One example of planning which —like the Teatro di Caserta—predated concepts usually ascribed to a later generation was the new Hannover opera, designed by Johann Friedrich Penther in 1746. Giusti's old opera house was replaced by a new theatre of modest proportions and of completely different form. Later architects took a logical approach toward acoustical satisfaction. The elliptical auditorium was one solution. Moreau's Paris opera was based on an ellipse which intruded beyond the proscenium opening, while the later Théâtre de Versailles had the ellipse truncated almost at its center. The end result of this experimentation was to be a house based on a circle like the older Italian houses, with the circle truncated by the proscenium rather than being completely within the auditorium enclosure. This form was to be common by the end of the century. Penther's Hannover opera was the first of its kind. His theatre plan was based upon the circle, with the center only a few feet from the orchestra pit, and with the circumference extending well within the stage house. There were four tiers of boxes, 16 in each of the lower three and 14 in the uppermost, and all box divisions were angled toward the stage in a pattern of mathematical precision. The divisions, furthermore, were only partial, as the supporting posts were positioned at the back of the boxes and the tiers were cantilevered out from them. The parterre was railed off from a separate semicircular amphitheatre which had no divisions. The stage was fitted with five pairs of multiple wing positions, plus a multiple backshutter; behind this, in turn, were three vistae in sharply forced per-

spective in the Olimpico manner. The total arrangement was not imitated abroad for almost forty years, but was then imitated everywhere.

The reputation of the popular Hanswurst, and the style of theatrical entertainment with which he was associated, had deteriorated over the years, and a new middle class provided an audience for moralistic, uplifting, and patriotic drama. In 1765 Ackerman, the famous German actormanager, persuaded the town fathers of Hamburg to tear down their tottering opera house, which had been built in 1678, and to erect in its place a proper modern theatre. Thus was born the single most renowned playhouse in Germany, which was to attract such men of talent as Lessing, and to influence the growth of the public theatre throughout Central Europe. It is regrettable that the form of the Nationaltheater remains obscure; it is thought to have been a simple structure, but it is unlikely to have been as simple as a few benches around a trestle stage. Probably it resembled contemporary theatres in Amsterdam and London.

In one of the many reconstructions of the Redoutensaal in Vienna the hall was converted to make the new opera house of 1772. This was an extremely large theatre in the Italian fashion, with 18 boxes in each tier of the deep U and a stage half again as large as the house.

In 1773, Victor Louis began a grand theatre in Bordeaux that was to have considerable influence upon the London stage. This playhouse has always been called the Grand Theatre de Bordeaux; the very term "Grand Theatre," when capitalized, is a Bordeaux referent. Louis's playhouse cer-

Fig. 160. Plan of the Redoutensaal opera, Vienna, 1772.

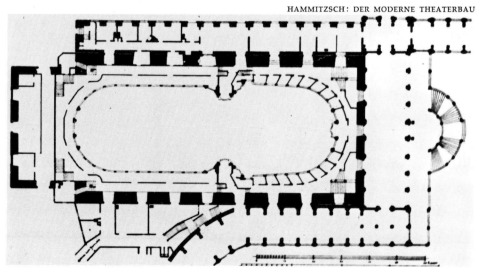

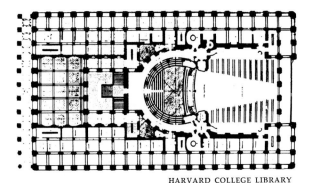

Fig. 161. Plan of the Théâtre de Bordeaux, 1780, by Louis, from Prudent and Guadet: *Salles de Spectacles construites par Victor Louis.*

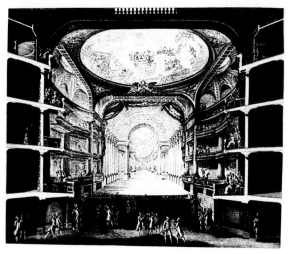

Fig. 163. Section of the Théâtre de Bordeaux, from Prudent and Guadet.

tainly was grand, and was designed with some unusual architectural features. The accepted style of Italian opera house design was based upon succeeding tiers of columns, each supporting the ones above and the beams for the gallery floors. The columns also dictated the locations for the box divisions, so to keep the posts as small as possible the divisions were numerous and the boxes consequently small. At Bordeaux, Louis supported the galleries with fewer and heavier posts in a monumental order reaching from pit to cornice. The columns were tied together by horizontal beams at each gallery level, and the gallery fronts were cantilevered out beyond the line of the columns. This made the individual boxes more commodious and gave a monumental appearance to the house chamber. The top gallery seats were placed between the pendentives of the domed ceiling, with a post-free view. The house plan was based upon a circle, one quarter truncated at the line of the orchestra pit. The weight of the ceiling pendentives was borne on four columns, one at either side of the apron and two in the back of the house.

The giant order was used earlier at Caserta and the truncated circle at Hannover; neither of these

houses, however, was as large as the Théâtre de Bordeaux, and the structural problems were different. At Caserta the ceiling was supported by pendentives resting on *each* vertical column, and the box fronts were not cantilevered. At Hannover the ceiling was suspended from trusses which ran from one exterior wall to the other, leaving the interior free of supports. In the larger Bordeaux house this was not practicable. Louis's plan was not entirely innovative, but it was the first to incorporate in one design a large number of the new ideas about effective large-scale playhouse construction. This grand and magnificently appointed playhouse was designed with the idea of providing every comfort and convenience, but the pit floor was still divided into a small section of seating *en amphithéâtre* and a large standing-room parterre. The front of the house occupied an area vastly larger than the actual auditorium, with salons and entrance foyers capable of handling the entire audience, evidence that the Berlin

Fig. 162. Exterior of the Théâtre de Bordeaux, from Prudent and Guadet.

Fig. 164. Interior of the Théâtre de Bordeaux, from Prudent and Guadet.

opera and De La Guépierre's Stuttgart design were influential.

Fig. 165. Drawing of the structural plan of the Théâtre de Bordeaux.

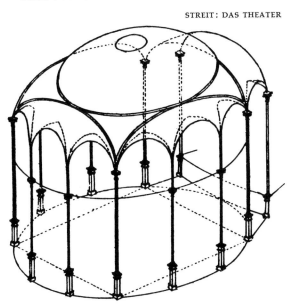

Fig. 167. Interior of the second Schouwburg Theatre, Amsterdam.

Variations on Louis's theme were introduced almost at once. In his Théâtre de Rheims, built soon after the construction of the Grand Théâtre de Bordeaux, Alphonse Gosset imitated Louis's use of few supporting columns, but instead of making them massive so that four could support the roof, he made them slender, resting the roof on pendentives which sprang from each column.

More typical of the public theatres of the late eighteenth century was the Schouwburg in Amsterdam. The original playhouse of 1638 had been entirely rebuilt in 1664 and again in 1774. The Italian influence was evident, together with the equally strong influence of French practice. The

Fig. 166. Drawing of the structural plan of the Théâtre de Rheims.

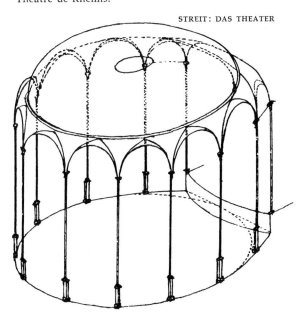

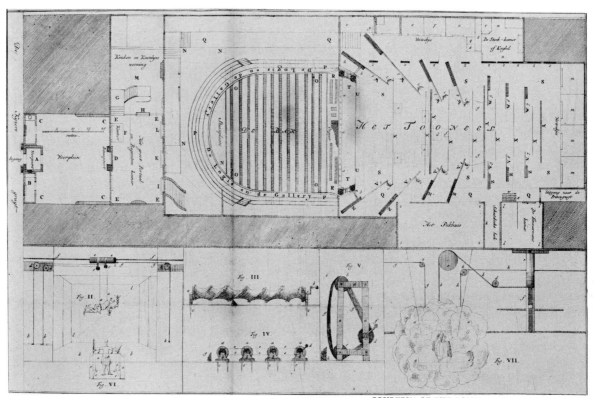

Fig. 168. Plan of the second Schouwburg.

Fig. 169. Interior of the Schouwburg, 1772.

Fig. 170.
Scene on the
Schouwburg stage
showing the use
of angle wings.

deep proscenium contained niches in which were placed statues of Comedy and Tragedy, an affectation that was to be popular from Berlin to Philadelphia, and the stage was set with all the necessary machinery for the mounting of bourgeois drama. The theatre was illustrated in great detail before its destruction by fire in 1772, and from this we have gained an impression of what scenic and architectural artistry was current in equivalent playhouses such as Drury Lane and Covent Garden.

The architect of the second Schouwburg solved the perennial problem of gallery supports and their interruption of sightlines to the stage. The house had two shallow side galleries; the lower was cantilevered out from the wall, leaving the

Fig. 171.
Interior of the
Schouwburg, *ca.* 1805.

Fig. 172.
Interior of
La Scala opera,
Milan.

HARVARD THEATRE COLLECTION

area below completely free of posts; the upper was suspended from the ceiling by chains which were wrapped in velvet. Thus there were no posts along the sides at all. Since the main floor was free of support columns, the pit benches were extended underneath the galleries, thus eliminating the first floor boxes entirely. This open plan was unique in its day and was not imitated elsewhere until the construction of the Sans Pareil theatre in London in the nineteenth century. The ground-plan of the Schouwburg indicates a late use of the angle wing and it includes illustrations of the chariots' run offstage, the tracks of movement of the wings, and the positions of the wing-light standards and the back scenes.

Since the principal opera company in Europe was resident in Milan, it naturally followed that the opera house used by that company was imitated abroad, although the plan was neither innovative nor of special interest. In 1778 the architect Piermarini designed La Scala opera house in the traditional horseshoe shape, either unaware of or uninterested in Victor Louis's design in Bordeaux. A forest of posts supported a beehive of boxes, 36 in each tier, and the scale was vast, from the enormous stage to the great auditorium. The influence of La Scala certainly was not in its shape (based on a circle whose circumference touched the or-chestra pit) nor in its size, but in the success of the house as a home for music. Acoustically the design was a good one, and, equally important, the capacity was the largest in Europe. Compared with Bordeaux, however, where the stage and house were supported by equally large ancillary spaces, La Scala was cramped.

It is the fate of many architectural visionaries to have their works either ignored or laughed at. Occasionally this is because of the lack of clarity with which the vision is presented. Claude-Nicolas Ledoux was a practicing architect with a revolutionary concept of theatre planning which he successfully translated into reality. Previous to Ledoux the most advanced theatre designs were those introduced at Hannover and at Bordeaux, in which few posts were used, and these were placed at the back of the boxes so sightlines would be unimpaired. This was not difficult to do once the idea was conceived, but the cantilevered tiers had to be shallow because of the wooden construction of the supporting members. Ledoux took theatre planning one step further and eliminated posts from the main part of the auditorium completely. In theory, this could have been attempted earlier if the trussed space had been enlarged to include the entire seating area and not just the auditorium core, but although the piers supporting the roof trusses of older theatres always rested upon the outer walls, those supporting the ceiling and the boxes rested on columns within the hall, because the seating was arranged vertically in layered tiers. Ledoux eliminated the layered tiers and constructed a single large amphitheatre where the first level of boxes were normally located. This amphitheatre extended over the house spaces at the rear of the pit seating, and rested on masonry vaulting so it needed no posts. The ceiling was suspended from the roof trusses which rested on the outer walls. This arrangement presupposed several things: first, that the audience was prepared to forgo the intimacy of sharing small boxes with their friends; second, that patrons were willing to exchange proximity to the stage for a clear view; and third, that sufficient land area was available for construction, because the amphitheatre took up more horizontal room than had the stacked tiers of the older style. While the first two suppositions presented little difficulty, the last created a problem which prevented the adoption of Ledoux's plan for commercial urban theatres.

The floor plan of the auditorium was influenced by the antique style. The parterre was small, an imitation of the ancient Greek and Roman orchestra; and the amphitheatre was large, and accommodated the majority of the audience in a shape which imitated the Roman playhouse, graded

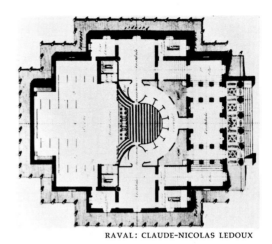

Fig. 173. Plan of the Théâtre de Besançon, 1778, by Ledoux.

banks of benches rising in semicircular tiers. Ledoux's new ideas were used in his Théâtre de Besançon of 1778. There he followed his concept nearly without exception, but he found that the democratic seating plan was not entirely favored. Low "box" partitions were built in the amphitheatre, but these disappeared from view when the house was filled with patrons and the classless theatre seemed to have arrived. The parterre was fitted with benches without any provision for standing room.

The amphitheatrical house plan broke with the traditions of a century. Formerly, the amphi-

Fig. 174.
Section of the
Théâtre de Besançon.

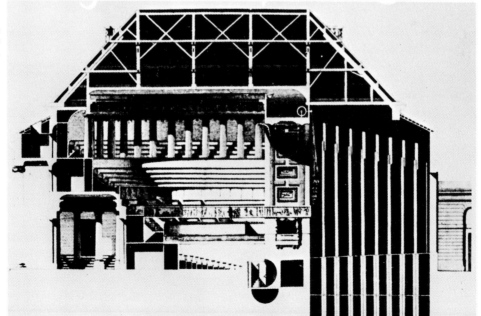

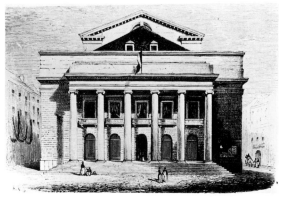

Fig. 175. Front of the Théâtre de Marseilles, 1785, by Ledoux.

theatre had been restricted to theatres designed for the courts, which served only one class—the aristocracy. The classical inspiration of the new plan was evident also in the inclusion of a columned gallery at the top of the house. It was behind these pillars that Ledoux hid the gallery patrons, although it should be noted that only a

Fig. 176. Plan of the Théâtre de Marseilles.

RAVAL: CLAUDE-NICOLAS LEDOUX

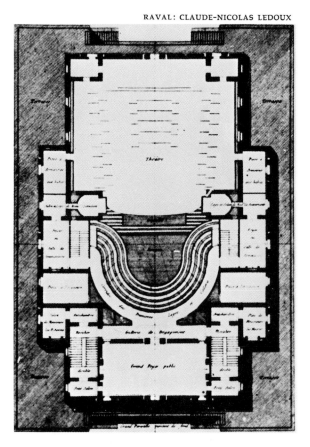

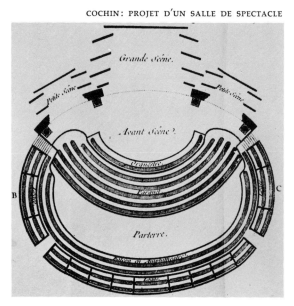

RAVAL: CLAUDE-NICOLAS LEDOUX

Fig. 177. Section of the Théâtre de Marseilles.

few rows of benches were provided so the view would not be blocked too much. The ends of the amphitheatre curve were pulled in sharp arcs to the sides of the house close to the proscenium so the patrons seated there could view the stage facing forward instead of over their shoulders. By restricting the projection of the amphitheatre toward the stage, Ledoux was left with a large uncluttered area within which he placed a vast arched proscenium.

The architect developed this theatre plan after considerable thought and experiment, and he was proud of it. It was so striking and successful that a similar theatre, with an even more open seating plan, was erected in Marseilles in 1785, and all Ledoux's subsequent projects included its essentials whenever theatre spaces were proposed. The old style of theatre design could never again be

Fig. 178. Plan of a triple proscenium project by Cochin, 1765.

COCHIN: PROJET D'UN SALLE DE SPECTACLE

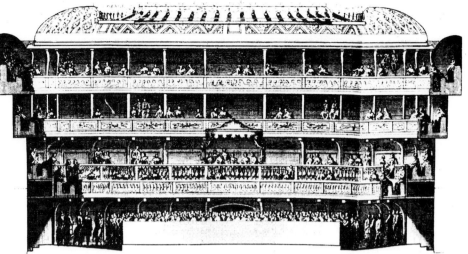

Fig. 179.
Section showing
the house of
Cochin's project.

COCHIN: PROJET D'UN SALLE DE SPECTACLE

COCHIN: PROJET D'UN SALLE DE SPECTACLE

Fig. 180.
Section through
the house and stage,
Cochin's project.

COCHIN: PROJET D'UN SALLE DE SPECTACLE

Fig. 181.
Section showing
the three
proscenia of
Cochin's project.

105

seriously considered as an architectural optimum, although this did not prevent subsequent architects from designing such theatres, partly because of urban site restrictions and partly because of traditional pressures.

There was one aesthetic difficulty with the designs of Ledoux and of other architects interested in the open Roman plan: while the concept was appropriate to operatic production or for dramatic spectaculars, less expensive and more intimate entertainments would be dwarfed. Amphitheatrical seating requires considerable space for the accommodation of even a moderate-sized audience, and while the omission of posts leaves the view unencumbered, the position of the average seat is remote from the stage. The older style of house, designed with boxes in succeeding tiers, could provide spaces for an equally large number of spectators in closer proximity to the performance. The desire for an unrestricted view and the necessity of maintaining some degree of intimacy were mutually exclusive because of the limitations of the structural materials available. When iron became available for construction, the large trussed balcony supported by occasional posts was found to be the solution to the problem.

Soufflot's friend, Charles-Nicolas Cochin, published a theatre project in 1765 which proposed a unique stage and house arrangement. The auditorium was composed in the form of an ellipse, but instead of having it truncated by the proscenium at one of the narrow ends, Cochin proposed that the ellipse face the stage the long way. This gave a wide, shallow house facing a wide stage. Since the stage acting area would be inordinately large were it to contain a single large proscenium, the architect proposed three proscenia. Unlike most projects this one did not die on the drawing-board; in 1779 Cosimo Morelli based his design for the new theatre at Imola on Cochin's plan, with an elliptical form that was truncated on the longer side and three proscenia. Behind each of the proscenia a set of scenes was arranged, simple ones for the sides and a more elaborate one in the center, which enabled every member of the audience to see one full setting. Action was intended to flow from one scene to another without pause and without changing any scene until all three could be changed. The two side scenes were static because they were too cramped for space to allow the wings to be withdrawn for additional reveals. Only the scene in the center proscenium could be changed in the normal manner. Most of the action was intended to take place on the small forestage, the actors entering from and retiring to whichever of the scenes was appropriate. Since the majority of favored plays of the period employed a few standard settings (the prison, the palace, the

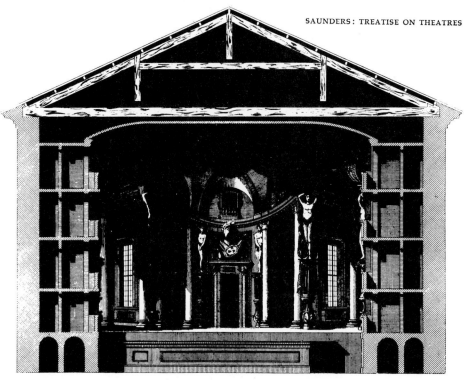

Fig. 182.
Stage of the
Teatro d'Imola
showing three
proscenia.

106

forest, the cavern, the cottage), few changes were necessary and some plays required only the three scenes already in position. The Teatro d'Imola was admired but not imitated, because it was more a curiosity than a fully workable playhouse. Three cramped scenic areas were not as flexible as one large one with movable parts, and the theatre could be used only within the context of the original design. Although the three-part stage was not a successful innovation, however, the shallow and wide design contributed to the changes in auditorium planning that developed as the century came to a close.

For many years Paris had had very few playhouses. Once the strict monopoly laws were loosened, however, there was an explosion of construction similar to the one in contemporary London. Even before the abolition of the laws some attempts had been made to provide additional playing spaces. During the Revolution there were twelve buildings constructed for or adapted to theatrical purposes; by 1830 the number had jumped to twenty-seven. From an aristocratic and middle class art form theatre grew rapidly into an entertainment for the people presented in covered, comfortable halls designed with an attention that previously would have been reserved for facilities for the monied classes. One of the first examples of the new theatre style was erected in 1787 by Victor Louis. It was later given the name Théâtre Français. The design of this official temple of dramatic art was based upon the old Italian opera house plan, with a few minor variations, although it was decorated in the then fashionable "Roman" style. A graded amphitheatre replaced the old style divided pit, and the shape of the auditorium was an extended circle, or horseshoe, with the circumference of the circle at the orchestra pit. This was very little different from San Carlo or La Scala. A slight innovation was made in the arrangement of the first tier of boxes above the main floor: a narrow shelf-like cantilevered balcony extended out from this tier and contained two rows of benches, behind which were the boxes of the first elevated tier. From this level a giant order of columns rose through two additional tiers to support the forward edge of the top gallery. This was a large, open amphitheatre of eight rows—post free—backed by a curved gallery of columns which supported the ceiling.

Fig. 183. Plan and interior of the Thèâtre Français, 1787, by Louis.

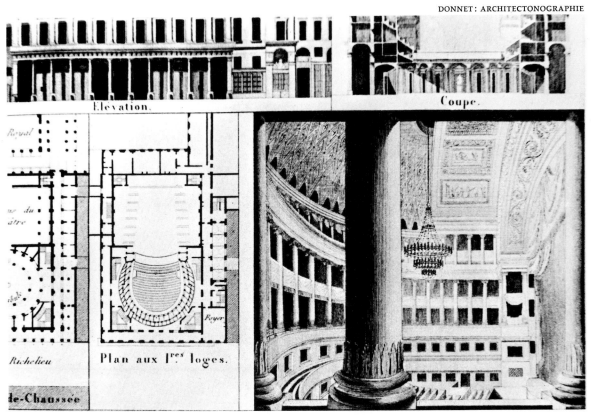

Fig. 184.
Views and plans
of the
Théâtre Français
as restored
in 1822.

What the design provided, then, was a house superficially resembling the designs of Ledoux, and not at all resembling Louis's own Théâtre de Bordeaux. Of necessity the audience had to be accommodated in raised tiers because of the restricted site. The semicircle of columns added a monumental appearance to the house, but they were so large and numerous (located at each box division) that sight lines were interrupted more than was necessary, and they proved to be a great annoyance. When the house was renovated in 1822 the columns were removed and cast iron

Fig. 185. Plan of the Théâtre Français in the late nineteenth century, from Prudent and Gaudet.

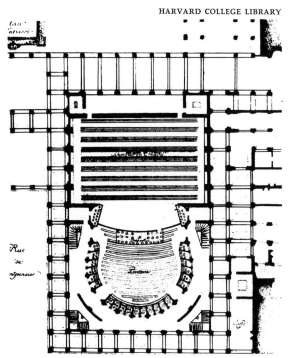

Fig. 186. Section of the Théâtre Français as rebuilt in the nineteenth century, from Prudent and Guadet.

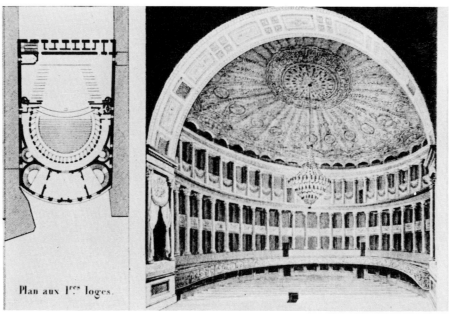

Fig. 187.
Plan and interior of
the Théâtre Faydeau,
1788, Paris, by
Molinos and Legrand.

Plan aux 1ʳᵉˢ loges.

posts substituted, which completely altered the appearance of the interior. The formal "Roman" magnificence was gone and a more delicate room took its place. The result was improved vision for the box patrons, even though the number of supports had to be increased from twenty-six to thirty-two.

Fig. 188. Interior of the Théâtre des Arts, from Prudent and Guadet.

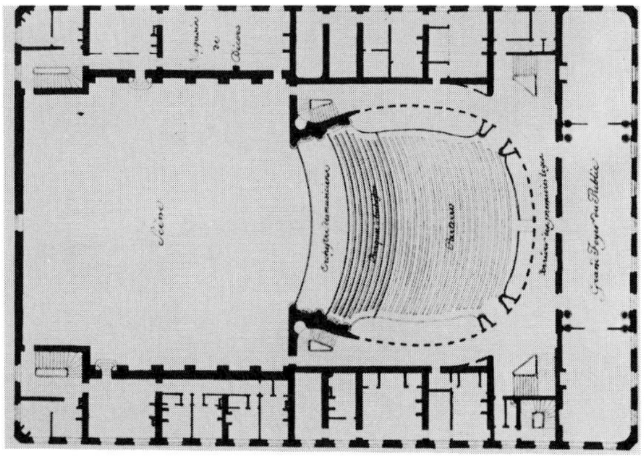

Fig. 189. Plan of the Théâtre des Arts, from Prudent and Guadet.

Fig. 190. Gallery plan of the Théâtre des Arts showing the seating placed between pendentives of the dome, from Prudent and Guadet.

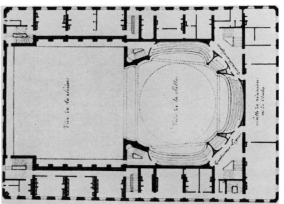

109

Another large house was the Théâtre Faydeau, on the Rue Faydeau, built in 1788 by Molinos in much the same style as the Théâtre Français. Here also large columns in the box divisions supported the top tier. Above this was another series of columns—behind the gallery seats—which supported the "paradise," two rows of benches crowded right underneath the cove of the ceiling. The Faydeau did not have a dome (an item which was impressive and decorative but which restricted the galleries) but a flat ceiling decorated like a *velarium*, or Roman awning.

Victor Louis was commissioned to design two other theatres, the Théâtre des Variétés, in 1790, and the Théâtre des Arts, in 1792. Of the two, the latter is the more interesting and influential, and reflects the innovations introduced in the Théâtre de Bordeaux. It had a tremendous domed ceiling, supported by eight columns grouped in pairs. The auditorium was extremely large, making the circular form impractical, and a more angular U was chosen. Shelf balconies were suspended between

Fig. 192. Interior of the Académie Royale de Musique.

the supporting columns, providing a post-free view. Gallery seats—as at Bordeaux—were fixed between the pendentives of the dome. After the fire which destroyed Moreau's opera in 1781, the Théâtre des Arts served as the home of the Académie Royal de Musique for some years. Its enormous stage and large audience capacity made this house an acceptable—if not perfect—home for spectacular and grand productions. When the new Académie Royal de Musique was constructed in 1820 the form of the Théâtre des Arts was copied almost exactly, except that a circular auditorium shape was adopted. Again, eight columns supported a great dome, and shelf balconies re-

Fig. 191. Plan of the Académie Royale de Musique, 1820, Paris.

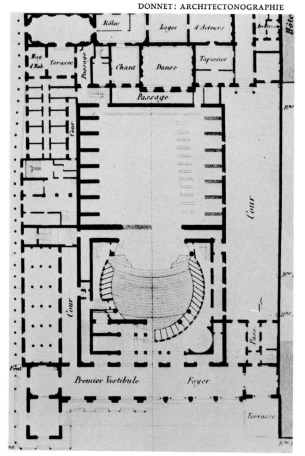

Fig. 193. Facade and section of the Académie Royale de Musique.

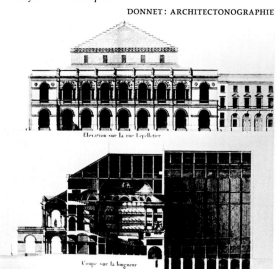

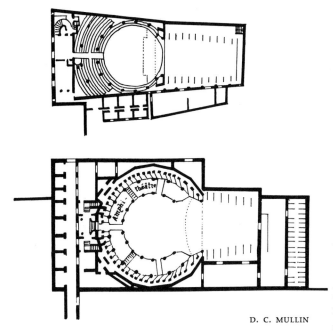

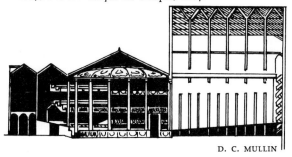

D. C. MULLIN

Fig. 194. Plans of the Cirque du Mont Thabor, 1807, and the Cirque du Temple, 1814.

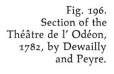

D. C. MULLIN

Fig. 195. Section of the Cirque du Temple.

placed the Italian box. The circumference of the circle that formed the house fell within the proscenium opening, which arrangement offers the least awkward view from the side seats. Unlike other theatres of the time, the parterre floor of the Académie was so steeply pitched that there was no room for slip boxes at the sides on the pit level. This reduced the capacity of the house, but made vision from the parterre superior to what was possible with the older style.

The success of Astley's Amphitheatre in London was not lost upon Parisian speculators. A similar, although larger and grander, structure entitled Cirque du Mont Thabor was built in 1807. A circle of fourteen giant corinthian columns rising from floor to cornice surrounded a large ring. While Astley's had boxes, in imitation of the regular playhouse, none were included here; instead the performing circle was surrounded on three sides by large banks of seats *en amphithéâtre*. The fourth side contained a modest proscenium and a small stage. Because of the enclosure of three-quarters of the ring, fully a third of the patrons found it difficult to view the stage, and some found it almost impossible. In 1814 the same company built the Cirque du Temple, in which the seating amphitheatre rose more nearly opposite to the stage, and only two rows continued the circular pattern.

In 1782 the Théâtre de l'Odéon was built by Dewailly and Peyre, and for a brief time it housed the Troupe de Molière. In 1807 a new Odéon was built by Chaigrin. This was a larger house. The auditorium was a circle whose center was close to the orchestra pit, and only two boxes at either

DONNET: ARCHITECTONOGRAPHIE

Fig. 196.
Section of the
Théâtre de l' Odéon,
1782, by Dewailly
and Peyre.

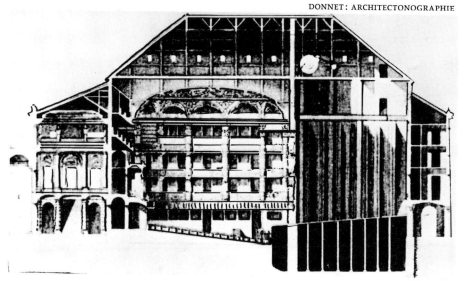

111

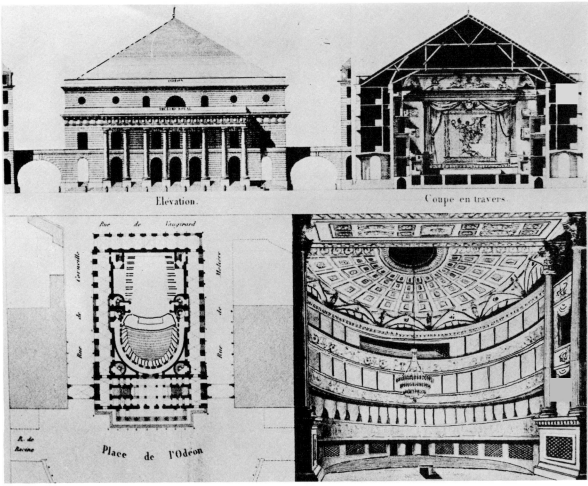

Fig. 197. Plan and views of the new Théâtre de l'Odéon, 1807, by Chaigrin.

side were beyond the diameter point in each tier. Two tiers of post-free boxes were arranged in a semicircle like the one in the Faydeau, a third tier had boxes at the sides and an amphitheatre at the rear, and a "paradise" was located above, under the coved ceiling. Unlike other buildings of its type, where the weight of the roof rested upon the load-bearing outer walls, the Odéon's great peaked roof was supported by trusses resting on the interior walls. This distributed the weight more evenly, and allowed lighter members to be used, and a lower cornice line.

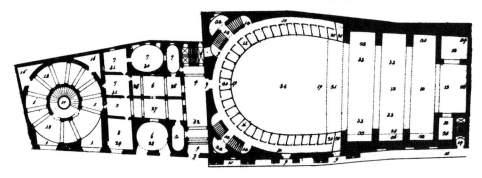

Fig. 198. Plan of the Teatro di Tor di Nona, Rome, 1785, by Barberi.

Fig. 199. Section to the stage, Teatro di Tor di Nona of 1795.

Whether the Empire style may be credited to the Revolution and Napoleon is debatable, because elements of this fashion were present before Louis XVI lost his head. Indeed, architectural rationale had often rested upon republican ideology. When the Consulate and the Empire seized upon the virtues of Augustan Rome, baroque monumentality and neoclassic elaboration gave way to a simpler and more austere "Roman" form and decoration because baroque and neoclassic had been so intimately connected with

Fig. 202. Interior of the Verona opera, *ca.* 1770.

royal houses that some new form seemed mandatory. Usually the Roman decoration of French theatres at the turn of the century relied upon a giant order of columns and a ceiling either domed or representing the awning used in the Roman theatre. Previous to the resurgence of antique influence, theatre proscenia were modest in size, with the house expanding beyond them into lyre, ellipse, or horseshoe shapes. In playhouses of the 1800's, however, the circle-based house plan demanded a different design. A circular plan that accommodates the same number of patrons as one of the other shapes must be a large circle indeed. If the circle is truncated so that all seats have a view of the stage, then the stage opening must be extremely large. Otherwise the house must have a decreased capacity in order to main-

Fig. 200. Italian system of box and pillar arrangement.

Fig. 201. Supporting structural arrangement developed by Victor Louis for his Paris theatres.

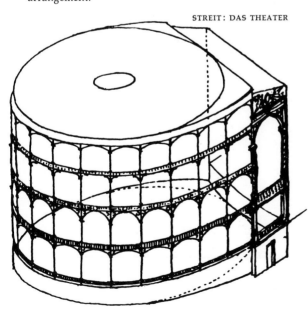

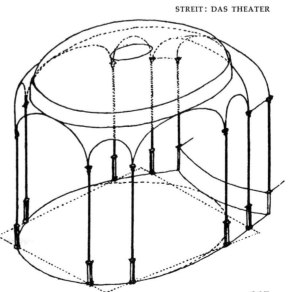

113

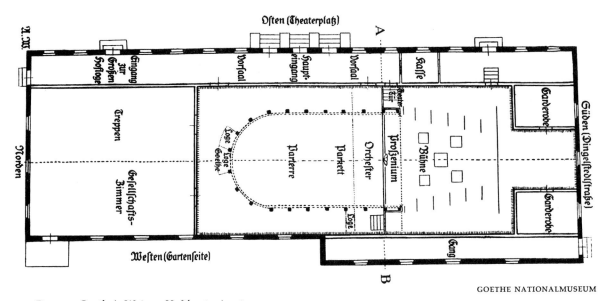

Fig. 203. Goethe's Weimar Hoftheater in 1800.

tain the modest proscenium, a method that was followed in Bordeaux, Wyatt's Drury Lane, and many other houses.

Whether the design change dictated by fashion influenced playwrights or whether the changes in dramatic entertainments ran parallel to those in architectural practice is not clear. What is plain is that the enlargement of the proscenium and the simpler decor of the house made the large, pictorial, and essentially Romantic style of stage production possible. Forces of Nature may be indicated in a small proscenium, but they may be felt only in a large one. Artists of the same period began to exploit space in a similar way. Man ceased to be a central figure, and instead became only a small part of a much greater world. Early romantic art was preoccupied with the concept of Man in isolation, facing forces larger than him-

Fig. 204. Exterior of the Weimar Hoftheater in 1800.

Fig. 205.
Reconstructed
model of the
Weimar Hoftheater
by A. Jericke.

self, a concept that never occurred to most artists of the eighteenth century. The early nineteenth century stage opening, then, was more than an architectural fashion. The movement toward post-free boxes with low divisions and open galleries made the patrons seated within such tiers feel closer to the main body of the house and therefore more susceptible of mass emotional responses. The enlargement of the proscenium and the reduction of the depth of the auditorium relative to the scene brought even the gallery patrons to within viewing distance of facial expression and atmospheric effects. Thus, the large speculative house of the early 1800's came close to reestablishing the contact between audience and actor that had been lost when the former intimate playhouses were outgrown and abandoned. The new contact, however, was not between audience and the individual, but between the audience and a scenic environment of which Man was only a part.

115

VII Yankee and Other Doodles

A magnitude of artistic expression depends upon a continuous culture and long history; when the pattern is broken it takes the arts many years to reassert themselves. Painting, sculpture, music, dance, architecture, and theatre depend upon money and time: money for the materials and labor, and time for execution and appreciation. These are abundant in areas of the world long settled by their present inhabitants, but are in short supply in places where cultures have been transplanted. Theatre arises when there is an audience sufficiently affluent to pay for the support of players and playhouses, and where there are enough persons with leisure to attend. These were not present in any of the colonies of Great Britain at first, and both remained in short supply for several centuries. When the necessity of spending time and energies only for survival becomes inbred, it is difficult to change that value system to include such non-survival matters as art.

For these and other reasons we find plays produced in early colonial cultures only in isolated instances and never for extended periods. Slow growth was true of the other arts as well as theatre. When Latrobe was building the Capitol in Washington, he found that no stone carvers of skill were available in America, and for the columns and capitals he would have to import Italian craftsmen. American painters of note received their training and most of their commissions in England. Acting companies were composed almost entirely of Englishmen until the nineteenth

century. Nowhere in America do we find the "stately homes" that one sees at the end of almost any English garden path. Even the nineteenth century excesses of the Vanderbilts cannot be compared to the country seats of the English and French new-rich. Playhouse design was subject to the same pressures as architecture in general. The first theatres in America were paltry affairs, and even the later theatres of more pretension were pale shadows of those of England and the Continent. Nowhere in North America do we find the complete "grand theatre" either contemplated or built until the twentieth century, and even these late-bloomers do not compare well with their counterparts abroad.

We tend to look with disdain at *nouveaux riches*, taking none of their interests or aspirations seriously, but no art of quality has survived without the patronage and interest of these maligned people. Excepting Greece, most of the beautiful things we cherish from the past were originally commissioned by persons who wished to display their recently acquired culture, position, or wealth. Without the absurd pretentiousness of Julian II we would have none of the magnificent statuary carved for his tomb, without the vulgar Medici there would be a less impressive Florence, and without the shipping and manufacturing interests of coastal France there would be no Grand Théâtre de Bordeaux.

The playhouses of the colonies were simple versions of the ones in use abroad, and the styles remained simple almost until the present day.

Usually this simplicity is ascribed to the Puritan and his horror of vain display, but the reasons are more complex. We are no longer puritanical, but we still generally refrain from making our theatre buildings beautiful as well as suitable. Whatever the reasons for this, the playhouses of the colonies must be considered in their own terms in order for an understanding of their design and function to follow.

The form of the first theatres in America is shrouded in almost as much mystery as those of sixth century Greece. We know only their approximate shape. The records of theatrical performances in the cities of the English colonies are mainly detailed accounts of touring companies that played the colonial circuit. Except for a passing reference or two, we have no information about the early playhouses, if, indeed, they were proper playhouses at all. It seems likely that the touring companies—and local talent as well—managed much as did companies touring English provincial towns: the town hall was rented, fitted up with a temporary stage and some benches, and was set with whatever scenes could be transported over bad roads. The results could hardly have compared favorably to theatrical productions in the London Patent theatres, but patrons were happy to get entertainment, and more frequently than not had little basis for comparison with which to make unflattering judgments.

Provincial theatres opened only when touring companies came through or when courageous local talent made a brave effort to overcome the difficulties of production. Although the London theatres produced many plays and employed many actors, it is certain that in the seventeenth and eighteenth centuries there were as many productions of plays outside London as within it. The majority of these were not presented by resident companies in local Theatres Royal, but by touring companies in available halls. When we consider the Colonial theatre scene, then, we must understand that the methods of mounting a stage and theatre as well as those of rigging a production must have been routine—even if they were not always pleasant tasks, or if the results were not spectacular. Since local halls throughout the British Isles and Colonies served for productions of contemporary plays, we may assume that simple staging was the rule, and not an exception, and a rule that had held true since the time of the Tudors.

Inigo Jones regularly mounted elaborate productions within the confines of the Banqueting House. Less elaborate arrangements were built elsewhere by local carpenters, as required. When we think of early theatrical performances in the colonies, therefore, we must not visualize touring managers laboring under unbearable difficulties while bringing culture to the benighted backwoods. They operated in a familiar manner which they used with equal ease and effectiveness at home and in the provinces. The arrangements must have taken advantage of the usual design of public halls of the period. Of the eighteenth century places of public assembly (town halls, churches, and market halls), only the simplest and smallest ones did not have some type of gallery at one end. Frequently there were galleries on three sides, for this arrangement was not restricted to the early theatre. Touring theatrical companies in England endeavored to play in these halls when possible, because the addition of a few benches on the floor and a stage at one end turned them into a recognizable approximation of an ordinary public theatre. When a suitable hall was not available, a duplicate of it could easily be erected within any open, covered building. If such a building was not available, the entire package could be built from the ground up, a course followed by the Hallams on more than one occasion.

These early "theatres" were of a modest design. First, there was a shallow gallery around three sides in the standard public hall, and at least at one end in the less elaborate ones. Second, the flat floor was filled with as many benches as could be crowded in. Third, a temporary stage was placed on trestles at one end of the hall. Fourth, proscenium doors (or curtained openings) were made in a two-dimensional flat proscenium which masked overhead and sides. Fifth, the drops and other canvas brought along by the company were framed and battened; the former were rigged with the tackle any seaboard town could supply, and the latter were set up in grooves on the temporary floor. Within a short time, then, a public hall, warehouse, loft, or other covered building could be converted into a playhouse with a minimum of expense and effort. The style and arrangement could have differed little from the first Little Theatre in the Haymarket, from Goodman's Fields, or from Davenant's playhouse at Lisle's tennis court. The tradition was a long one,

Fig. 206. Reconstruction of the exterior of the Southwark Theatre, Philadelphia, 1766.

coming directly from the trestle stage and gallery common in Shakespeare's time.

Early playing spaces in the Colonial towns usually are referred to as theatres, but it seems clear that these were temporary theatre arrangements, not playhouses as we think of them. We know little about them except their locations and when they opened. A temporary theatre was built in Williamsburg in 1716 about which we know little except that it was the first in Colonial America. In New York, a large room above a commercial establishment located off Pearl Street was turned into a playing space in 1732. A playhouse was built in Charleston in 1736, only to be abandoned soon after. A second theatre was built in New York in a converted warehouse on Nassau Street in 1750, and this was described as having a stage five feet high and wings made out of paper. A similar stage was erected on Pine Street in Philadelphia in 1749. A second theatre was built in Williamsburg in 1751 which was described as a homely structure of wood with pit benches and a few boxes. Still another New York theatre was put up in Nassau Street (after the first theatre of that name had been demolished) in 1753, and yet another at Cruger's Wharf in 1758. A hall of some type was knocked together at Society Hill in Philadelphia in 1759, and a fourth theatre was built in New York at Beekman Street in 1761. The same year a playhouse was built in Newport, and New England was further invaded by the erection of a "school" for moral discourse in Providence in 1762. Most of the fore-

going were built by the Hallams for their touring company, and all would certainly be considered shoddy by modern standards, equivalent to the tackiest summer-stock barn.

The first permanent theatre in the American colonies was the Southwark, built in Philadelphia in 1766. While there are no plans available for this playhouse, there is an old woodcut which gives us a view of what may be the exterior of the building. The illustration is not contemporary with the original structure but was probably based upon information or an illustration now lost, or upon detailed observation in secondary sources no longer available. Although the value of the print is suspect, it does illustrate a structure which would be suitable for the time and place. The "Southwark Theatre" as shown is essentially a meeting house, complete with bell tower.

The next playhouse of note was built in John Street, New York, completed in 1767. Some details of this playhouse have been left to us in contemporary accounts. The precise form and elaboration are a matter of question, although the comment was made that the interior was just like a meeting house. There was a pit, a gallery around three sides, boxes, and all accounts agree that the interior was crude. The building was set back from the street, connected to it by a long shed intended to shield incoming patrons from the weather. For many years a series of prints labeled "Interior of the John Street Theatre" have been

Fig. 207. Reconstruction of the front of the John Street Theatre, New York, 1767.

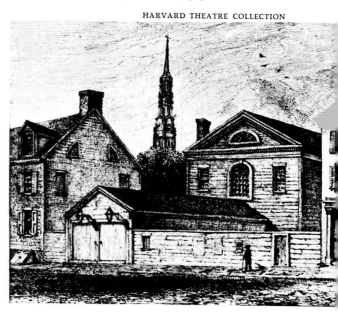

reproduced, and even though they have been thoroughly discredited, they are still seen occasionally. The "John Street" prints were pirated from a single retouched woodcut of a performance given by and for boys in an English public school. The hall illustrated still stands, and it has nothing whatever to do with America or the New York stage. Another print, depicting the front of the building from the street, is a later reconstruction, though it is possible that it does resemble the theatre.

An attractive and substantial brick theatre was built in Annapolis in 1771 to replace a temporary hall; this is credited with a capacity of 600. While there are no plans of the interior, the long, narrow design suggests that the arrangement was similar to that of contemporary English playhouses of modest size. A new theatre was erected in Charleston in 1773, and additional ones in later years. It was not until 1791, however, that an American theatre was built of which we have any interior views. The Chestnut Street Theatre, Philadelphia, begun in 1791 by Thomas Wignall and Alexander Reinagle, was completed in 1793, but the plague prevented its opening until the following year. This indeed was a proper playhouse, and resembled the usual public meeting house not at all. It was modeled after the Theatre Royal, Bath, the plans having been sent from England to the American promoters. The novelty of such a playhouse created much interest, and as a consequence enough information is available for us to recreate its appearance fairly accurately. The auditorium was not straight-sided as the earlier playhouse interiors almost certainly were; it was

Fig. 208. Original design for the facade of the Chestnut Street Theatre, Philadelphia, 1793.

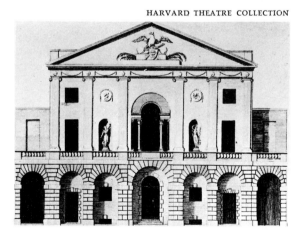

Fig. 209. Interior of the first Chestnut Street Theatre, 1794.

an extended horseshoe circle, in keeping with the current English and Continental fashion. Although the Chestnut Street Theatre was no Covent Garden, it was commodious and well appointed. Columns graced the front, and marble steps led to the galleries. The building was 90 feet wide, 134 feet long, and had an apron stage 71 feet wide with a proscenium opening of 36 feet containing proscenium doors with windows above. The theatre held over 2,000 patrons in three galleries and a pit filled with backless benches.

Other theatre construction followed hard upon the heels of the Chestnut. In 1794 Baltimore opened the first Holliday Street Theatre, a rambling structure of wood, designed to replace the temporary playhouses built in that city in 1781 and 1786.

The superiority of Philadelphia was short-lived. Charles Bulfinch was commissioned to build a theatre in Federal Street in Boston, and he designed a small elegant playhouse based on the form of the Théâtre de Bordeaux. The building was 61 feet wide, 140 feet long, and 40 feet high. The auditorium was the quarter-truncated circle considered by contemporary theoreticians to be the best form for seeing and hearing. Since the auditorium was a small one (based on a circle only 36 feet in diameter inside the line of the boxfronts), the domed ceiling was on pendentives resting upon four columns, one at each side of the proscenium and one between each third of the group of boxes. There were three large boxes which were really small galleries in the first tier above the floor, and a top gallery above, with seats in the pendentives of the dome. The front of the house boasted several salons, and a large

Fig. 210. Chestnut Street Theatre, with arcade added by Benjamin Latrobe in 1820.

Assembly Room was provided on the second floor, 36 feet by 58 feet. This was dressed with mirrors, columns, and chandeliers in an elegant fashion.

If Boston could accept theatre could Newport do less? In spite of previous prohibitions the City Fathers relented in 1793 and allowed Alexandre Placide to convert an old brick market into a

Fig. 211. View of the second Federal Street Theatre as it appeared in the early nineteenth century.

Fig. 212. Exterior of the Newport Theatre as it appeared in the early nineteenth century.

Fig. 213. Detail of a watercolor of the Haymarket Theatre, Boston, after a lost original.

playhouse. Like most English markets of the seventeenth and eighteenth centuries, it had arcades and stalls on the lower floor and public rooms above. These must have been adapted for theatre purposes with few changes except for the introduction of a stage. While this was hardly a pretentious edifice, it served Newport well for over half a century. It is no longer a theatre, but it still stands.

In 1796 a second theatre was opened in Boston —the Haymarket—a wooden building on the edge of the Common away from the center of the city. Little is known about it except that it was comfortably and suitably arranged, whatever that may have meant to our hardy forebearers. An old print shows us a box-like exterior of clapboard which indicates nothing of the interior arrangements.

New York's first permanent playhouse was the Park Street Theatre, begun in 1795 but not completed until 1798. The building was large—80 feet wide and 165 feet long—and was constructed of stone after designs of Marc Isambard Brunel. The new playhouse was fitted elaborately; con-

Fig. 214. Front of the second Park Street Theatre, New York, 1821 (on the right).

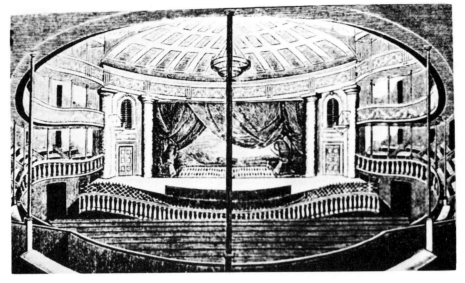

Fig. 215. Interior of the second Park Street Theatre in 1805.

HARVARD THEATRE COLLECTION

temporary accounts relate that it had a carpeted and spacious lobby, warmed by fireplaces, and three tiers of boxes with an open top gallery. Unlike contemporary English theatres, the upper boxes were not supported by pillars from below, but were cantilevered from the wall. With the establishment of this permanent theatre New York, like Philadelphia, saw the last of temporary and graceless barns and converted warehouses. A more settled political and economic situation, a larger populace, and more sophisticated tastes, all encouraged a theatre architecture of consequence.

In 1807 the English architect J. J. Holland remodeled the Park Theatre with a lavish hand. Audience comfort was paramount, and coffee rooms, seating, and lighting were all improved so much that the house became the resort of fashionable society. A new Park was opened in 1821—designed by Hugh Reinagle—after the old Park had burned. It is the second Park which was illustrated in the famous watercolor from the New York Historical Society. The dimensions of the building were the same as its predecessor, and the capacity was approximately 2,500. The exterior was simple to the point of severity, but

HARVARD THEATRE COLLECTION

Fig. 217. Facade of the Tremont Theatre, Boston, in 1827.

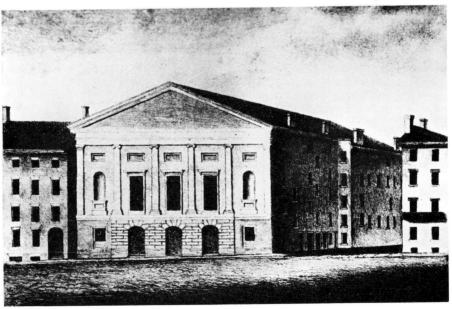

Fig. 216. (left) Interior of the second Park, painted by John Searle.

Fig. 218. View of the Walnut Street Theatre, Philadelphia, 1812.

Fig. 219. Front of the second Chestnut Street Theatre.

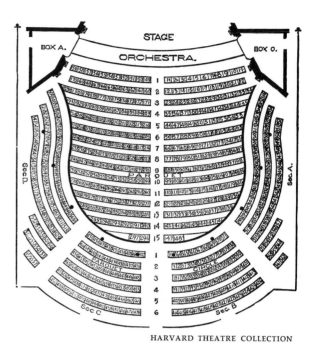

Fig. 220. Plan, presumably of the second Chestnut Theatre.

the interior was more elegant. Slender iron columns covered in gold leaf held up the tiers of boxes.

When the Federal Street Theatre in Boston was destroyed by fire it was rebuilt at once, reopening in 1798 as an even more elaborate and distinctive building. Distinction was not the prerogative of only the old Colonial cities, however; the new cities of the Republic emulated their theatrical enterprise. The Green Street Theatre in Albany was built in 1812, and in 1825 an even more elaborate playhouse was completed, the Albany Theatre. In 1819 another new theatre was built in

Boston on Tremont Street, with a modest brick facade hiding an amphitheatre which catered to the public taste for vaudeville and skits. It was used for a while as a circus for equestrian entertainment, and finally became a home for dramatic performances under the name of the City Theatre.

In Philadelphia, the Chestnut Street Theatre also was destroyed by fire, a fate which overtook the old playhouses almost as frequently as financial collapse. After a makeshift period in the old Walnut Street Theatre, Philadelphians subscribed generously for the rebuilding of the Chestnut, and demanded a more elaborate build-

Fig. 221. Interior of the Chatham Street Theatre, New York, 1825.

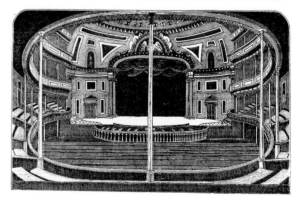

Fig. 222. Front of the first Bowery Street Theatre, New York, 1826.

Fig. 223. Drop curtain for the first Bowery, painted by H. Liebenau.

ing than the old one had been. The new Chestnut was similar to the old one, but more spacious and comfortably appointed. Cast iron posts held up the tiers, the first such use of iron in America. Other theatres were constructed in other cities of the United States as their populations and wealth grew. Permanent theatres were built in Pittsburgh in 1832, in Cincinnati in 1820, and many in New Orleans, of which the most famous was the St. Charles.

Progress in American theatre architecture was truly remarkable considering the tacky and awkward beginnings. In New York the second Park

was followed by the Chatham Theatre in 1824, and in 1826 the first Bowery Theatre was completed by the Greek revival architect Ithiel Town. The facade of this theatre was one of the finest examples of the Greek revival style in America, and was considered by English contemporaries to be superior to that of Covent Garden. The interior was huge, accommodating an audience of 3000. This playhouse burned in 1828, but was rebuilt at once in the same style, with a new Doric facade. The new playhouse was equipped with the finest and largest auditorium in the United States and fitted with machines equal to those in

Fig. 224. Front of the second Bowery, 1828.

Fig. 225. Front of the Lafayette Theatre, New York, 1828.

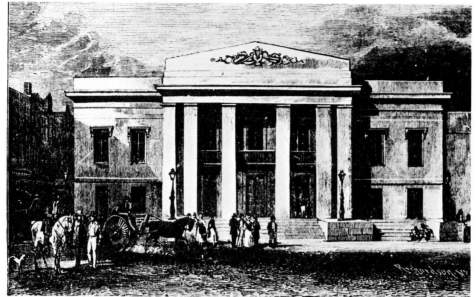

Fig. 226.
The National
Opera House
(National Theatre),
New York, 1833.

Fig. 227. Interior of Niblo's Theatre, New York, in 1854.

126

any theatre in London. In the Lafayette Theatre of the same year, New York was given an even grander playhouse. The stage of this playhouse was comparable to any in Europe, 120 feet deep, with wing space up to 100 feet wide. Gas lighting was introduced at the Bowery, but in the Lafayette the new medium was exploited to better advantage. The old standing wing-lights were abolished and gas pipes were rigged overhead to replace them. With this arrangement, the light upon the actors' faces came from above instead of from the sides, contributing to the realism of the scene rather than detracting from it. The overhead sources also allowed a more even spread of light over the stage as opposed to having the most intense light near the wings. The wing-light stand had prevented wing movement that would expose them to view, so when the stands were removed, the wings could be thrust on or withdrawn with more flexibility than was previously possible; cottages and palaces no longer had to be the same size, and the acting area could be altered as required.

New Yorkers made several attempts to establish opera in the city, but with little success. In 1833 an elaborate and luxurious National Opera House was built to house Italian opera; it included several features new to the Americas. The first requirement of the management was that the pit be eliminated so rowdy or inelegant people would be dissuaded from attending. This also allowed premium prices to be charged for former pit places. The separation between pit and first tier was removed, and the sloping floor of the lower section was continued through what would have been the first tier in the older style. This new parterre was fitted with upholstered chairs and sofas instead of with benches, and was fully carpeted. For the first time in democratic America, the second tier was divided entirely into boxes. The restrained and elegantly proportioned facade of the National—together with the beautiful neo-Grec front of the Bowery—helped give the New York playhouse a dignity possessed by few other buildings in the country. Unfortunately, the opera venture was not a financial success and the National Opera House was forced to close. It reopened in 1836 as the National Theatre and led the precarious life of a speculative playhouse.

Taking a cue from London, where family gathering places had been highly successful, New York entrepreneurs opened the Columbia Gar-

Fig. 228. Interior of Castle Garden, New York, in 1854, as designed by Calvin Pollard.

Fig. 229. Exterior of the Astor Place Opera House, New York, 1847, by Ithiel Town, from a contemporary newspaper woodcut.

Fig. 230. Interior of the New York Academy of Music, from a contemporary newspaper woodcut.

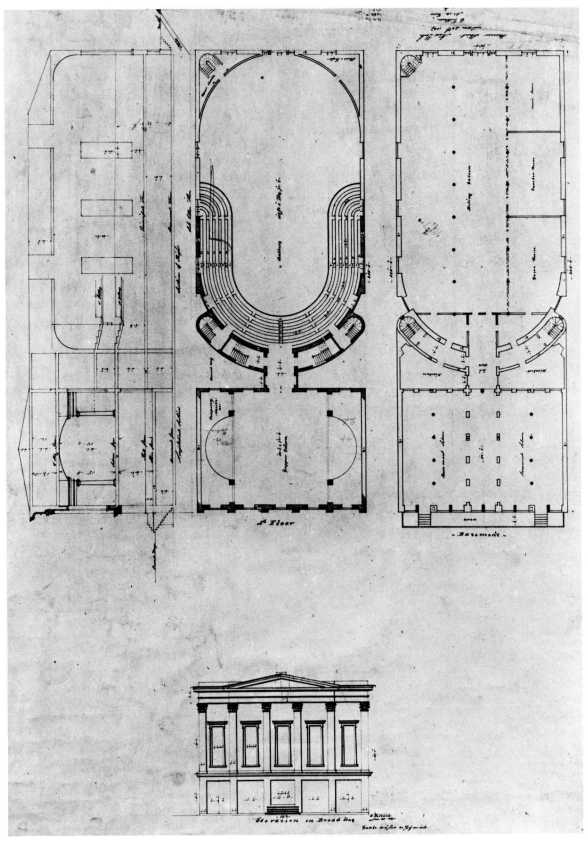

L Floor

- Basement -

Elevation on Broad Way

128

Fig. 232.
Exterior of
Booth's Theatre,
New York, 1869,
from a contemporary
magazine
illustration.

dens in 1823, a combination park, tea house, playground, and trysting place. This was so successful that more pretentious buildings were added, including a theatre for pantomimes and concerts, in 1830. This Niblo's Theatre was a favorite meeting place for the fashionable for many years, even as the old Columbia Gardens was sold for houses and shops. While of little architectural interest, Niblo's was the first of a type of hall that was to become very popular: a clean, pleasant, middle class center for family entertainment. In 1844 Calvin Pollard was asked to redesign the interior of the old fort at the tip of Manhattan, Castle Garden, to make it a larger version of Niblo's. He installed a great amphitheatre that seated more than 6,000 people, arranged in a three-quarter circle around a podium stage. The design was not suitable for drama, but nevertheless Castle Garden was used for opera, ballet, and plays, as well as for concerts and lectures.

Fig. 231. (left) Plan of a theatre on Broadway by Calvin Pollard, probably Brougham's Lyceum, 1847.

The immense spaces of the new theatres would seem to have exhausted the potential audience, but apparently this was not the case. In 1847 the new Broadway Theatre opened—modeled on the Haymarket in London—with a capacity of over 4,000. In the same year another attempt was made to construct an opera house for the city's elite. A magnificent new building, designed by Isaiah Rogers in the Greek revival manner, was built in Astor Place; this was the Astor Place Opera House, remembered more clearly for the riot than for its architectural excellence. The interior was designed according to the best acoustic principles, and was constructed entirely of wood. There were no plaster walls, only wooden paneling, including the sounding-board ceiling which was covered with painted canvas. The experiment was a remarkable success even though as a financial venture it was not, because the building was too small to make sufficient money to cover the expense of operatic production. Still, optimism prevailed, and the large New York Academy of Music was built, in 1854, as an opera house with a capacity of 4,600.

In 1850 a peculiar and popular lecture hall-playhouse-concert hall was completed by Calvin

Fig. 233. Interior of Booth's Theatre, from a contemporary magazine illustration.

Pollard to be known as Broughham's Lyceum. This magnificent and elaborate structure included a ball-room, a lecture room, salons, and a vast apse-ended auditorium with seating arranged in a deep U shape. This rapidly became the new fashionable resort of the city's upper class, echoing the success of Wyatt's earlier and similar Pantheon in London.

130

Not until 1868 was the experiment in American theatre form to come to a conclusion that was to be satisfactory enough to be a standard for many years. In that year Edwin Booth completed his Booth's Theatre, a large and expensively decorated solid stone structure in the second Empire style. Several new features were included by Booth that others rushed to imitate. For the first time the stage was no longer raked, but flat. All vestiges of the apron stage were banished, and the audience faced a 76 foot proscenium behind which all the action took place on a stage 55 feet deep. For the first time, also, the stage was not rigged with grooves which required flats to be mounted in a regular pattern; instead, the wings were held in position by braces pegged to the floor, and thus could be placed at any convenient angle. Booth's Theatre boasted yet other innovations; portions of the stage floor were given over to elevator traps run by hydraulic rams, and the stage house was of sufficient height that drops could be flown entirely out of sight instead of being rolled or tripped. The height from the stage floor to the gridiron was 76 feet, a respectable distance even in modern theatres framed in steel. Audience comfort in the winter was guaranteed by central hot-air heat. With the completion of Booth's, the American theatre had made its transition from the ancient to the modern. Few additional changes were introduced in the following years. The American playhouse had found its pattern.

VIII Bourgeois Baroque

By the time the fabric of Europe had been stitched back together after twenty years of war, egalitarianism was here to stay, in spite of the Holy Alliance. Vestiges of aristocratic pretension were not allowed to die, however, but were snapped up, enlarged, and improved upon by the middle class. Competition in the once exclusive preserves of art and architecture spurred the aristocracy to a ruinous race with the bourgeoisie, a race they were to lose. There was no vulgarity to which the nineteenth century aristocrat would not stoop, but he found that he was outmaneuvered and anticipated by the merchant prince who had learned his lesson in a harder school.

Thus, while the popular theatre was democratic, other, more pretentious entertainments such as ballet and opera were the exclusive playgrounds of the new-rich. This was partially because of the expense of maintaining ballet and opera companies and the consequent high price of tickets, but it was also partly the result of snobbery. The old royal operas and court theatres had been designed to delight and astound the eyes of all, and to provide an appropriate setting for royal receptions. In these, the royal box was cavernous, festooned in velvet, carpeted in Savonnerie, hung with crystal, and trimmed with Sèvres. The magnificence of these houses reflected the royal gold standard. By the middle of the nineteenth century, however, the royal box was no longer flanked by tiers of simply trimmed boxes. The new merchant prince demanded and

received more for his money. Pomped-up boxes proliferated until it became difficult to tell who was prince of what. The few magnificent salons which formerly had served all, but which dwindled into dark corridors to the tiers, were replaced with equally grand box-foyers, second lobbies, loge salons, and dress circle promenades. The patrons were treated royally. They could afford the display and cared more for it than for the performance, a situation which has changed little to the present day. In this race to provide amenities, architects followed the line of least resistance.

The first grand theatres were part of a search for civic monumentality; the later opera houses were little more than wedding cakes, enriched by all that the earth could provide. More usually than not, the basic form was baroque. Stairways swirled from floor to floor, while endless vistae of corridors and salons glistened in every direction. If the initial inspiration was baroque, the final product was a baroque fantasy. The affluence of the nineteenth century enabled architects to follow their inclinations to the most preposterous conclusions. Seventeenth and eighteenth century spaces and forms, no matter how gorgeously trimmed, were characterized by formality and order. Nineteenth century exuberance manifested itself in the picturesque. The result was a blinding and bewildering richness of varicolored marble, gilt, stucco, bronze, fringe, plush carpet, swagged drapery, and pendulous bubbles of gasoliers. Ludwig II of Bavaria built—among other things—a Gallery of Mirrors larger and more elaborate than the one in Versailles; he was called Mad Ludwig for his pains. Bourgeois monarchs of railroads and steel mills went to grand theatres and opera houses that were trimmed to an excess that Ludwig's treasury could not afford, and they called it Art. This was all done with such outrageous and blatant crassness that we revolted against it a few generations ago, but we now find it extremely funny and even a little charming.

The popular playhouse was another matter. The theatre changed seating from galleries fitted with benches, to boxes filled with chairs, and, in the revolutionary upheaval, to galleries once more. The number of boxes diminished as the number of posts necessary to support the galleries decreased, but the logical end of this type of construction had to await a structural material that would allow almost post-free galleries. Ledoux found one answer in his amphitheatre arrangement, but it was inefficient and suitable only for theatres built on large plots of land. An appropriate form for the urban playhouse, built on a city lot of restricted size and unrestricted price, had to await structural iron. Early experiments

with cantilevered galleries were not economically satisfactory because the galleries had to be shallow; neither wood nor stone had the tensile strength necessary for overhangs of more than a few feet. Ledoux's amphitheatrical method of seating was preferred to the older box and gallery, but with masonry construction the main amphitheatre had to be supported by vaults. Additional seating in the Greco-Roman style, placed behind and at the sides, was also supported by vaults, within which audience circulation areas were accommodated. The most efficient house arrangement—both for construction and for the best use of the land—would be an amphitheatre above the pit instead of behind it. With the introduction of structural iron the solution to this age-old problem was within reach. Thin strips of metal, arranged in girders, made it possible to extend galleries far out over the heads of patrons in the amphitheatre below. These galleries, supported only at a few points by posts, created a second amphitheatre within reasonable proximity to the stage. The possibilities were limitless, because the size of the galleries depended entirely upon the intended capacity of the house. This freedom led to an extravagance of construction. The first Bowery Theatre, built in New York in 1826 (and lighted by gas) had a capacity of 3,000 many of whom were accommodated on a great cast iron amphitheatrical balcony; the Broadway Theatre, New York, completed in 1847, was modeled after the Haymarket Theatre Royal in London, but on an enlarged scale that seated 4,000; and one has only to glance at prints of the Boston Theatre of 1854 to see the expansion of spaces and seating made possible by cast iron.

The Age of Wonder produced not only the iron necessary for democratic seating but also the gas that changed the entire atmosphere of theatrical performances and made realistic productions possible. When candles or oil were in use, audiences were accustomed to wick trimmers and snuffers clambering about during the performance, whacking ladders against the gallery fronts and reaching out of boxes to trim the sconces. Realistic illusion was difficult to maintain while oil smoked and candle wax dripped from the upper galleries. The seasoned pit patron wore his finery only when he planned to sit in the middle, far from the sources of illumination. Early Venetian theatres adopted the central

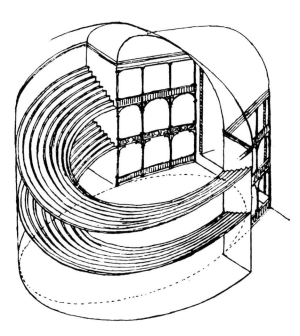

STREIT: DAS THEATER

Fig. 234. Gallery arrangement in a nineteenth century auditorium.

133

Fig. 235.
Interior of the
Boston Theatre in 1854.

GLEASON'S DRAWING ROOM COMPANION

chandelier, which was lowered from a well within the roof. This was withdrawn again at the start of the performance so that the auditorium was darkened. Lights within the boxes, however, remained lit. Some court theatres adopted the same method, and a few public theatres did also, but most playhouses relied upon sconces and small chandeliers suspended from the pillars which supported the boxes, positions from which the lights could be reached for trimming, snuffing, and replacement. With the introduction of gas, the central chandelier became less troublesome and more effective: the threat of dripping wax and oil was eliminated, and the lights could be turned on or off as required; "gasoliers" could be fed by a single line and could be controlled by a single valve; and not only could the house now be free from drips and noxious vapors, but also it could be dimmed without laborious, time-wasting machinery. (The dim, of course, was not to a blackout, because the necessary pilots on the gasolier prevented a reduction to complete darkness.) When this change in the position and intensity of the principal source of light became common, the managers of popular theatres found there was less to distract audience attention from the stage and the patrons were therefore less

prone to excuse practices that detracted from the verisimilitude of the performance. Since the house was now dark, the forestage, lighted only by inadequate footlights, had to be abandoned, and the actors withdrew within the proscenium, behind which the stage lights were located. Thus began the eye-glued-to-the-picture syndrome we blame on television.

The large auditorium spaces in the eighteenth century house were roofed by great trusses which rested on the outer walls. Within the high peaks, workshops were located in which to lay out and paint scenic drops. This space was usable only if it communicated directly with the stage by being open through from the house above the proscenium, and only if the auditorium ceiling was flat. In the eighteenth century domed ceilings intruded into the trussed area, making much of it useless as a work area. Nineteenth century additions of exhausts for gasoliers and for auditorium air circulation cut the space still further, and the introduction of central heating finished what workspace was left, so scene rooms for drop manufacture, painting, and storage had to be built elsewhere. Early theatre groundplans show little space for scenic storage and drop painting; later ones show an increased amount of floor space given to these functions, particularly as more three-dimensional pieces came to be used in production. In the nineteenth century theatre, the backstage areas frequently were larger than the audience spaces—not for the great scenic vistae of former years, but for work space.

It is a common trait with human beings that the more they get the more they want. As innovations were introduced into theatre planning it became impossible to return to simpler arrangements. Except for the most poverty-stricken local variety house, no audience of the nineteenth century would tolerate the conditions common in the seventeenth century playhouses. Comfort and convenience were taken for granted, and each convenience cost more money to install and to maintain. Charles I commissioned the Masking House to be built because smoke from the torches was ruining the Rubens paintings on the ceiling of the Banqueting House, but he did not give a thought to the smoke-filled eyes of the audience. Later gallery gods hooted if a wax candle needed snuffing. Patrons of Wren's Drury Lane sat in their outer clothing to keep from freezing, and if the windows were closed they suffocated in their own stench. Nineteenth century patrons demanded and received fresh, heated air, and could sit comfortably away from drafts, drizzle, and damp. Lavatory facilities were unknown in the seventeenth century, and the Queen's Theatre, Haymarket, was elaborately appointed with a single indoor privy for the entire audience. Theatre construction costs, then, soared out of all proportion to the actual size of the building. It became impossible to consider placing a few benches in a hall, because sofas and upholstered chairs had been introduced, as well as the luxury of carpets. Architects entered into the modern business of engineering and subcontracting; plumbing, gas piping, upholstering, carpentry, iron casting, stone and brick-laying, stucco and composition work, all attained an equal footing with stage rigging and scenic grandeur. As central heating was introduced, checkrooms had to be provided for wraps. As orange-girls were discouraged, coffee and tea service had to be provided. In order to make money, money had to be spent for appointments and comfort. The municipal grand theatres provided all that anyone could want, but they were built with public funds. The private theatres were hard hit by the rising expectations of audiences, and what might have been a highly lucrative operation in the eigh-

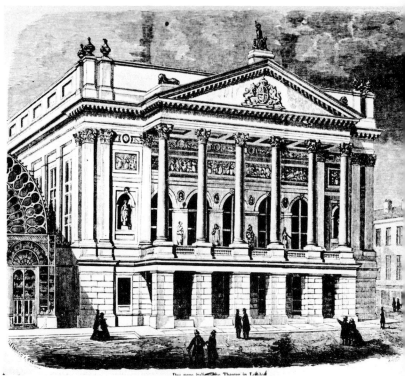

Fig. 236. Front of the Royal Italian Opera House, Covent Garden, 1847. From a contemporary magazine illustration.

teenth century was a chancy business in the nineteenth century. In spite of the vastly increased audiences and greater affluence, private theatres opened and closed regularly. Houses built in the earlier part of the century had to be rebuilt (enlarged, and embellished with conveniences), or they were reduced to catering to the cheapest audiences—or forced to close entirely. Increased capacity was one way to beat the system. In addition to the American theatres noted previously, another elephantine example was Covent Garden, enlarged in 1846 to 6 tiers, 108 boxes, and a capacity of 4,000.

New architectural requirements also included an elaborate and complex arrangement of machines and stage areas. The original mechanized stage—initiated by Torelli and typified in the Drottningholm playhouse—had been enormously complex in its time. A review of the elements of this system will enable us to compare it with nineteenth century practice. The seventeenth and eighteenth century playhouses were built to hold a precise system of machinery, always completely rigged, which enabled a set series of actions to be completed. The wings were

Fig. 237.
Interior of the
Royal Italian Opera
House, from a
contemporary mag-
azine illustration.

mounted on chariots, which were moved simultaneously by means of lines attached to a long
cylinder with various-sized wheels on it, sup-
plemented by counter-weights. This system enabled the wings to move off, the large drops to be
gathered up and let down, and the short overhead
borders to be changed, all at the same speed and
time. When scenery was composed of wings,
drops, and borders, the entire assemblage could
be rigged permanently, only requiring the attach-
ment of whatever individual pieces the performance demanded. The palace, the wood, the
prison, the drawing room, the garden, and the
street, all required exactly the same rigging. In
addition to these sets of lines, many plays of the
period called for clouds to be lowered and raised
and heavenly beings to be flown to and from
the stage. A "glory" also was common, in which
an elaborate arrangement of clouds would descend, open, and reveal the Heavenly Host or the
Olympian Host, or a Host of Angels. A permanent installation for these effects usually was included in the set of machines rigged over the
stage and took up a fixed amount of space. Stage
equipment also included at least one, and usually
several, traps so risings and disappearings from
the nether regions could be simulated.

The eighteenth century theatre, then, required
a stage for the actors to work upon, a level beneath the stage for the wooden machinery which
operated the scenic changes, and a space above
the stage for additional machines for borders,

drops, and cloud effects. Other minor devices
were installed as needed and dismantled when
no longer required. There was no fly space as we
think of it in modern terms, because all overhead
areas were masked by borders, and drops were
rolled, tripped, or furled like sails, not raised un-
furled into an open area above.

Early stage production occasionally used
pieces which sat on the stage floor in the center.
These pieces could not be shifted by the usual
means and had to be handled by stagehands; they
either were hidden by shutters or drops placed
downstage of them when they were shifted off, or
they were changed right in front of the audience
without embarrassment. These pieces were in the
minority in the seventeenth and eighteenth centuries, but in the following century they were in
the majority. The rise of Romantic drama destroyed the old permanent-rig system, because
each play demanded so many special effects that
a single permanent arrangement of machines
could not handle them. Machines had to be built
especially for each production, and the larger and
more elaborate the playhouse, the more complex, elaborate, and expensive the stage requirements. By the last quarter of the nineteenth century, technical operations had changed entirely
from what they had been in the eighteenth century. The machinery for the simultaneous shifting of wings remained, but was manufactured of
iron and was therefore less bulky. The long cylinder windlass was banished, because it took up

space under the stage needed for other things. The stage overhead developed into a fully elaborated fly loft, with enormous spaces for the raising and lowering of flat drops. The numerous sets of lines rigged for this purpose were handled from banks of fly galleries fastened to the side walls, one above the other up to the trusses of the roof. The understage area was changed from a single level filled with cylinders and capstans to a substage several stories deep. This was filled with permanent vertical supports for the stage floor, with removable horizontal flooring at each level. This made it possible to rig "bridges" in slots, upon which entire ships could sink beneath the waves, crews and all, or vast assemblages of the damned be brought from fiery regions below. Earthquakes, in which the ground opened up and swallowed cities, could be simulated by using elevators—operated by counterweights—which sank below carrying all the scenery with them. If required, the entire stage floor could be removed and tanks installed for aquatic ballets or naval combats.

It was the increase in bulky stage scenery mounted in the center of the floor that dictated the increased loft and cellar space. Without the additional space it would have been impossible to rig such demanding productions realistically, while with them it was possible to erect extremely elaborate and convincing settings, all of which rose, sank, moved from side to side, shifted, and changed with acceptable fidelity. Previous centuries had seen individual performances with such spectacular effects, but these had been specially rigged at tremendous expense and only for special events which allowed long preparation. The nineteenth century popular theatre managed the same thing daily, week in and week out. Reading nineteenth century scripts, we tend to think the demands were preposterous and the effects silly, and that the methods were probably slipshod, obviously make believe. This was not the case in the better houses. Designers, technicians, mechanics, and engineers worked to fulfill the requirements in a manner which delighted and astounded audiences sophisticated in such matters. Today, even the simplest effect brings gasps of delight from audiences inured to dull realistic interiors. In earlier years when spectacle was taken as a matter of course, the work of the technicians and designers had to be of a very high order indeed; now we equip large theatres in such

an elaborate fashion only in preparation for the production of opera, perhaps the only remaining theatrical form that demands large settings and elaborate technical effects. Operas from the nineteenth century, of course, are musical versions of ordinary romantic melodramas, the type of play that was seen regularly without music on every stage in the western world.

Only in England did the development of the mechanical stage lag behind. When the Italians—and later the French—adopted the chariot-wing system, the English stood fast to the older wing-in-groove; when all other European playhouses were using the large painted drop for a scenic background, most English and American theatres retained the split backshutter for the backscene and wings pushed on by stagehands for the sides. The prompter's silly little whistle brought the movement of scenic pieces into what it was hoped would be concerted action. More frequently than not, worn shutters stuck in grooves and the scene changed as if palsied. Only the largest English and American theatres had the substage caverns or multistory lofts required for really spectacular work, and designers developed ingenious methods of producing much from little space. The "French" system of chariots and

Fig. 238. Interior of Selwyn's Theatre, Boston, 1867, from a contemporary magazine illustration.

Fig. 239. Interior of the Princess's Theatre, London, 1876, from a contemporary magazine illustration.

sub-stage machinery was not introduced into London until 1863, at the Lyceum, and even after that, the foreign fashion was slow to be accepted. The European ability to build vast theatres depended upon state subsidies, but British and American theatres were built with private speculative capital. Only in the case of the London Patent houses did the King's purse contribute to

Fig. 240. Interior of the Grand Theatre (The Bolshoi), Moscow, 1861, from a contemporary magazine illustration.

the finances. Only occasionally, and usually in the twentieth century, have private theatres in English-speaking countries been constructed with the volume of stage space allotted to the usual nineteenth century European opera or state theatre.

The custom of building large houses that could contain thousands of people cannot be blamed entirely on the architects and managers of the nineteenth century. Late eighteenth century theatres had already expanded in size. The increase in capacity compelled the actors to play down center in order to be heard. Playing in that location started as a necessity and ended as a habit, and theatre architects of later years assumed this to be an immutable law of the theatre. Thus, when cast iron—and later steel—became avail-

Fig. 241. Interior of Stratford's Opera House, Brantford, Ontario, from a contemporary flier.

able for construction, we find great wraparound galleries still being used so the maximum number of patrons could be squeezed into the minimum space. Additional seats could be fitted only by undulating the curve of the gallery, which explains the use of horseshoe and lyre shapes long after baroque was out of fashion. Patrons seated at the rear of these houses could see well, but those at the ends of the horseshoe had difficulty in seeing more than the front of the stage, and, in the more extreme cases, of seeing the stage at all. As the apron was abolished, the stage boxes decreased in importance; managers continued to seat distinguished guests in them to show them off to the remainder of the audience, but the locations no longer were preferred. Eventually the

BRANDER MATHEWS: THE THEATRES OF PARIS

Fig. 242 (above)
Front of the new Paris Opera
by Garnier, 1874, from a
contemporary magazine illustration.

Fig. 243. (right)
Grand staircase of the Paris opera.

Fig. 244. Interior of the Paris opera, from a contemporary magazine illustration.

boxes were only extensions of the proscenium decoration. The more ludicrous examples of this style were located in America, although other nations were not immune.

Perhaps the single greatest example of the architectural and decorative concepts of its time is the Paris Opera, completed by Charles Garnier in 1874, which was intended to be an expression of all that was grand and beautiful in the second Empire. Like all great monuments, it was the culmination of a style, and within a few years of its opening it was old-fashioned. The Paris Opera was—as it is still—the largest in the world. The spaces are immense, and the majority of them are never seen by the audience. There is an extravaganza of salons, escaliers, rotundas, withdrawing rooms, and triumphal entrances. It is in reality what de la Guépierre's Stuttgart Opera was designed to be, heavenly splendor brought to earth, and it is more frivolous, ornate, and vulgar than anything built by Mad Ludwig of Bavaria. The

Paris Opera had no technical innovations; the facilities for production were larger and more complex versions of those which had been in use for generations. The auditorium was extremely large, a refinement of the one in the Théâtre des Arts of half a century earlier. Eight giant columns grouped in pairs supported the dome, which was a great bulbous affair with a spectacular gasolier hung from the center. While the design of the Théâtre des Arts seems to have made no impression abroad, the larger and gaudier Paris Opera drew instant reactions.

The Beaux-Arts baroque was exported to London, New York, and elsewhere, but made little impression in Germany where the neo-Grec style had been used in most of the first state theatres, and as the playhouses were rebuilt or altered the style was continued. Many German architects were directly inspired by Papa Biedermeier, but the better ones drew upon more classical sources or the Renaissance. The result in many instances

Fig. 245. Section through the Paris opera, from a contemporary magazine illustration.

was strikingly handsome. New theatres occasionally were given a touch of French decorative exuberance, but this was not the rule.

The vastness of the larger theatres demanded extraordinary amounts of stage rigging to handle the spectacles for which the stages were built. Some of the best engineering brains labored over methods to make elaborate changes quickly. The more one placed on a stage, the more had to be removed before the next scene; the larger the pieces which were used outside of the chariot-and-drop system, the more difficult it was to move them without complicated combinations of platforms, weights, and lines. The engineers of the later part of the century used hydraulics—when funds permitted—to shift the large constructions on the stage floor, and to avoid the use of heavy platforming. Since the expense of an hydraulic system was considerable, such innovations usually were reserved for the largest theatres and opera houses. Hydraulic stages were used not only as elevators to lower scenes, but also as platforms which could be raised above the stage floor. This provided a series of ready-made levels which would bear almost any amount of weight. The advantages of such a system are im-

mediately obvious to even the most casual theatre-goer. True, the understage area was pre-empted by hydraulic pistons, cylinders, tanks, pipes, and valves, but the areas below the stage were no longer needed for complicated machinery nor for vast open spaces to house mechanical devices which would lower individual bridges. Hydraulic elevators could be broken up into almost any combination of sizes and shapes; a small part of the stage could be raised, or all of it could be raised, a foot or twenty feet. More sophisticated systems allowed the elevator tops to tilt in any direction, providing ramps as well as levels. The limitations of the system are not as immediately apparent. Any mechanical system composed of large parts presupposes a pattern of arrangement. Many plays would fall into the pattern quite readily, others would be less accommodating, and some could not be used at all. One could not have a trap wherever one wished, but was constrained to accept a trap wherever the elevator arrangement would allow one of the appropriate size.

Hydraulic systems of an extremely complex nature were installed in some European houses, but most of the ones used were relatively simple,

141

Fig. 246. Cutaway drawing showing the hydraulic machines and elevators rigged in the Buda-Pest opera, together with the new roll-up cyclorama.

designed for the movement of large and heavy loads or for the readjustment of the entire stage to a different level. The movement of the elevators was slow, and the initial equipment was unreliable: at any moment the stage might sink gently out of sight because of a leaky valve. Not

Fig. 247. Hydraulic elevators on a nineteenth century stage.

until the advent of the electric motor of large capacity was the small stage segment to come into its own, and even then the limitations inherent in the system made its selection a difficult one.

Once the circular galleries had replaced the tiers of boxes, and the new mechanical stages had replaced the old, theatre architecture did not settle down into a new pattern that would be saisfactory for some time. Instead, continued experiment brought some architects to other thresholds. Much theorizing had been done on auditorium shape, and many projects were developed by proponents of the Roman style. Ledoux was but one of many who attempted to reconcile practical theatre needs with a semicircular pattern. Perfect semicircles were possible in small court theatres like Gripsholm or the Hermitage in St. Petersburg, but not quite practical in larger houses because the proscenium would have to be very large if sightlines were not to be completely obscured. Inspiration for a solution to this dilemma came from the Greek theatres at Priene or Athens. In these—unlike those in which the seating was arranged in an arc greater than 180 degrees, with the arms enclosing the dancing circle—the slopes into which they were built forced the amphitheatre into an extended clamshell shape, a much reduced segment of a circle.

Karl Schinkel made some experiments in this Greek form when he designed a reconstruction of Langhan's Nationaltheater in Berlin, built in 1774. Schinkel borrowed the large amphitheatres resting on vaults from Ledoux, but he reduced the segment considerably. In his own Neue Schauspielhaus of 1817 he attempted a similar study, but without conclusive results. It was Gottfried Semper who developed a logical and revolutionary plan which was to change the course of theatre design.

Richard Wagner—supported by funds from Mad Ludwig—built a special theatre, the Bayreuth Festspielhaus, suitable for the performances of his operas. Almost every axiom of standard theatre architecture developed over the previous century was broken. Semper worked on the original project but was dismissed, and the resulting building—while mainly his inspiration —was worked out between a more compliant architect (Otto Brückwald) and Wagner himself. None of the elements of the new building were new, but all were gathered together in one house for the first time. Wagner wanted none of the old-style hall with its tiers of boxes filled with

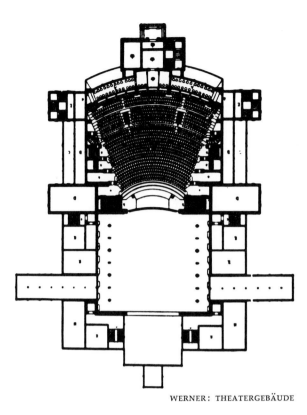

Fig. 248. Plan of the Bayreuth Festspielhaus, 1876, by Bruckwald.

Fig. 249. Exterior of the Festspielhaus.

patrons who ogled each other—He wished undivided attention to be given to his music-dramas; Semper-Brückwald obliged by making the auditorium a diminished segment of a circle, so every seat faced the proscenium directly, and from no seat could the faces of other patrons be seen. Wagner wished the performances of the musicians to be restricted to music and not to distracting gesticulation; the architects provided him with a sunken orchestra pit dropped so far beneath the stage that the players could not be seen at all. The sonorities of Wagnerian orchestration required a melding of orchestral tones in which individual instruments had no place; the sunken pit with its carefully shaped chamber made this possible. Wagner wished every patron to see and hear; the architects—following trends introduced by Schinkel and Semper himself—gave him a steeply raked amphitheatre from which every patron could see most of the stage width and all of the stage height without being blocked by heads or posts. Wagner wrote about gods and men; the architects included a double proscenium which divided the forestage into two distinct areas: when singers worked within the

more forward of the two, they were aesthetically separated from the mortals in the "real" world on the stage, and through perspective illusion achieved greater physical and psychic stature. Wagner wished for great forests, cavernous castles, and the chasms of the Rhine; the architects gave him the highest stage house in Europe, so drops of truly enormous proportions could be flown entirely out of sight.

Fig. 250. Interior of the Festspielhaus, from a contemporary magazine illustration.

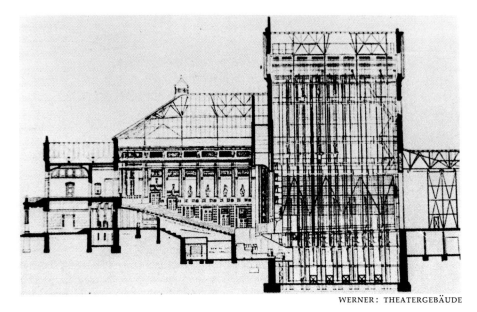

Fig. 251. Section of the Prinzregententheater, Munich, 1901, by Max Littmann.

This theatre plan changed the course of play-house design at a single stroke. Houses continued to be built in other styles, but the advantages of the Festspielhaus for producing and viewing realistic drama were so obvious that they could not but sweep the field. The brilliance of the design is manifest not only in the elements noted above, but also in the grasp of aesthetic problems arising from it. One of the values of the old tiers of boxes was the breaking up of what would otherwise be intolerable expanses of bare wall, which would create acoustical problems and are an aesthetic horror. The Festspielhaus walls were broken up by great splays which protruded into the house volume. The effect of these is difficult to describe,

but is immediately apparent when one looks at views of the interior. Without the side splays, the house would fall into the dreary pattern of so many houses of later years which were imitations of Bayreuth without comprehension of its aesthetic: stiff banks of seats set within a blank box. Brückwald—and Wagner—understood what we are only now beginning to relearn: that a well scaled, mobile, and interesting wall surface is mandatory to the effective articulation of a theatre interior.

After the erection of the Festspielhaus in 1876 other architects in Germany took the revolutionary plan to heart at once, and copies of the new building sprang up in Worms, Munich, Char-

Fig. 252. Plan of the Prinzregententheater.

Fig. 253. Interior of the Schillertheater, Berlin, 1906.

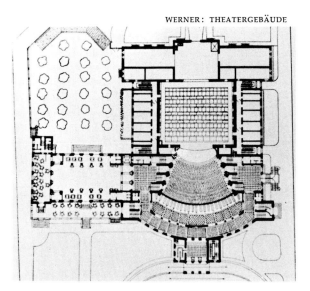

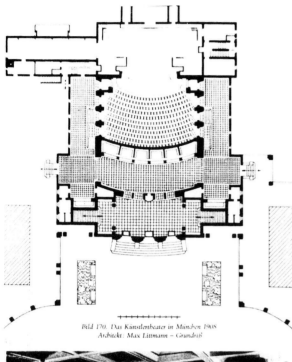

Bild 170. Das Kunstlertheater in München 1908
Architekt: Max Littmann – Grundriß

Fig. 254. Plan and interior of the Kunstlertheater, 1908, Munich, by Max Littmann.

lottenburg, Weimar, and Berlin, each with local variables included, and each worked out with varying degrees of success.

Realism in the mounting of forests, castles, and chasms of the Rhine is one thing, but a realistic box set is something quite different. Wagner's enormous loft and great stage spaces were perfectly suited to mounting the sets required for his operas. For realistic interior settings in the popular theatre, however, Wagner's solution was no solution at all. The old shifting machinery was almost unusable, because the machines developed over the centuries had been designed to move two-dimensional wings and borders. Even the elaborate bridge and mechanical elevator systems could not handle the changes of full-sized real-

istic interiors, complete with furniture and properties. The only immediate solution was to allow intervals during which the curtain was lowered while the scenic change took place. It was no longer amusing to watch a crew change from prison to palace, because the new system meant interminable waits in utter boredom. Inevitably these intervals became too long even to masquerade as intermissions. An ingenious means to speed up changes was introduced by Steele MacKaye in the Madison Square Theatre, New York, in 1880. Instead of keeping the large stage loft free for flying rigs that could no longer be used, MacKaye installed an enormous double-deck elevator that filled most of the backstage area. Each of the levels was an acting platform. While a complete realistic setting appeared before the audience on the upper platform, the lower one was being set in the basement. When needed, it rose to the acting position, raising the previous one to the level above. There the first setting was removed and another placed in its stead, which in turn could be lowered, and the second setting returned to the basement where still another set could be rigged in its place. The possibilities for change were limited only by the storage areas above and below. The entire elevator was

Fig. 255. Section and interior of the Kunstlertheater.

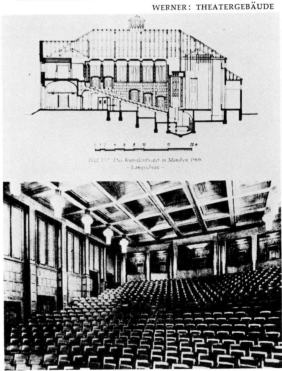

Bild 171. Das Kunstlertheater in München 1908
– Langschnitt

145

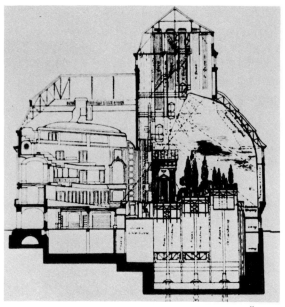

Fig. 256. Section of the Dresden Hoftheater, 1918, showing the large elevators on which scenes were mounted. The elevators were lowered to the basement where changes were made by lateral movement of full-stage wagons.

counterbalanced by weights attached to steel cables, and was moved by electric motors. The method worked, but it was extremely expensive to install and had some built-in limitations which prevented it from being imitated by other producers. Its major fault was that exterior scenes could not be shown with the same degree of fidelity as interiors because numerous borders were required to mask the trusses supporting the floor above. Even if the exterior was mounted on the topmost of the two levels, the necessary sky drops and other masking pieces interfered with the raising of the elevator to reveal the second scene rising below, requiring a scenic wait that defeated the purpose of the whole system.

The problem remained, and solutions were sought with increasing ingenuity. A new method that mounted entire scenes on giant wheeled wagons showed promise. In theory these could be rolled offstage with all scenic elements, furniture, and properties mounted on them, and a new wagon fully set could take its position before the audience. In practice this was not so quick an operation as it may appear to be on paper. Such wagons are extremely heavy, slow to start and hard to stop, and they rumble loudly enough to drown out the intermission music entirely. A logical and elaborate extension of this principle

was installed within the famous Dresden Hoftheater of 1914. There, rolling platforms were mounted on elevators which could be lowered into the sub-stage area. A transfer could then take place and a new wagon with a new scene raised to stage level. In theory this might seem a superior method of handling the extraordinarily cumbersome materials required by realism. In practice, however, it proved only that the audience had to wait for the elevator to go down, for the exchange to be made, and for the elevator to rise again. This method ruled out changes of locale between scenes, and required intermissions for changes to be completed. German audiences were accustomed to viewing one act and then retiring to restaurants for supper—perhaps interminable changes contributed to the emergence of this reflective pause. The new systems were a far cry from the old wing and drop in which scenes could be changed in seconds and as frequently as desired.

By 1914 the new theatres were almost unrecognizably different from those of a century before. The old patterns of house design and scene handling that had served the theatre since the seventeenth century had been broken. A new style was introduced which was to sweep all before it in as radical a change as the one from the old trestle platform to the Italian scenic stage. Even the new form did not settle at once into an acceptable pattern, but was experimented with endlessly, producing new combinations for different production methods and styles. The twentieth century brought with it a fan-shaped auditorium, a steeply raked amphitheatre, electricity, the possibility of controlling light on the stage to a degree never before possible, and a mechanical stage of great expense and complexity.

IX New Horizons

Ironically, as the mechanically elaborate theatre rose to the height of perfection, a reaction to mountainous scenery was developing parallel to it. As early as 1840 Ludwig Tieck and Karl Immermann designed a "Shakespearian" stage which eliminated most of the cumbersome stage materials common at the time. The Tieck-Immermann stage really was closer to the Olimpico than to the Globe, but the purpose was clear: to provide an almost bare platform upon which a progression of scenes could take place without scenic waits. The "simple stage" movement was principally designed to make Shakespearian production less costly, and experiments in modest, formal settings continued with Perfall and Savitts in Munich and with William Poel and the Shakespeare Stage Society in London. This small but vocal minority was joined, near the end of the century, by such visionaries as Adolphe Appia and Gordon Craig. Appia deplored the cumbrous castles and painted Rhines of the usual nineteenth century Wagnerian production, and advocated a more imaginative, simpler, more expressive, and vastly less expensive method of design, which was to be dependent upon atmosphere created through the manipulation of light and apparent space instead of upon scenery and real space. Craig was more radical still, crying for much greater simplification than had been previously attempted.

The efforts of both men were to stimulate new thinking about the function of scenery and decoration in the theatre, and to lead directly to a reevaluation of the theatre structure as a place in which to view drama. The nearest parallel to this questioning of accepted standards was at the turn of the nineteenth century, when the preachments of such men as Ledoux had brought auditorium design away from the pigeonhole box system to a more open plan. The cry of the reformers at the turn of the twentieth century was more than an echo of previous thought, however, because the demand was now for a more "free" stage, in the physical sense as well as in the sense of being liberated from state interference. Wagner's Festspielhaus was the first true architectural manifestation of the free internal organization of theatre spaces. The normal social divisions of the galleried theatre had to be abandoned when the galleries were abolished, and the division of the pit into distinct areas of preference gave way to Wagner's single-unit seating in unsegregated, democratic ranks of undivided rows.

The free open spaces of the new theatre concept, however, were requested by Wagner not so that audience members could react as intelligent individuals, but so that the audience mass could become submerged more effectively in the emotion of the music-drama. We noted in an earlier chapter that the development of the more open house plan made audience participation in Romantic theatre simpler, and enhanced the effect of spectacle-drama. The Wagnerian theatre plan, and later most of the "free," "mass," and "epic"

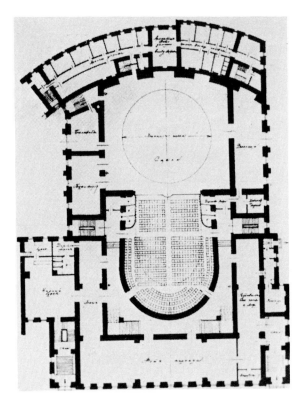

Fig. 257. Plan of the Moscow Art Theatre, 1902.

theatre styles, were authoritarian in concept. The audience was to submit passively to the will of the producing artist, and was to be carried to supreme emotional heights which would transcend daily experience. This quasi-religious interpretation of the function of drama found favor among many artists and critics of the turn-of-the-century and later, and was to have a profound influence on the development of theatre architecture up until World War II.

The Wagnerian democratic plan was united with the simple stage in several theatres designed by the German architect Max Littmann. The first of these, the Munich Künstlertheater of 1907, had many of the attributes of the Wagnerian auditorium, but was fitted with a stage entirely different in form and function. The theatre had no giant loft, great proscenium, or deep mechanical stage, but a relatively shallow and unadorned acting space specifically designed for the "relief stage" technique. In this—similar in principle to the modern "end" stage—the actors were intended to work against simplified settings, operating independently of the scenery instead of amid and in conjunction with it. This movement

paralleled that of Art Nouveau, a highly decorative means of expression which emphasized background rather than surrounding environment.

In spite of Appia, Craig, Wagner and Littmann, the resources of the mechanical stage continued to be developed. In 1896, in the Residenztheater in Munich, Karl Lautenschläger introduced the first revolving stage outside of the Orient. This was the beginning of a technical revolution which would be imitated by those who could afford it and discussed admiringly by those who could not. The advantages of the revolving stage are apparent at once. Several scenes may be mounted permanently on a large movable disc, each shown to the audience in turn as the disc revolves. The only pause necessary is the time needed to turn from one setting to the next, and all scenes remain in place to be reused as needed. The revolve is eminently suited to plays in which settings repeat, such as those of Shakespeare. The problems inherent in the revolve are not quite so obvious as the advantages, but nonetheless are present. The turntable must be very large indeed if the settings for a complex play are to be accommodated, and it also must be very large if the major portions of each setting are to be located near the proscenium opening. A small circle with a sharp arc requires the offstage sides of the setting to be farther upstage than may be desirable, and a revolving stage of appropriate size requires an enormous area and is expensive to build and to install. As further experiments with revolves were made this became apparent at once, and turntables have increased to enormous proportions in the stages in which they are now being installed. Since few present day commercial houses contain anything but the most rudimentary equipment, the typical Broadway and West End production, wishing the advantages of a turntable, makes use of temporary discs mounted on the stage floor, manufactured as each production may require them. These are seldom satisfactory and are no substitute for the built-in revolve of large dimensions.

The combination of hydraulics and sliding stages used in the Dresden Hoftheater of 1914 (later the Dresden Schauspielhaus), was not repeated. Instead, a new general plan was adopted which holds favor to the present day. It became obvious that the only way to permit maximum flexibility on the stage was to increase its free area so that any combination of shifting devices could be used as required. Thus, the new German the-

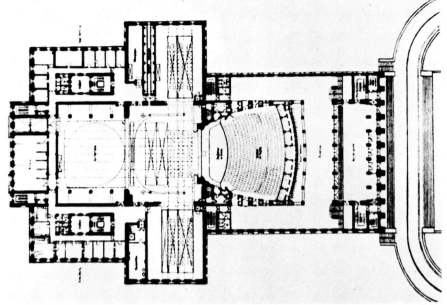

Fig. 258
Plan of the Dessau
Landestheater, 1938,
showing the large area
given over to scenic
change machinery.
Note the wagons off
stage to the right
and left, as
well as
the full-stage revolve,
also mounted on a
wagon.

atres of the post World War I period had not only large working stage areas fully equipped with the latest in hydraulics, but also enormous wing spaces and backstage areas. These were included so that great sliding stages—as large as the entire acting area—could be run on and off. In the largest theatres of this type an entire sequence of full-stage wagons—each with a complete setting —could be navigated on and off, one succeeding the other as the scenes progressed. The literal, pragmatic middle class found literal realism to its taste, and the vastly expanded production facility made this possible; with such an arrangement any number of realistic settings can be mounted in sequence, and the enlarged ancillary spaces allowed the great settings to be constructed and stored. Carpenter shops, metal shops, electrical shops, hydraulic and electro-mechanical rooms all took as much space in the new houses as formerly had been considered sufficient for the entire building. In some of the German and Russian state theatres, particularly, the playhouse grew from an accommodation for audience, actor, and scenic artist into a vast factory. The patron was encouraged into doll-like passivity, the actor swallowed in cavernous settings, and the scenic artist turned into an engineer whose primary concern was the articulation of all the elements that would enable the ponderous scenery to be moved.

The commercial theatre never has been able to imitate the production style or the technical facil-

ities of state theatres and opera, and, in America particularly, the commercial house has even developed a distinct form quite different from what is common in the state theatres abroad. As the prices of urban land increased, the theatre audience had to be compressed into the smallest possible space. This pressure had been felt long before the twentieth century, but architects had to await steel framing before they could develop a truly efficient design. American (and many London) theatres of the twenties and thirties had an orchestra level extending in a clamshell shape from wall to wall and only slightly raked. The

Fig. 259. Section of the Ziegfeld Theatre, New York, showing the degree of balcony overhang possible with steel construction.

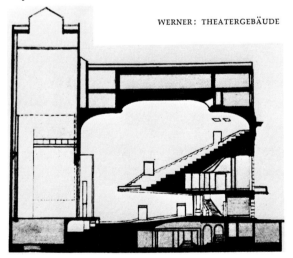

149

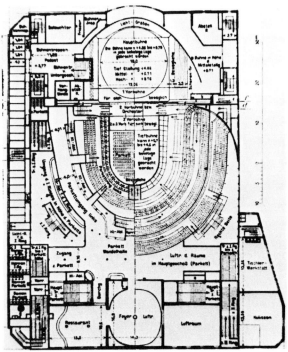

Fig. 260. Plan of the Grosses Schauspielhaus, Berlin, 1919, by Poelzig.

depth of the seating was limited by the ground area available on the normal city lot; the large numbers of patrons were accommodated on deep cantilevered balconies which were laid down in repetitions of the orchestra-level shape, but were much more steeply raked so that persons seated in them could see the stage. Patrons in balcony seats could see most of the proscenium (though usually not all) and almost nothing of the remainder of the house, the full height of the audi-

torium was visible only to those who sat in the first few rows of the balconies and to those in the forward section of the orchestra, chandeliers and frescos could be seen from the main floor only by tipping the head back until the neck cracked, and the remainder of the house could be viewed only by turning around. Most of those seated in the balconies had little view of other seating areas, and thus had no sense of the audience as a corporate body. Except from the first rows, indeed, balcony patrons could not see the main floor at all. Each level—except those in the forward part of the orchestra—was compressed within a low-ceilinged chamber of claustrophobic proportions, and audiences sat squeezed together in narrow seats, knees jammed up against the back of the seat in front. Some of the playhouses were designed for resident companies and thus were equipped for modestly complex production. Others—the majority—were purely speculative enterprises and contained as little as could be gotten away with. Companies that booked in had to manufacture what machinery they required or do without. Most did without. The logical and absurd end of this business was the play which used only one set and required nothing to be changed except properties. Thus, realism in the commercial theatre was reduced to its fundamentals, and those fundamentals were seen to be utterly barren of interest or theatricality.

Such commercial establishments not only provided none of the production facilities taken for granted in even the poorest nineteenth century vaudeville house, but also offered virtually no accommodation for patrons except seats. Foyers,

Fig. 261. Section of the Grosses Schauspielhaus.

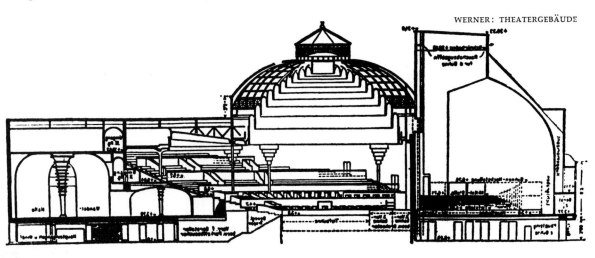

lobbies, stairways, and corridors were the bare minimum required by fire regulations, so intermission audiences found themselves spilling out onto the sidewalks. This situation was not much different from what was suffered in previous centuries, in spite of the "modernism" of the picture frame stage and of water closets.

There were several exceptions to the general trend which presented interesting solutions to production and aesthetic problems. None of the exceptions had much influence on general theatre architecture, however, and they remain only curiosities. Lessons were learned from their development, but—as usual—the lessons have gone unheeded by most. Variants were of both the mechanical stage and the simple stage types. The most ambitious of the former was the great circus-style playhouse built in 1919 for Max Reinhardt by Hans Poelzig, the Grosses Schauspielhaus, also called the Theatre-of-Five-Thousand, although it seated considerably less. The plan developed from Reinhardt's successful use of the circus format for prewar productions of such plays as *Oedipus Rex*. The interior of this new (or reconstructed, for it was rebuilt from an old circus hall) theatre was designed to resemble a vast stalactite-filled cavern. The seating was arranged in a U shaped amphitheatre with a large open orchestra partly composed of elevators. A large proscenium stage was fitted with a revolve and backed by a sky dome. As in the festival theatres of the Renaissance, the stage was intended to be used as a thematic center for the play being produced; the action of the play was to be carried out into the open orchestra. This early thrust stage was only partially successful. The great expense of producing in epic proportions required that the house be filled to a capacity above the average percentage. Such a production style required numerous technicians and large casts of extras, and the number of plays which could be staged in the pageant fashion was limited. At one point, seating was installed in the open acting area of the orchestra and productions were limited to the proscenium stage. Since the theatre was not designed for this, much of the audience had only a partial view of what was performed, and found it extremely difficult to hear. The enterprise was a failure, although it struggled on for many years, and it seemed an imaginative approach that promised much.

Another interesting variant in design—this time of a simple stage—was used by Jacques

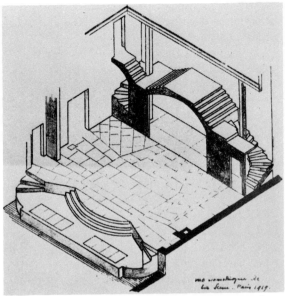

Fig. 262. Isometric drawing of the basic stage of the Théâtre de Vieux Colombier, Paris.

Copeau in his Théâtre du Vieux Colombier. Copeau opened this small, old proscenium house in 1913. Within a few years he sought freedom from the restraints of the pictureframe, and removed the proscenium entirely. In the stage area he had built a permanent architectural unit which had several acting levels incorporated within it to form a simple, multipurpose stage. Copeau's aim was simplification of the realistic stage to its essentials, while at the same time retaining maximum mobility for the actor. The acting levels and general form of the architectural stage were suited to numerous plays, and additional trims could be added to the basic unit by the insertion of panels and set-pieces to conform to almost any acting situation. Copeau soon discovered that a multiform and changeable architectural unit is more cumbersome and restrictive than ordinary scenery constructed in the usual manner for each production. If one is to have an architectural stage it must be extremely simple, and the "changes" must take place in the minds of the audience. Any other arrangement becomes unwieldy, monotonous, and eventually unusable. In other words, one may have either the Italian scenic stage or the bare Elizabethan platform, but there is no satisfactory way in which they may be combined, as exponents of the multiple stage for Shakespeare have discovered. Eventually Copeau removed his architectural unit. The lesson has been lost on many theorists, but most practical

151

theatre technicians learned the lesson well. Reinhardt's and Copeau's experiments have not been repeated until recently, and now are coupled with other arrangements in the modern thrust stage to make the dramatic potential of the form practical.

Almost every possible variable in the arrangement of audience, actor, and acting space was enquired into by the avant-garde Russian directors of the twenties. Actors played amid the audience, above it, behind it, and below it. The audience was placed around the action, on either side of it, beneath it, and was scattered around in little clumps. The scenic conventions of the previous 400 years were abandoned completely, and a freely associative series of experiments took their place. The old architecturally designed playhouse was challenged by open rooms in which seating could be arranged in whatever manner was appropriate for the moment. The result of these experiments was disappointing. Serious new drama did not evolve from new staging, as had been hoped, nor did different actor-audience relationships. Old patterns were broken deliberately, but nothing of consequence rose to take their place. At best these experiments proved that drama does not depend upon realism—or any other style—for its effect, and at worst showed that gimmicks and tricks do not make drama.

Except for Germany and Russia, experiment between the wars was minimal. There was a great deal of talk, to be sure; aestheticians and cultists proclaimed the doom of the realistic stage and of the proscenium theatre that after a brief three quarters of a century seemed to have outlived its usefulness. The Italian stage had not been replaced by another working method for 250 years. Was the widely acclaimed picture frame—which had not entirely replaced the old style until World War I—so soon dead? Complaints about the proscenium echoed the dissatisfactions voiced when the form was first introduced: the audience was cut off from the action—both literally and aesthetically—and the realistic scenery, realistically used, tended to pull the actor back into the stage house where his voice was lost and his face could not be read except by those in the front rows. These objections were not new, but they were reiterated with greater and greater force, especially in countries where there had been little experiment with fluid new forms, as in Germany and Russia. In spite of the complaining by

theorists, audiences continued to favor the proscenium form and the plays written for it. The late Victorians and Edwardians found their objectivity and good manners complemented by the proscenium, which completely separated the action from the audience. The actor was not amid the audience, imposing his character and personality, but was withdrawn so that these elements intruded into one's consciousness no more than one allowed. The self-satisfied passivity of the bourgeois found the proscenium a friendly and comforting barrier between the illusion on the stage (a picture of reality) and the reality of the audience (a distillation of illusions).

Max Reinhardt's experiments with the open stage showed that he understood that one element of the old style theatre architecture was important enough to be adapted to a new form. A theatre is a place in which both actors and audience are gathered in order to participate in a dramatic experience. In the early English theatre the actor could leave the scene and enter the house enclosure because the galleries circled the forepart of the stage, the portion upon which much of the general action and all the intimate scenes took place. The Italian style house had no proscenium at all—the boxes merely ended and the scene began—and the shape of the opening included the performer within the house volume. Reinhardt attempted to improve upon the past by combining the stage and the house. In the Grosses Schauspielhaus much of the action was thrust out onto the space surrounded by the audience. Whatever the faults of the Theatre-of-Five-Thousand, the performance and the patron were under the same roof and thus shared a sense of participation and immediacy which the proscenium theatre cannot match.

When Reinhardt opened a second theatre within the old Redoutensaal, he chose to erect not a separate stage but an acting area distinguished only by a few screens decorated in the style of the remainder of the hall. Some set pieces were placed in front of the screens, but Reinhardt found that the more he used these, the less successful the effect, particularly when they contrasted with the baroque decor. He followed the same inspiration when he toured his production of *The Miracle*, an elaborate musical pantomime that was presented in Europe and America. For the American opening, Norman Bel Geddes decorated the theatre interior as a gothic cathedral, and used the aisles for processions. The audience was within the place depicted and did not view it as a separate picture. The enclosure effect in both the Redoutensaal and *The Miracle* productions was favorably commented upon at the time, but was not imitated by other producers. The Redoutensaal was limited by its baroque decor, and *The Miracle* was an extremely expensive business not calculated to succeed—even if one could visualize designs—in more routine productions which did not require a company of 600.

During the same period between the wars other producers, directors, and designers of imagination attempted to break the pattern of realistic production, but with small success. Works by the expressionistic playwrights were hardly amenable to serious development within a structural style antithetical to their whole purpose. Elmer Rice's *Adding Machine* was produced in New York with a large but perfectly realistic adding machine on the stage (at the author's direction), a reduction to absurdity that was amusing but pointless. Staging of the expressionistic plays was done, ironically, within the existing proscenium framework—a *picture* of an artistic concept instead of the truth of the concept—and so lost its impact. Later attempts by cubist and surrealist painters to contribute to ballet and opera decor also failed, and for the same reason. The backdrop (for this was as much as the painter who was unfamiliar with the theatre dared contribute) was comfortably enclosed within a frame, remote and *there* instead of present and *here*. Audiences were not included in the world of the form; the form was made a precious and packaged exhibition that could be regarded only as quaint and curious. The battle raged, as it continues to rage, between the illusionistic picture frame and the enclosure theatre with the thrust or end stage. In modern experiments with contemporary art forms, however, the error of the twenties has not been repeated. Now, in most instances, the concern is for a total environment both through the arrangement of the hall and through technical tricks like projections.

Innovation and experiment continued, were written about and discussed, but the commercial theatre had found a pattern which it accepted as standard, and theatre architecture as an expressive art died for an entire generation. Once a restrictive formula was introduced which was deviated from only as the commercial situation changed, architects gave way to engineers and decorators. Whether the decor was Louis Quinze or Art Moderne, the concrete and steel was the same. Lobbies and salons became pointless little boxes tucked into odd corners and tricked out with whatever decorative scheme the client took a fancy to. The "bourgeois baroque" style passed away with the First World War, but only in the legitimate theatre. Some deep, responsive chord must have been struck. While the steel and concrete inhibited swirls and undulations, the movie palace used applied decoration to provide all the glorious excesses common to the theatres of the nineteenth century: stucco, plush, colored glass lighting fixtures wrought like lilies, and all the other glorifications of the humdrum were piled on with an hysterical abandon. No playhouse architect of the twentieth century would have dared erect a Roxy Theatre, perhaps New York's (and America's) most delicious expression of Hollywood rococo.

A phenomenon peculiar to America was the rise of the little theatre and the university theatre. Regional drama had been supplied from the earliest times by local resident companies across the country, and, in later years, by touring companies following the various circuits. With the collapse of the touring empires after the introduction of the motion picture, a vacuum was left in many places on the continent. Productions would still leave New York and play in the major cities, but the small cities and towns saw little in the way of live performance. Native dramatic societies took the place of professional companies, styling themselves after the art theatre movement, and occasionally offering "art" drama to their patrons. In areas where there were no cities large enough to attract touring companies, the local land grant university frequently assumed the burden of offering both training in theatre and productions for the public.

While the beginnings of these two types of regional theatre were modest, they developed into enterprises of major proportions. Since the only real source of theatrical expertise in the United States was New York, many of the theatres built for the civic and university societies were imitations of those current on Broadway. The leaders of these movements soon found, however, that the Broadway house was inappropriate for their purposes: it was too large and too

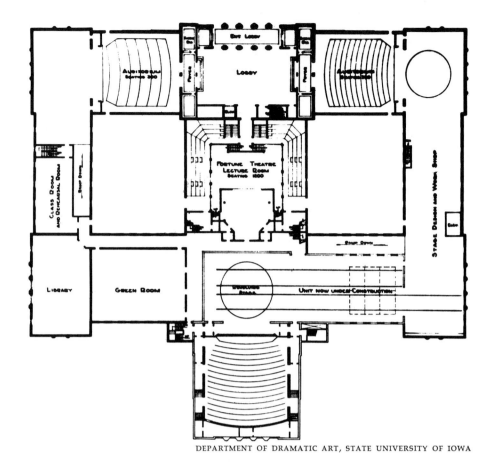

Fig 263.
Project plan for a
multiple theatre,
State University
of Iowa, 1935.

DEPARTMENT OF DRAMATIC ART, STATE UNIVERSITY OF IOWA

expensive to operate. Regional audiences were smaller, and local operating budgets minimal. Thus, the civic and university theatres eventually developed an architectural style quite different from the commercial theatre which was to have considerable influence on the playhouses constructed after the Second World War.

The dream of academic technicians, educated in European experiments, was to reconstruct in America the modern European playhouse capable of handling complex productions in an efficient manner. Perhaps the most ambitious plans were the ones laid at the State University of Iowa. There, the dream was to construct a drama center to serve the nine states of the Mississippi Valley. Various projects were developed—some of them including an example of each theatre plan used through the ages—but the final version was a

THEATRE ARTS BOOKS

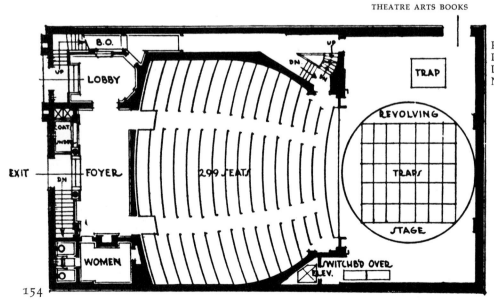

Fig. 264.
Plan of the
Little Theatre,
New York, 1912.

154

single theatre of the proscenium style that seated five hundred. The plan was unique, however, because it allowed as much offstage space as several Broadway houses combined, and included not only built-in stage wagons but also a revolving stage. These were facilities of which few other playhouses possessed on this side of the Atlantic. A steeply pitched auditorium guaranteed good sightlines from each seat, and a double proscenium like that at Bayreuth allowed a style of production impossible on the usual picture frame stage.

The Little Theatre, New York, was built in 1912 by Ingalls and Hoffman to hold only 299 seats. The stage, though small, was almost the size of the auditorium, and was fitted with a revolve that was fully trapped. The auditorium was dished rather than raked, as the first rows were placed on the flat and succeeding ones raised more sharply as they reached the rear of the house. The name and the intimacy of the theatre influenced designs throughout the country, even though the plan did not provide the additional spaces necessary for production preparation. Civic groups found at once that proper mounting of plays required large areas for scene construction, costume manufacture, storage, and house uses—areas which the Broadway house neither required nor offered. An early civic playhouse which attempted to provide all the facilities needed was the Cleveland Playhouse, built in 1927 by Small and Rowley. The plan for this theatre was unique: it provided two playing spaces instead of one. The civic theatre which depends upon box office receipts requires a series of productions calculated to appeal to the average public taste. Interested volunteer help, on the other hand, can be encouraged effectively only if some exciting and experimental work is encouraged. A main auditorium containing 580 seats, and a laboratory auditorium containing 169 seats accommodated both needs. These were supported by appropriate ancillary spaces for production preparation, and by comfortably arranged public areas. Many civic and community theatres were forced to make do with halls, gymnasia, or with movie houses. Some were fortunate enough to be able to afford to rent or purchase old theatres built for touring companies. These, at least, had some stage area although the audience capacities were greater than needed or desired. When possible, however, civic

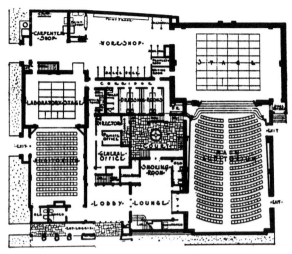

Fig. 265. Plan of the Cleveland Playhouse, 1927.

Fig. 266. Section of the Cleveland Playhouse.

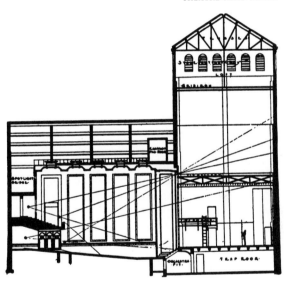

as well as university theatres built playhouses designed for their requirements, and many of these—when finances permitted—followed the style initiated at Iowa and Cleveland. Later complexes costing millions of dollars were to be influenced strongly by these initial endeavors.

155

X Yesterday, Today, and Tomorrow

There was much speculation and planning in Europe during the twenties, some of it resulted in actual theatre facilities. An equal amount of fervor, if not of results, was evident in Britain and America. Great plans were afoot, as anyone could plainly tell, and only the right moment was awaited for handsome and elaborate playhouses to spring from the earth like flowering dragon's teeth. German and Russian experiments in new staging techniques were studied with avidity, and a new dawn for English-speaking drama was about to break. The tension was all the greater because Britain and America had not experimented much, and the time was ripe for all the old conventions to be swept away. Apostles of the New Stagecraft in the United States were proclaiming the millennium on the one hand, while demanding efficient and standardized practices on the other, practices which had become common on the continent a generation before. The New Stagecraft, with its emphasis upon carefully developed realistic components, seemed, somehow, to negate the artistic freedom noticeable abroad. Many beautifully illustrated works about Continental practices showed what could be done, but somehow domestic efforts were hesitant, abortive, or simply not forthcoming. This was partly because of a lack of artistry, but it was also because of a lack of playhouses in which bold and striking designs could be mounted. The Broadway theatres lacked any but the most rudimentary facilities, and regional playhouses were no more than copies of New York commercial houses. There were no well-appointed theatres, equipped with sufficient space or mechanical equipment, to make striking settings practicable. The New Movement in Europe was, essentially, a new romanticism. Settings were simplified versions of those popular a century before—not in design but in concept. Man once more was pitted against vast forces, if not of nature then of mechanical civilization, or of himself as a corporate being. The movement depended upon simple expressions within large frameworks, a grand simplicity entirely Romantic in inspiration. Such romanticism—exemplified by the influential designs of Craig and Appia—could only be applied if large enough stages were available. Unfortunately, all the large stages built in the early nineteenth century had been torn down to make way for the wretched little commercial boxes discussed previously.

Whatever dreams were in the minds of the theatre enthusiasts during the twenties evaporated during the Great Depression. Proposals were shelved until such time as the financial picture improved. The trouble was not that the financial situation was bad, but that it was bad for such a long time. Dreams can be held in abeyance for a short time, but an entire decade was too long. Not until the financial revival of the late thirties was it possible to plan new theatres with any expectation that they would be completed, and even this short burst of new hope was dashed by

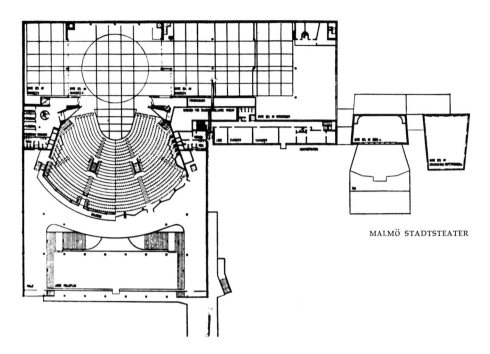

Fig. 267.
Plan of the Malmö
Municipal Theatre,
1941.

MALMÖ STADTSTEATER

the prospect of war. For an entire generation, then, there was almost no playhouse construction. The exceptions were so isolated that they drew immediate notice. The State University of Iowa Theatre made a stir not so much because it was unique—although, for the United States it was that—but because it indeed got built, and for $75,000 of hard Depression currency. It could not

Fig. 268.
Plans showing the
various forms of
the adaptable
auditorium, Malmö.

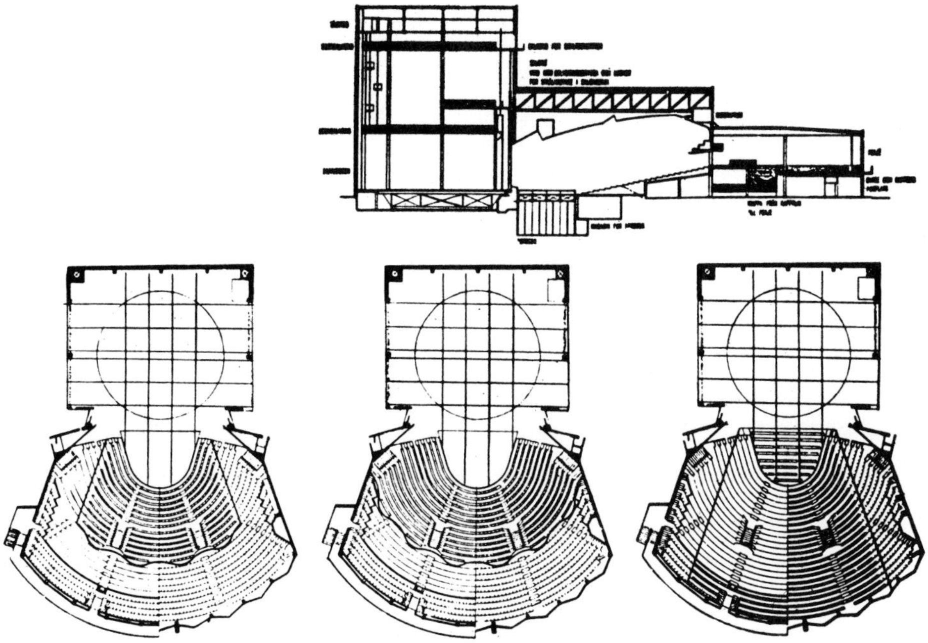

MALMÖ STADTSTEATER

157

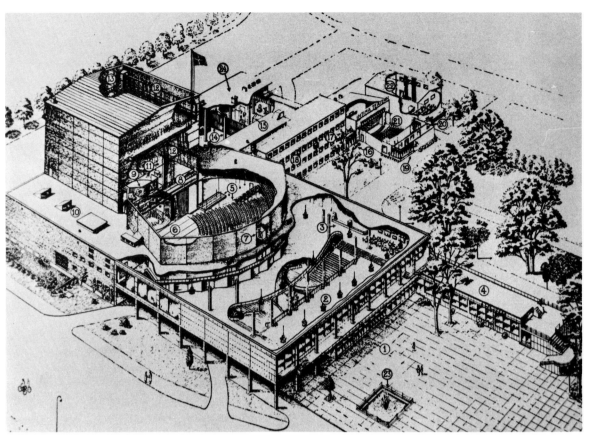

Fig. 269. Bird's-eye view of the Malmö theatre.

be duplicated today for ten times that amount. The Malmö Municipal Theatre, in Sweden, was another significant exception, built during the war years when everyone else was busy with other matters, even in Iowa. The Malmö theatre plan was one of the first attempts at compromise among several different production style requirements, an initial example of the flexible theatre. The Malmö design is an interesting one, not so much because it succeeded or failed, but because it was so much more thoughtfully considered than many of the flexible designs erected in the last ten years. The shape chosen for the auditorium was closer to the Greco-Roman than that of any theatre since the Grosses Schauspielhaus. The orchestra was composed of elevators which would enable it to be used as a thrust forestage, as a level for additional seating, or as an orchestra pit. The auditorium was so constructed that—with the removal of selected seats—large panels could be drawn out from their places in the side walls to cut down the size of the house. Several shapes were possible in the arrangement of the panels, so the seating could be adjusted not only to accom-

modate fewer patrons, but also so they would be arranged in a pattern suitable for several different styles of actor-audience relationship. Acoustical differences in the panel arrangements, also, made the house more or less suitable for concert performances. Although much theorizing had been done about variable house configurations, this was one of the few times an investment had been made in the theories. Unfortunately, while the panel movement mechanism worked well, the aesthetic problems involved prevented the variable house from being as much of a success as was originally hoped. The variable orchestra, also, was only moderately successful. When used in conjunction with the full stage scene it worked well enough, or when used as an orchestra pit. As a thrust upon which action was to take place, separate from the stage scene, however, it presented problems: it was not sufficiently large to be self-contained as an acting platform, and access problems had not been well thought out; and in particular, the forestage was completely dominated by the great figured front curtain and the proscenium opening.

In spite of the problems inherent in the design, the Malmö theatre almost succeeds because the total structure is effective and harmonious as a design. Spacious lobbies, workrooms, storage areas, and the addition of a small experimental theatre made the complex particularly well suited to the urban area for which it was built.

Some of Moscow's grandiose plans for regional culture palaces bore fruit in quite startling ways, but the entire scheme was not completed because of the intervention of Hitler's armies. As early as the twenties, international competitions were held for several of the planned complexes, and some of the world's most talented architects submitted ingenious designs, which, had they been built, would have placed the Soviet Union in the forefront of theatre architecture. The elements which were constructed, however, were revolutionary only by courtesy, because the plans finally accepted were pedestrian in spite of their great size and "Moscow-classical-gothic" decoration. The exciting and innovative submissions of foreign architects were set aside in favor of routine wedding cakes by Soviet architects more familiar with Party views on art.

While the foregoing observations on theatre architectural plans of the thirties may seem a lament for time wasted and opportunities lost, it was all for the best. All the new romanticism died in World War II. A more precise, colder, and infinitely more pragmatic attitude toward art and life came out of the struggle. If great new theatres had been built during the forties they would no longer have served. Times, attitudes, and ideas about the function of the arts had changed, and the changes seemed to split theatre into several pieces. The architecture of the playhouse—a matter once understood—was reexamined during the fifties by serious artists, and a curious reaction was the result. Theatres were unnecessary. Almost all of the most stimulating, innovative, and successful new drama depended not upon a certain relationship between audience and actor, nor upon a kind of stage organized to move scenic pieces, but upon the actor relating with other actors and the audience placed around in any suitable manner. An effort to stage *Camille* in any terms other than those in which the play was conceived must lead to an artistic lapse. With *Endgame*, on the other hand, it simply does not matter, as long as one may see and hear. This new development was considerably different from the Soviet experiments of the twenties. The older experiments led to nothing, because the innovations were external. The new drama, however, was internal, and has led to chaos.

The result of the changes since World War II has been architectural schizophrenia. A single playhouse design is no longer thought appropriate for the drama. Previously the only dichotomy was between large and spectacular operatic production and the smaller, more intimate dramatic style. The opera and the theatre have required separate facilities since the advent of realism, although the distinctly different appeals of each type of entertainment resulted in differently organized buildings at a much earlier period. Such a relatively simple division of functions is no longer useful. The Cleveland Playhouse contained two theatres, one large and one small, but both in the proscenium style. Now there must be several stages of different types, each appropriate to a particular kind of dramatic exercise. The breakdown of accepted patterns has left architects high and dry. Clients demand theatre designs that will serve several different aesthetic functions. This leads to attempts to combine within one structure the attributes of several, and the results, predictably, have been disappointing, ludicrous, or unusable. It is only natural that architects defend the designs they submit, that clients favor the designs they have requested, and that public relations men puff the theatres they are paid to help fill. If one relies upon such evaluations, one will find that all theatres are beautiful, eminently suited to dramatic production of any type, and—like soap—are endlessly new and improved. Discussion of theatres constructed within the recent past must necessarily be evaluative and subjective in nature. Lest one consider that such evaluation be mere prejudice, we should review some of the lessons of the past 400 years of theatre construction, relating these to modern styles.

The several styles range from the purely theatrical (in which we do not pretend that we are not in a theatre) to the familiar realistic. One of the variables is the arena, in which the audience entirely surrounds the action. Early experiments with this form were made at the Penthouse Theatre, University of Washington, the Tufts Arena Theatre, Tufts University, the Théâtre en Rond, Paris, and the Victoria Theatre, Stroke-on-Trent, England. The arena provides an acting platform limited in physical size but unlimited in aesthetic projection. It is one in which the most intimate drama can be displayed with truly remarkable effect: even the most fumbling dramatic effort assumes an immediacy that would not be possible in the proscenium theatre. In ironic contrast, some commercial producers discovered that the arena demands little in the way of expensive stage decoration, and the result is the summer music circus arena tent, a form with peculiar—but operable—systems of its own.

Another variable is the end stage, a platform at one end of a rectangular hall. In this form, the proscenium is omitted entirely—as in Jacques Copeau's Théâtre du Vieux Colombier—and no pretense is made of realistic illusion. At its best, the end stage provides an acting area of large but open proportions on which productions employing large casts may be mounted without the restraints of the arena form. At worst, it is a proscenium theatre with the arch deemphasized. Much has been done to exploit the large open platform of the end stage by means of film, projection, screens, and freeform solids. The well-designed end stage has few associations with the traditional proscenium theatre, and thus allows a freedom of production technique that would seem pretentious or precious in the older style.

Yet another variable is the thrust stage, or the acting platform with audience located around three sides in the Greco-Roman manner. It is less limited to intimate drama than the arena, and the fourth wall may be set or not, as required, lending a semirealistic atmosphere when necessary, but leaving the fourth wall invisible when it is not needed. The end stage and the thrust stage have been exploited most successfully for the possibilities they allow for pageantry. The acting platforms provided in the most familiar examples of these two types have not been as satisfactory for productions of an intimate nature. Paradoxically, the quite specific arena form can be made to seem limitless and generalized in production, while the more generalized end and thrust stages are much more specific in outline and therefore self-conscious in application to movement and business.

Other variants, such as the caliper stage, have been considered, but none has been developed to a point which would make them distinct theatre styles. In the search for novelty it is possible to work out variables of the arrangements noted above, but until well-thought-out examples have been constructed, it is difficult to discuss them.

The multiplication of staging possibilities opens a Pandora's box of contention. Fragmentation of dramatic method may create renewed interest in the theatre, but it also leads architects (and clients) into untried forms difficult to assess. To select a favored medium is to accept the limitations inherent within it. Most producers are unwilling to do this, and for good financial reason: at the Stratford Festival audiences have gotten tired of straight Shakespeare and demand other diversions, even though the diversions may not be suitable to the thrust stage; producers within arena playhouses have found that intimate drama must be played with contrasting types in order to maintain audience interest, even though the contrasting scripts are not suitable. For practical considerations, various attempts have been made to create a theatre design flexible enough to provide the aesthetic of several different types of playhouses, and thus to permit differing productions with equal effect. None of the flexible theatres has been really successful in incorporating the best features of each of the styles. Necessarily, the compromises required have prevented the multipurpose theatres from fulfilling what is required of them. No two stage types can be combined without limiting the effectiveness of both, and diminishing the value of each.

Each of the production forms has specific requirements. The proscenium cannot effectively be combined with an apron stage unless the transition between the two is handled in much the same manner used in the eighteenth century. Earlier architects resolved the difficulty by abandoning the proscenium arch entirely, simply ending the progression of boxes or galleries at a fixed point without any additional framing. The picture frame proscenium prohibits additional stage areas (forestage or side stages) unless the proscenium is of the multiple frame type (as in the Festspielhaus) or of the deeply coved triumphal arch type (Second Schouwburg). The thrust stage requires an architecturally neutral fourth side. This cannot be a proscenium with a drawn curtain (as in the Malmö Theatre), because the arch and curtain make their own statement which is unrelated to the thrust form. The fourth side must be architectonic and visually complete within itself, as at the Stratford Festival or the Tyrone Guthrie Theatre. The arena must be full-round with each of the seating divisions identified as part of the whole, unified in design and form. A thrust stage design modified so that an additional seating section or unit may be installed in the open fourth does not make an arena theatre; such an addition is isolated and separate from the identity of the remainder of the hall. It is, literally, on stage, and patrons will avoid such seating when possible. Variants of the end stage—with seating placed on an additional side—fragment the audience into aesthetically unrelated portions, and response suffers as a consequence, because production focus becomes diffused. The empty room laboratory—within which nothing is fitted permanently—is a partial solution to some of the difficulties, and serves reasonably well under laboratory conditions. It is impossible, however, to arrange comfortable and suitably appropriate seating plans for a more pretentious production under these circumstances. No manipulatory seating unit has yet been designed which will provide the proper aesthetic for all staging arrangements. In at least one of the several arrangements, the patron is shortchanged. All of the elements of auditorium design contribute to proper staging and to the appreciation of productions mounted within the theatre. Each theatre design and style developed through the centuries presupposes a distinct production pattern, philosophical point of view, and aesthetic reaction. No single element can be altered without changing the whole; changing one of the parts merely makes the remainder irrelevant and incongruous.

One of the less fortunate results of the intrusion of engineers into theatre architecture has been the tendency to shape the auditorium to conform to technical requirements of one kind or another. A theatre auditorium is a unit of space occupied by a number of seated persons participating in a dramatic experience of a specific kind. The entire rationale of the hall is to provide an aesthetically appropriate volume within which this experience may take place. There are a limited number of ways in which the components of such a hall may be articulated, and any deviation from the basic requirements diminishes the artistic effectiveness of the architectural space, which in turn reduces the dramatic intensity of the performance, and eventually a point is reached where the hall is so unsuitable for theatrical production that it is abandoned. The range of flexibility is not a wide one, and the point of no return may be reached before anyone is quite

aware of it. The basics of theatre auditorium design have—in large measure—been clearly established for some time. Each patron should be able to see and hear the actor, and should also be able to see as much of the scenic development as is appropriate for the type of theatre and production method. It is not necessary for every patron to see each corner of every flat. One no longer goes to the theatre to see flats; indeed, in some production methods none are used.

While it is not difficult to arrange seating so the foregoing conditions are met, it is more difficult to do so in a manner which will be appropriate for a theatre enclosure meant for dramatic exercise. Each seat must be as close to the source of dramatic action as possible so the actor's natural voice, his facial expressions, and his small movements may be grasped. Recognition of this basic requirement has led to a reduction in the size of the average theatre, and many now consider the optimum capacity of a theatre for live dramatic entertainment to be between 500 and 600. The capacity of the house, however, is only one of the factors which determines the aesthetic appropriateness of the auditorium. The apparent intimacy of the hall is another. The physical location of the patron 30 feet away from the stage may be made to seem closer or farther away by the arrangement of the house volume. If the seat seems remote, its actual proximity is irrelevant. The apparent location of each patron is determined by his relationship to the walls, ceiling, and stage front. Since the arrangement of seats for a production method is usually the most fixed item out of several variables, then the disposition of the other elements must be considered with some care.

Lighting technicians have, for many years now, recommended that selected positions be arranged within the auditorium for the location of lighting instruments to illuminate the stage from the front at proper angles. One of the characteristics of theatres of the recent past was the slot from side to side in the ceiling from which light could be directed. The use of low-powered instruments required that the slot and the ceiling be lower and closer than might otherwise be desirable. The use of a slot is not incompatable with proper ceiling height and disposition, but it must be fitted into an arrangement that is aesthetically appropriate. The aesthetic must not be sacrificed merely to provide a lighting position.

161

Acoustical engineers create further difficulties, sometimes through no fault of their own. Some architects consult with acousticians as the auditorium is being planned; others do so only after the shape of the enclosure has been determined, and the acoustical expert is expected to fit his designs and materials into what spaces are left. A fashionable method to relieve acoustical problems is to suspend panels from the auditorium ceiling. Such "clouds" are acoustically reflective, distributing sound evenly throughout the hall according to their placement. While the science of cloud composition and arrangement has been developed to a degree where good acoustics are now more the rule than the exception, the panels create aesthetic problems. This is more because of their arrangement than their presence. Acoustic panels frequently descend as they approach the stage, providing a ceiling that apparently is higher at the rear of the house than at the front. While this may give acoustic satisfaction, it makes the distance between seats and stage seem greater than it is because of the diminishing perspective effect of the sloping cloud surfaces. The perspective effect is multiplied by the fragmentary appearance of the cloud arrangement, and the patron only modestly distant from the stage finds himself peering down a tunnel even though the actual ceiling line is quite different. Air movement equipment may also intrude into the spaces that should be left as part of the aesthetic volume, and all technical requirements together constitute a major threat to the proper arrangement of the theatre interior. There is, of course, no single proper way to make such an arrangement. All depends upon the number of variables mentioned. It is the good taste, the sense of theatre, and the architectural expertise of the designer which make the theatre auditorium appropriate, and not a single formula.

Critics of the proscenium frequently confuse that word with picture frame, the *bête noir* of the modernists. It is the picture frame stage which requires all action to be inside it, and which separates such action from reality by the very fact of its presence. Booth's Theatre of 1868 had a proscenium remarkably like those gesso and gilt confections which hung over the mantle in any Victorian home. The vast New York State Theatre, Lincoln Center, has a proscenium like the frame of a television set. Both perform the same function; they separate the world of illusion from that of reality, although on which side of the arch the illusion takes place is a matter of conjecture. It is not the proscenium that makes such a distinction, but the manner in which it is treated. "Proscenium" now implies a rectangular opening within which certain scenic functions may be contained. If such scenic backgrounds are necessary or desirable, then the proscenium is required, but need not be a decorated mask, and may be simply a suspension of the house line at a designated point. If the opening is large enough, the rise of the curtain will display something which is not a keyhole or a letter-slot at all, but a great void within whose confines anything (or nothing) may be placed. An appropriately proportioned auditorium matched by a large but unobtrusive opening is one of the most flexible styles of theatre architecture. This is particularly true if the stage is designed to provide changes of level with ease. There are reasons why the proscenium should be abandoned for some styles of production, but these reasons must derive from a proper understanding of the aesthetics of each type, not from the whim of fashion. Many of the excuses given for abandoning the proscenium—as those given for embracing the thrust or arena—are specious.

Each item included within the audience view must be selected according to two fixed points: will this element fit into the production style(s) to be offered; and will it contribute toward an aesthetic which increases the theatricality of the enclosure? We are usually more concerned with the former than with the latter, an easy error to make. With a theatrically oriented house it is no problem to arrange a dramatic performance regardless of the appurtenances of the stage. The best equipped stage, on the other hand, will not provide the proper atmosphere necessary for a theatrical experience if the house is poorly designed.

The volume of space within which the actor works is of equal importance to that in which the audience member sits. Consideration of the actor enclosure is particularly important in theatres of the single room type, like the arena and thrust stages. While the audience chamber requires a volume of one size and shape, the actor working on a stage may require something quite different. One difficulty with the open platform—whatever its shape—is that the acting area includes all the visible space above it. In situations where reflected light makes the open volume of space above the stage apparent, the resulting enclosure seems inconsistent with the realistic atmosphere attempted on the stage. It is ludicrous to see a carefully demarcated floor line of living-room proportions and an overhead free area of boundless dimensions. In the proscenium the appropriate limit is supplied by the teaser trim, a ceiling, or some other means of preventing the eye of the patron from traveling outside the world of the production. Some similar arrangement must be included within the designs of open stage theatres so the space apparent in the production is that amount required by the script and no more. Professional music circus arenas employ a ring suspended over the acting area and decorated appropriately for the production, trimmed at a level suitable for the play. The "stage room," therefore, is separate from the room within which the audience is contained, yet is still a part of it. Similar arrangements may be used in thrust or arena stages as required.

The abandonment of the old box, pit, and gallery and the adoption of the raked amphitheatre add a new problem—barren side walls. Wagner's theatre, and a few others, treated the side walls so they seemed mobile. Now that architectonic decoration is no longer fashionable we are faced with the same difficulty without having any solutions. European theatres following older traditions still mount box-like gallery sections down the sides of the auditorium, and these projections serve the same purpose as the tiers of boxes they replace. The performer is never faced with a bare wall. American and British practice reject the aristocratic box for the democratic shelf balcony, thus baring the side walls. More frequently than not, these walls have been "decorated" with irrelevancies fancied at the time of construction. The arena and thrust stage eliminate the problem of side walls almost entirely, but the end stage and the traditional proscenium continue to be plagued, and the question is begged by the continued use of applied decoration. Although we no longer see Art Moderne panels, we do find ourselves enclosed by brick, wire mesh, striated concrete, vertical slats, or plywood panels. These surfaces are seldom related to the human scale needed to make them part of an architectural enclosure intended to be occupied by human beings, but are composed of bits and pieces related only to each other. Where such elements do not in-

trude and distract they are irrelevant and dull. Properly articulated wall surfaces are integral parts of the audience enclosure and should not be capable of being redone in isolation without destroying the entire aesthetic of the house.

In some of the new theatre centers we find architects and clients who no longer reject the lessons of the past, but who select from it things of value for modern theatre patrons. The disadvantages of the modern cantilevered balcony are now clear to those who examine theatre architecture with a critical eye unclouded by biases. The result has been a reversion to shallower balconies or galleries, in some instances with arms extended down the sides of the hall. This relieves the barren side wall problem, and also serves to open up the main floor, freeing it from the overshadowing balcony ceiling. An altogether more spacious (and, paradoxically, more intimate) interior results.

Audience accommodations in the front of the house are also receiving attention. It is a poverty-stricken modern arts center indeed which cannot boast of a graciously proportioned lobby in which most of the patrons can find room during intermissions. In some instances, these spaces have been coupled with open stairways that relieve the horizontal emphasis and which stress the human scale of the entire design. The new theatre centers are spacious and magnificent to a degree not dreamed of a generation ago. Much of this is because of the combination of artistic activities under one roof. The presentation of fine arts in a single center enables clients to erect a structure of monumental proportions whose public spaces (because of the multiple function of the building) can be scaled much larger than would be possible in individual structures.

The new theatre centers are built for the same reasons as the Iowa and Cleveland theatres: to provide entertainment, artistic stimulation, and training for audiences within a defined area. Because of the separate requirements of entertainment and training, both municipal and university complexes include large and small theatres. Because of the diversity of types, many centers also include several styles of playhouse; the larger may be of the traditional proscenium variety, but the smaller frequently is of another pattern entirely. Some provide several theatres, each of a different kind. The new Krannert Center for the University of Illinois, for example, includes a large concert hall, an opera theatre, a proscenium drama theatre, a freeform studio theatre, and a Greek-style amphitheatre out-of-doors; the Canadian Center for the Performing Arts, Ottawa, includes a large auditorium, a proscenium theatre, and an arena; the Benedicta Arts Center, College of St. Benedict, includes a large auditorium, a flexible drama theatre, and an arena; the Hopkins Center, Dartmouth College, includes a large auditorium, a proscenium theatre, and a "student" theatre with a thrust stage; the John F. Kennedy Center for the Performing Arts, Washington, includes a concert hall, an opera house, an extended stage drama theatre, and a studio playhouse. The examples are numerous and the demands upon the architects are similar. Each complex of the multiple theatre type requires a large capital outlay. A fully mechanized flexible theatre may, on the other hand, cost more than a multiple theatre facility which does not require elaborate and expensive machinery.

With the foregoing generalizations in mind, we may examine the theatres we find about us and evaluate them in relation to their designed purpose, their effectiveness as enclosures for dramatic entertainment, and their use of available budget and materials. Such evaluations necessarily must rely upon subjectivity. It is the eye of the sensitive critic that may separate the effective artist from others not certain of means and materials. The large culture complex built for municipal or university communities poses special problems not faced by previous generations of architects, who were concerned with theatres alone. Frequently money is thought to be the key to appropriate design: enough of the former must guarantee the latter. This, of course, is not the case. Expensive vulgarity is no less vulgar than the inexpensive. The humdrum and the dreary have been with us as long as the exceptional and the beautiful, and certainly in far greater amounts.

While the majority of current plans show the confusion in which contemporary production finds itself, without doubt this will resolve itself within the next decade. From this point in time it seems most likely that flexibility will be required of any theatre plan expected to serve a community well. Since theatre is one of the most conservative of man's institutions it is extremely unlikely that the more extreme projects will be realized in more than a few instances.

Appendixes

Appendix

I *Chronological List of Theatres and Architects Mentioned in the Text*

Date	Location	Theatre	Architect(s)
1548	Paris	Hôtel de Bourgogne	
1576	London	Blackfriars	
1576	London	The Theatre	
1577	London	The Curtain	
1585	Vicenza	Teatro Olimpico	Palladio
1586	Florence	Teatro Mediceo	Buontalenti
1590	Sabbioneta	Teatro di Sabbioneta	Scamozzi
1592	London	The Rose	
1594	London	The Swan	
1598	London	The Globe	
1599	London	The Red Bull	
1600	London	The Fortune	
1607	Darmstadt	Schlosstheater	
1608	Mantua	Teatro Ducale	Vianini
1614	London	2nd Globe	
1614	London	The Hope	
1616	Florence	2nd Teatro Mediceo	Parigi
1617	London	Cockpit-in-Drury Lane	
1618	Parma	Teatro Farnese	Aleotti
1621	Paris	Théâtre de Marais	
1622	London	Banqueting House	Jones
1626	Vienna	Theatre in the Hofburg	
1628	Bologna	Teatro del Torneo	Coriolano
1629	London	Salisbury Court	
1630?	London	Cockpit-in-Court	Webb?
1632	El Buen Retiro	Teatro	Lotti
1634	Rome	Teatro Barbarini	
1635	Paris	Petit Bourbon	
1636	Pesaro	Teatro del Sol	Sabbattini
1637	London	Masking House	Jones
1637	Venice	Teatro San Cassiano	Ferrari

1638	Amsterdam	Schouwburg	van Campen
1639	Venice	Teatro San Moise	
1639	Bologna	Teatro della Sala	
1640	Bologna	Teatro Formigliari	Sighezzi
1641	Paris	Palais Cardinal	
1641	Venice	Teatro Novissimo	
1641	Ulm	Stadttheater	Furttenbach
1652	Regensburg	Theater	J. Burnacini
1652	Vienna	Opera	J. Burnacini
1654	Venice	Teatro SS. Giovanni e Paolo	
1655	Venice	Teatro San Samuel	
1656	London	Rutland House theatre	Webb
1657	Florence	Teatro de la Pergola	
1657	Munich	San Salvator	Santurini
1659	Paris	Salle-des Machines	Vigarani
1660	Rome	Teatro di Tor di Nona	
1660	Paris	Palais Royal	Lemercier
1660	Modena	Teatro del Torneo	
1661	Fano	Teatro da Fano	Torelli
1661	London	King's Theatre, Vere Street	
1661	London	Duke's Theatre, Lincoln's Inn Fields	
1661	Venice	Teatro San Salvatore	
1662	Fano	Teatro della Fortuna	Torelli
1663	Oxford	Sheldonian Theatre	Wren
1663	London	Theatre Royal, Bridges Street	Webb?
1664	Dresden	Komödienhaus	von Klengel
1664	Amsterdam	2nd Schouwburg	
1667	Venice	Teatro San Giovanni Crisostomo	
1667	Vienna	Opernhaus auf der Cortina	L. Burnacini
1671	London	Duke's Theatre, Dorset Garden	Wren?
1671	Rome	Teatro di Tor di Nona #2	Fontana
1673	Paris	Théâtre Guénégaud	
1674	London	Theatre Royal, Drury Lane	Wren?
1676	Venice	Teatro San Angelo	
1678	Dresden	Komödienhaus	Mauro
1689	Paris	Comédie Française	d'Orbay
1697	Weimar	Schlosstheater	
1697	Dresden	Kleine Komödienhaus	
1705	London	Queen's Theatre, Haymarket	Vanbrugh
1714	London	Lincoln's Inn Fields #3	Shepherd
1716	Williamsburg	Williamsburg Theatre	
1719	Dresden	Neues Opernhaus	Mauro & Pöppelmann
1720	Bologna	Teatro Filarmonico	F. Galli-Bibiena
1720	London	Little Theatre, Haymarket	
1732	New York	Pearl Street Theatre	
1732	London	Theatre Royal, Covent Garden	Shepherd
1732	Rome	Teatro d'Argentina	Teodoli
1735	Mantua	Teatro da Mantua	F. Galli-Bibiena
1736	Charleston	Dock Street Theatre	
1736	Emilia	Teatro Reggio	
1737	Naples	Teatro San Carlo	Medrano & Carasale
1738	Metz	Théâtre de Metz	
1738	Dresden	Hofoper	Zucchi
1740	Turin	Teatro Torino	Sarda
1741	Vienna	Burgtheater	Selliers

1742	Berlin	Komödienhaus (opera)	Knobelsdorf
1742	Berlin	Saaltheater	Knobelsdorf
1746	Hannover	Opera	Penther
1748	Bayreuth	Opera	G. Galli-Bibiena
1749	Philadelphia	Pine Street Theatre	
1750	New York	Nassau Street Theatre	
1751	Williamsburg	Williamsburg Theatre #2	
1752	Munich	Residenztheater	Cuvilliés
1752	Caserta	Court theatre	Vanvitelli
1753	New York	2nd Nassau Street Theatre	
1754	Lyon	Grand Théâtre de Lyon	Soufflot
1756	Bologna	Teatro Communale	A. Bibiena
1758	New York	Cruger's Wharf Theatre	
1759	Stuttgart	Opera	de la Guépierre
1759	Philadelphia	Society Hill Theatre	
1761	New York	Beekman Street Theatre	
1761	Newport	Newport Theatre	
1762	Providence	"School for moral discourse"	
1764	Paris	Opéra, Palais Royal	Moreau
1765	Hamburg	Nationaltheater	
1765	London	Sadler's Wells	
1766	Philadelphia	Southwark Theatre	
1766	Drottningholm	Court Theatre	Adelkrantz
1767	New York	John Street Theatre	
1770	Versailles	Théâtre de Versailles	Gabriel
1770	London	Pantheon Theatre	J. Wyatt
1771	Annapolis	Annapolis Theatre	
1772	Vienna	Redoutensaal opera	
1773	Charleston	Charleston Theatre	
1774	Berlin	Nationaltheater	
1774	Amsterdam	3rd Schouwburg	Witte
1775	London	Theatre Royal, Drury Lane	Adam
1776	Rheims	Grand Théâtre de Rheims	Gosset
1778	Milan	Teatro alla Scala	Piermarini
1778	Besançon	Théâtre de Besançon	Ledoux
1778	London	King's Theatre, Haymarket	Adam
1778	Imola	Teatro d'Imola	Morelli
1780	Bordeaux	Grand Théâtre de Bordeaux	V. Louis
1781	Gripsholm	Court Theatre	Palmstedt
1782	Paris	Théâtre des Arts	V. Louis
1782	Paris	Théâtre de l'Odéon	Dewailly/Peyre
1785	Marseilles	Grand Théâtre de Marseilles	Ledoux
1785	London	Royalty Theatre	Wilmot
1787	Paris	Théâtre Français	V. Louis
1787	London	East London Theatre	Dixon
1788	Paris	Théâtre Faydeau	Molinos/Legrand
1789	London	King's Theatre, Haymarket	Novosielski
1790	Paris	Théâtre des Variétés	V. Louis
1790	London	Theatre Royal, English Opera House	
1791	London	Theatre Royal, Covent Garden	Holland
1793	Philadelphia	Chestnut Street Theatre	Wignall/Reinagle
1793	Newport	Newport Theatre	
1794	London	Theatre Royal, Drury Lane	Holland
1794	Baltimore	Holliday Street Theatre	
1794	Boston	Federal Street Theatre	Bulfinch
1795	New York	Park Street Theatre	Brunel

1796	Boston	Haymarket Theatre	Brunel
1798	Boston	2nd Federal Street Theatre	Bulfinch
1802	London	Adelphi Theatre	
1806	London	Sans Pareil Theatre (former Adelphi)	
1807	Paris	Cirque du Mont Thabor	
1809	London	Theatre Royal, Drury Lane	B. Wyatt
1809	London	Theatre Royal, Covent Garden	Smirke
1810	London	Regency Theatre	
1812	Albany	Green Street Theatre	
1814	Paris	Cirque du Temple	
1816	London	Theatre Royal, English Opera House	Beazley
1817	Berlin	Neues Schauspielhaus	Schinkel
1818	London	Royal Coburg Theatre (Old Vic)	
1819	Boston	Tremont Street Theatre	
1820	Paris	Académie Royal de Musique	
1821	London	Theatre Royal, Haymarket	Nash
1821	New York	2nd Park Street Theatre	Reinagle
1824	New York	Chatham Street Theatre	
1825	Albany	Albany Theatre	
1826	New York	Bowery Street Theatre	Town
1828	New York	Lafayette Theatre	Crain
1830	New York	Niblo's Theatre	
1833	New York	National Opera House (National Theatre)	
1844	New York	Castle Garden	Pollard
1846	London	Royal Italian Opera, Covent Garden	
1847	New York	Broadway Theatre	
1847	New York	Astor Place Opera House	Rogers
1850	New York	Brougham's Lyceum	Pollard
1854	Boston	Boston Theatre	
1854	New York	Academy of Music	
1868	New York	Booth's Theatre	
1874	Paris	Opéra	Garnier
1876	Bayreuth	Festspielhaus	Semper/Brückwald
1880	New York	Madison Square Theatre	
1907	Munich	Künstlertheater	Littmann
1912	New York	Little Theatre	Ingalls/Hoffman
1913	Paris	Théâtre du Vieux Colombier	
1914	Dresden	Hoftheater	
1919	Berlin	Grosses Schauspielhaus	Poelzig
1927	Cleveland	Playhouse	Small/Rowley
1936	Iowa City	State Univ. of Iowa Theatre	
1941	Malmö	Municipal Theatre	
1962	Hanover, N.H.	Hopkins Center	Harrison/Abramovitz
1964	St. Joseph, Minn.	Benedicta Arts Center	Hammel/Green/Abrahamson
1968	Urbana, Ill.	Krannert Center	Harrison/Abramovitz
1968	Ottawa	Canadian Center	Affleck/Desbarats/Dimakopoulos Lebensold/Sise

Appendix
II Alphabetical List of Cities with Chronological List of Theatres in Each, as Mentioned in the Text

ALBANY
Green Street Theatre, 1812
Albany Theatre, 1825

AMSTERDAM
1st Schouwburg, 1638
2nd Schouwburg, 1664
3rd Schouwburg, 1774

ANNAPOLIS
Annapolis Theatre, 1771

BALTIMORE
Holliday Street Theatre, 1794

BAYREUTH
Bayreuth Opera, 1748
Bayreuth Festspielhaus, 1876

BERLIN
Berlin Opera (Komödienhaus), 1742
Berlin Saaltheater, 1742
Nationaltheater, 1774
Neues Schauspielhaus, 1817
Grosses Schauspielhaus, 1919

BESANÇON
Théâtre de Besançon, 1778

BOLOGNA
Teatro del Torneo, 1628
Teatro della Sala, 1639
Teatro Formigliari, 1640
Teatro Filarmonico, 1720

BORDEAUX
Grand Théâtre de Bordeaux, 1780

BOSTON
Federal Street Theatre, 1794
Haymarket Theatre, 1796
2nd Federal Street Theatre, 1798
Tremont Street Theatre, 1819
Boston Theatre, 1854

CASERTA
Caserta court theatre, 1752

CHARLESTON
Charleston Theatre (Dock Street), 1773

CLEVELAND
Cleveland Playhouse, 1927

DARMSTADT
Schlosstheater, 1607

DRESDEN
Komödienhaus, 1667
Komödienhaus, 1678
Kleine Komödienhaus, 1697
Hofoper, 1719
Hofoper, 1738
Hoftheater, 1914

DROTTNINGHOLM
Court theatre, 1766

EL BUEN RETIRO
Court theatre, 1632

FANO
Teatro da Fano, 1661

170

FLORENCE
Teatro Mediceo, 1586, 1616
Teatro della Pergola, 1657

GRIPSHOLM
Court theater, 1781

HAMBURG
Nationaltheater, 1765

HANNOVER
Hannover Opera, 1746

HANOVER, N.H.
Hopkins Center, 1962

IMOLA
Teatro d'Imola, 1779

IOWA CITY
University Theatre, 1936

LONDON
Blackfriars, 1576
The Theatre, 1576
The Curtain, 1577
The Rose, 1592
The Swan, 1594
The Globe, 1598
The Red Bull, 1599
The Fortune, 1600
2nd Globe, 1614
The Hope, 1614
Cockpit-in-Drury Lane (Phoenix), 1617
The Banqueting House, 1622
Salisbury Court, 1629
Cockpit-in-Court, 1630?
Masking House, 1637
Rutland House Theatre, 1656
King's Theatre, Vere Street, 1661
Duke's Theatre, Lincoln's Inn Fields, 1661
Theatre Royal, Bridges Street, 1663
Duke's Theatre, Dorset Garden, 1671
Theatre Royal, Drury Lane, 1674
Queen's Theatre, Haymarket, 1705
Lincoln's Inn Fields Theatre, 1714
Little Theatre in the Haymarket, 1720
Theatre Royal, Covent Garden, 1732
Sadler's Wells Theatre, 1765
Pantheon Theatre, 1775
King's Theatre, Haymarket, 1778
Royalty Theatre, 1785
East London Theatre, 1787
King's Theatre, Haymarket, 1789
Theatre Royal, English Opera House, 1790
Theatre Royal, Covent Garden, 1791
Theatre Royal, Drury Lane, 1794
Adelphi Theatre, 1802
Sans Pareil, 1806
Theatre Royal, Drury Lane, 1809
Theatre Royal, Covent Garden, 1809
Theatre Royal, English Opera House, 1816
Royal Coburg Theatre, 1818 (Old Vic)
Theatre Royal, Haymarket, 1821
Royal Italian Opera House, Covent Garden, 1846

LYON
Grand Théâtre de Lyon, 1754

MALMÖ
Malmö Municipal Theatre, 1941

MANTUA
Teatro Ducale, 1608

MARSEILLES
Grand Théâtre de Marseilles, 1785

METZ
Théâtre de Metz, 1738

MILAN
Teatro alla Scala, 1778

MODENA
Teatro Torneo, 1660

MUNICH
San Salvatore, 1657
Cuvilliestheater, 1750
Residenztheater, 1752
Künstlertheater, 1907

NAPLES
Teatro San Carlo, 1737

NEWPORT
Newport Theatre, 1761
Newport Theatre, 1793

NEW YORK
Pearl Street Theatre, 1732
Nassau Street Theatre, 1752
2nd Nassau Street Theatre, 1753
Cruger's Wharf Theatre, 1758
Beekman Street Theatre, 1768
John Street Theatre, 1767
Park Street Theatre, 1795
2nd Park Street Theatre, 1821
Chatham Street Theatre, 1824
Bowery Street Theatre, 1826
Lafayette Theatre, 1828
Niblo's Theatre, 1830
National Opera House (National Theatre), 1833
Castle Garden, 1844
Broadway Theatre, 1847
Astor Place Opera House, 1847
Brougham's Lyceum, 1850
Academy of Music, 1854
Booth's Theatre, 1868
Madison Square Theatre, 1880
Little Theatre, 1912

OTTAWA
Canadian Centre for the Performing Arts, 1968

OXFORD
Sheldonian Theatre, 1663

PARIS
Hôtel de Bourgogne, 1548
Théâtre de Marais, 1621
Petit Bourbon, 1635
Palais Cardinal, 1641
Salle des Machines, 1659

PARIS CONTINUED
Théâtre Guénégaud, 1673
Comédie Français, 1689
Opéra, Palais Royal, 1764
Théâtre des Arts, 1782
Théâtre de l'Odéon, 1782
Théâtre Français, 1787
Théâtre Faydeau, 1788
Théâtre des Variétés, 1790
Cirque du Mont Thabor, 1807
Cirque du Temple, 1814
Académie Royal de Musique, 1820
Opéra, 1874
Théâtre du Vieux Colombier, 1913

PARMA
Teatro Farnese, 1618

PESARO
Teatro del Sol, 1636

PHILADELPHIA
Pine Street Theatre, 1749
Society Hill Theatre, 1759
Southwark Theatre, 1766
Chestnut Street Theatre, 1793

PROVIDENCE
School for Moral Discourse, 1762

RHEIMS
Grand Théâtre de Rheims, 1776

ROME
Teatro Barbarini, 1634
Teatro di Tor di Nona, 1660
Teatro di Tor di Nona, 1671
Teatro d'Argentina, 1732

ST. JOSEPH, MINN.
Benedicta Arts Center, 1964

STUTTGART
Stuttgart Opera, 1759

TURIN
Teatro Torino, 1740

ULM
Stadttheater, 1641

URBANA, ILL.
Krannert Center, 1968

VENICE
Teatro San Cassiano, 1637
Teatro San Moise, 1639
Teatro Novissimo, 1641
Teatro SS. Giovanni e Paolo, 1654
Teatro San Samuel, 1655
Teatro San Salvatore, 1661
Teatro San Giovanni Crisostomo, 1667
Teatro San Angelo, 1676

VERSAILLES
Théâtre de Versailles, 1770

VIENNA
Teatro Olimpico, 1585

VIENNA
Theatre in the Hofburg, 1626
Opera, 1652
Opernhaus auf der Cortina, 1667
Burgtheater, 1741

WEIMAR
Schlosstheater, 1697

WILLIAMSBURG
Williamsburg Theatre, 1716
Williamsburg Theatre, 1751

Appendix *III* *Alphabetical List of Architects Discussed in the Text*

Adam, James	Drury Lane, 1775; King's Theatre, 1778
Adelkrantz, Carl	Drottningholm, 1766
Aleotti, Giambatista	Teatro Farnese, 1618
Beazley, Samuel	Theatre Royal, English Opera House, 1816
Brückwald/Semper	Bayreuth Festspielhaus, 1876
Brunel, Marc Isambard	1st Park Street Theatre, 1795
Bulfinch, Charles	Federal Street Theatre, 1794 & 1798
Buontalenti	Teatro Mediceo, 1586
Burnacini, Giovanni	Vienna opera, 1652; Regensburg theatre, 1652
Burnacini, Lodovico	Opernhaus auf der Cortina, 1667
Campen, Jacob van	1st Schouwburg, 1638
Coriolano, Girolamo	Teatro del Torneo, 1628
Crain, Peter	Lafayette Theatre, 1828
Cuvilliés, François de	Residenztheater, 1652
Dewailly/Peyre	Théâtre de l'Odéon, 1782
Dixon, Cornelius	East London Theatre, 1787
Ferrari, Benedetto	Teatro San Cassiano, 1637
Fontana, Carlo	Teatro di Tor di Nona, 1671
Furttenbach, Josef	Ulm Stadttheater, 1641
Gabriel, Jacques Ange	Théâtre de Versailles
Galli-Bibiena, Antonio	Teatro Communale, 1756
Galli-Bibiena, Fernando	Teatro Filarmonico, 1720; Teatro de Mantua, 1735
Galli-Bibiena, Guiseppi	Bayreuth opera, 1748
Garnier, Charles	Paris opera, 1874
Guépierre, Philippe de la	Stuttgart opera, 1759
Gosset, Alphonse	Grand Théâtre de Rheims
Holland, Henry	Drury Lane, 1794; Covent Garden, 1791
Hoffman/Ingalls	Little Theatre, 1912
Jones, Inigo	Banqueting House, 1622; Masking House, 1637
Klengel, Kaspar von	Komödienhaus, Dresden, 1667
Knobelsdorf, Georg von	Komödienhaus, Berlin, 1742
Langhans, C. F.	Nationaltheater, Berlin, 1774

Ledoux, Claude-Nicolas	Théâtre de Besançon, 1778; Théâtre de Marseilles, 1785
Lemercier	Théâtre du Palais Royal, 1660
Littmann, Max	Künstlertheater, 1907
Lotti, Cosimo	Teatro El Buen Retiro, 1632
Louis, Louis-Nicolas (Victor)	Théâtre de Bordeaux, 1780; Théâtre des Variétés, 1790; Théâtre Français, 1787; Théâtre des Arts, 1782
Mauro, Alessandro	Komödienhaus, Dresden, 1678; Dresden opera, 1719
Medrano, Antonio	Teatro San Carlo, 1737
Molinos/Legrand	Théâtre Faydeau, 1788
Moreau, M. de	Opéra, Palais Royal, 1764
Morelli, Cosimo	Teatro d'Imola, 1779
Nash, John	Theatre Royal, Haymarket, 1821
Novosielski	King's Theatre, Haymarket, 1789
Parigi, Giulio	Teatro Mediceo, 1616
Piermarini, Guiseppi	Teatro alla Scala, 1778
Poelzig, Hans	Grosses Schauspielhaus, 1919
Pollard, Calvin	Brougham's Lyceum, 1850; Castle Garden, 1844
Reinagle, Alexander/ Wignall	Chestnut Street Theatre, 1793
Reinagle, Hugh	2nd Park Street Theatre, 1821
Rogers, Isaiah	Astor Place Opera House, 1847
Sabbattini, Nicola	Teatro del Sol, 1636
Santurini, Francesco	San Salvator, Munich, 1657
Sarda, S. M.	Teatro Torino, 1740
Scamozzi, Vicenzo	Teatro di Sabbioneta, 1590
Schinkel, Karl	Neues Schauspielhaus, Berlin, 1817
Selliers, Josef	Vienna Burgtheater, 1741
Semper/Brückwald	(see Brückwald)
Shepherd, James	Lincoln's Inn Fields, 1714; Covent Garden, 1732
Sighezzi, Andrea	Teatro Formigliari, 1640
Smirke, Robert	Covent Garden, 1809
Soufflot, Charles	Théâtre de Lyon, 1754
Teodoli, Girolamo	Teatro d'Argentina, 1732
Torelli, Giacomo	Teatro della Fortuna, 1662; Teatro da Fano, 1661
Town, Ithiel	Bowery Street Theatre, 1826
Vanbrugh, Sir John	Queen's Theatre, Haymarket, 1705
Vanvitelli, Luigi	Court Theatre, Caserta, 1752
Vianini	Teatro Ducale, Mantua, 1608
Vigarani, Gaspare	Salle des Machines, 1659
Webb, John	Cockpit-in-Court (?), ca. 1632; Rutland House Theatre, 1656; Theatre Royal, Bridges Street (?), 1663
Wignall/Reinagle	(see Reinagle)
Wilmot, John	Royalty Theatre, 1785
Witte, J. E.	3rd Schouwburg, 1774
Wren, Christopher	Duke's Theatre, Dorset Garden (?), 1671; Theatre Royal, Bridges Street (?), 1663; Sheldonian Theatre, 1663; Theatre Royal, Drury Lane (?), 1674
Wyatt, Benjamin Dean	Drury Lane, 1809
Wyatt, James	Pantheon, 1770
Zucchi, Andrea	Dresden opera, 1738

Appendix
IV Observations on the Nineteenth Century Stage

(Condensed from "Theatres, Halls, and Audiences," by Dion Boucicault, *North American Review*, CCCXCV, October, 1889)

In 1854 Tripler Hall, on Broadway, New York, was burned. It stood on the site now occupied by the Grand Central Hotel. In the same year were built the Metropolitan Theatre and the Lafarge Hotel, covering the same ground. This theatre measured one hundred and fifty feet in width by one hundred and fifty feet in depth. The curtain opening was sixty feet in width—by far the largest in the world. After struggling vainly for five years, the elephantine theatre came to grief. I pointed out to Mr. Lafarge its unwieldy size as the cause of its failure;—no management could successfully deal with such a leviathan. He confided the building to me, and I scooped out the interior down to the foundation, leaving only the walls and the roof standing, and within this space a theatre was erected about the size of the Star. We called it the Winter Garden; it was successfully managed until its destruction by fire in (I think) 1866 or thereabouts.

In 1857 the Academy of Music in Philadelphia was built. The object which inspired its proprietors was to have a theatre which should surpass in size any theatrical building in the world. So, on the plans of this monument were traced the outlines of the Scala, the San Carlo, the Covent-Garden Opera-House in London, the Boston Theatre, to show how very much larger was the Philadelphia monster. Amongst the eminent stars that made their appearance there during its opening season came Charles Mathews, the English Comedian. He pronounced the Academy a magnificent affair as a theatrical monument, but suggested that every spectator be provided with a telescope and each actor with a speaking-trumpet.

In 1864 the Albert Hall in London was projected, dedicated to the Prince Consort, then recently dead; this hall was to be devoted to concerts, to fine-art meetings, and exhibitions. When the plan was set forth, it was found that the auditorium was to be of proportions so enormous than Langham Church steeple and spire, if set in the midst of the pit, would not reach the proposed ceiling. I ventured to point out that such an auditorium would be found unfit for speech; and even for music it would present all the objections that singers and instrumental performers find in open-air concerts. These objections were set at nought; and the Albert Hall was opened by the Prince of Wales in the presence of ten thousand spectators. We cannot call them an audience, as not a word his Royal Highness uttered on this occasion could be heard. The result verified all the objections raised. Then came the remedies. Amongst others, a huge *velarium*, or swinging canvas ceiling, was suspended with lines over the orchestra; but these contrivances failed to mitigate the trouble, for the trouble was and is, simply, that the human voice can fill an area containing only a certain number of cubic feet, and the eye of the spectator can see only within the scope of human vision. These limitations seem to be self-evident, but our ambition and pride continue to ignore, or, at least, to disregard them.

The most powerful and articulate voice, when used in speech, can fill an enclosed area of 320,000 cubic feet—that is, a room eighty feet in breadth, eighty feet in length, and fifty feet in height; and to fill even this space perfectly the speaker should be aided by certain conditions, which are to be found in the peculiar arrangement of a theatre. Let us assume that the stage and auditorium, taken together, represent an enclosure one hundred and twenty feet in length, eighty feet in breadth, and fifty feet in height. The speaker would stand at a point with eighty feet in front of him, and forty feet behind him, this forty feet representing the stage. But this forty feet is contracted, practically, by the hanging scenery above his head, which packs that space closely, excepting twenty-five feet, which is the height left clear on the stage. At the sides scenery on frames stands in the entrances, packed so closely as to leave about thirty-six feet clear. Thus the speaker finds himself boxed in an area thirty-six feet in width, twenty-five feet in height, and forty feet deep. From this chamber he directs his voice into the auditorium eighty feet in depth, eighty feet in width, and fifty feet in height. The auditorium, packed with an audience and brilliantly lighted, generates considerable heat, while the stage remains at a much lower temperature; this state of affairs causes a current of air to flow continuously from the stage to the auditorium. It carries the voice of the speaker with it. The draught is very sensibly felt by the spectators at the moment when the curtain is raised, and its presence may be detected by the movement of the curtain, which tends invariably to distend, or "bag," towards the audience, under the pressure of the colder air on the stage, so that in some cases the curtain must be anchored down or held on sliding rings at the sides, that run down on fixed wires or rods; without which tension the curtain would be blown out over the orchestra.

With all the advantages enumerated for the conveyance of the voice in theatres, which no other form of auditorium affords, still we have never discovered the principles applicable to the proportions of a great hall by which the voice is spread and conveyed evenly and in the most perfect manner to all parts. After the building is completed, it is, confessedly and notoriously, a matter of accident, and a question to be solved by experiment, whether it is "good for sound." When it proves to be defective, no one can explain why it is so, or where the defect lies, or prescribe a remedy. Echoes will be discovered nestling in one spot; reverberations confusing the voices will be found in another; a person seated thirty feet from the speaker will hear with difficulty, while his voice reaches one seated seventy feet away distinctly. This hall, containing 300,000 cubic feet, is easily filled by the voice, while in this smaller one, not containing 200,000 feet, the speaker is at great trouble to make himself heard. If acoustics were an exact science, would there be, could there be, any doubt or error in these matters? By experiment we are led to believe that the domed, the arched, the groined roof is bad for sound.

The exorbitant buildings to be devoted to music and the drama, now either in process of erection or under advisement, in Chicago and in Madison Square and Seventh Avenue, New York, are, by the description we hear of the proposed large capacities, liable to disappoint the hopes of their projectors. Let us parade a few poor and perhaps sordid facts concerning buildings for this purpose, which, after all, must eventually arrive at the fundamental question—will they be self-supporting? Will they pay?

I have frequently heard the management of a theatre complain that it was too large. I have never heard a manager complain that his house was too small.

A large theatre requires for the production of the same work a greater number of musicians in the orchestra; a greater consumption of gas; a greater number of attendants; a larger number of supernumeraries and ballet; a larger staff of carpenters, property-men, and gas-men; a larger amount of canvas and wood for the larger scenery; a larger quantity of furniture on the stage. There is an increment in every department. It is, therefore, much more costly to carry on than a small theatre. The same entertainment does not look so well on the large stage, unless it be a spectacular play, and the public do not patronize a performance in proportion to the size of the theatre in which it is given. The popular places of public entertainment have always been medium-sized or small.

The stature of the actor should determine the size of the stage on which he appears, and the distance at which his features can be perfectly seen may determine the proportions of the auditorium. The measure of the spectator's eye may be taken as a standard for his ear, for within that scope the actor will be heard: the two senses are, so far as a theatre is concerned, of equal capacity. I am led to believe that a group of more than two thousand persons is not so susceptible to the psychic influences exerted by artists as a group of less than that number. There is a limit to the genius of the actor as regards its reach over his audience; and no auditorium should exceed in size that limit.

(N.B.—the Chicago building "devoted to music and drama" referred to by Mr. Boucicault was, of course, Adler and Sullivan's Auditorium Theatre. Ironically, the Auditorium was—as it still is—noted for its perfect acoustics in spite of its great capacity.)

Appendix
V Illustrations of Technical Apparatus, Sixteenth to Nineteenth Centuries

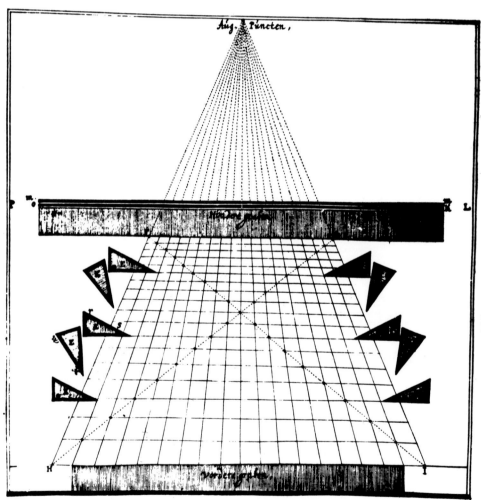

Fig. 270.
Plan of a scene using *periaktoi,* by Furttenbach.

FURTTENBACH: ARCHITECTURA RECREATIONIS

FURTTENBACH: ARCHITECTURA RECREATIONIS

Fig. 271. Section of a stage by Furttenbach, showing fixed borders, lights, and *periaktoi.*

Fig. 272. Sketch illustrating the different developments of *periaktoi* by Sabbatini and Furttenbach.

D. C. MULLIN

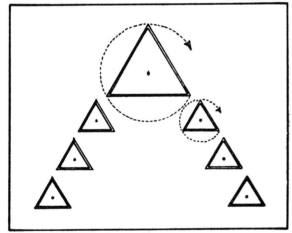

SABBATTINI

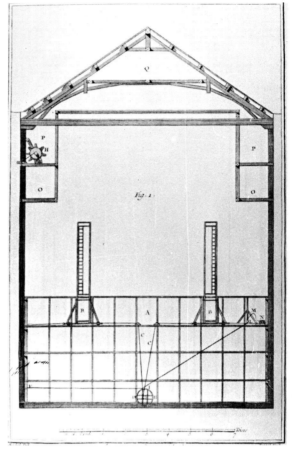

DUMONT: RECUEIL DES PLANCHES

Fig. 273. Section through the stage of Moreau's opera, showing mounted chariots and the mechanism which moves them.

Fig. 274. Stage section of the Dresden opera of 1749, showing chariots, borders, and a zig-zag run for cannonballs to simulate thunder.

HAMMITZSCH: DER MODERNE THEATERBAU

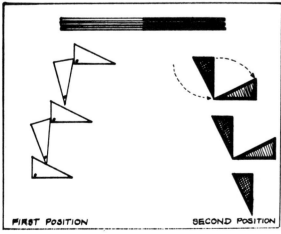

FIRST POSITION   SECOND POSITION

FURTTENBACH

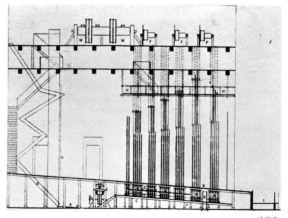

Fig. 275.
View
under the stage,
Drottningholm,
showing the
main windlass.

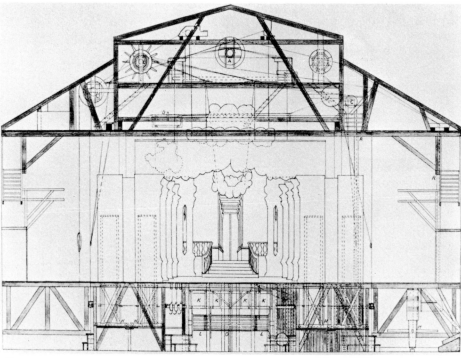

Fig. 276.
Section through
the Drottningholm
stage, showing
wings on chariots
and hanging
cloud machines.

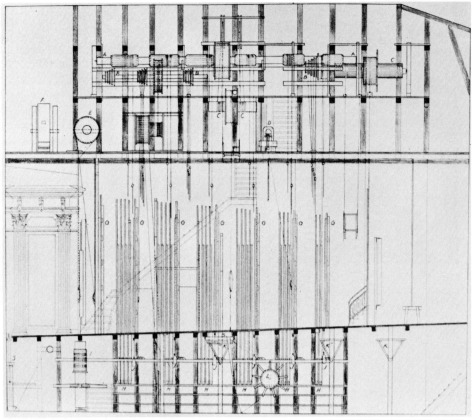

Fig. 277.
Cross-section of
the Drottningholm
stage showing the
relative positions
of all machines.

Fig. 278.
Below the stage,
Gripsholm, showing
the main windlass
and the chariots
on their tracks.

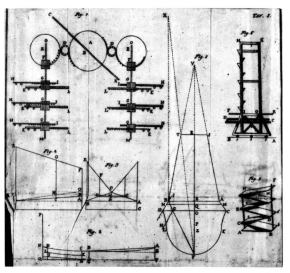

LAMBERTI: LA REGOLATA CONSTRUZIONE DE TEATRI

Fig. 279. Illustration of a method of moving chariots through the use of gears.

Fig. 281. (right) Section of an English stage showing the "bridges" mounted between the groove positions.

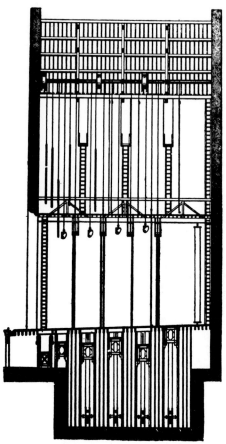

SACHS: OPERA HOUSES AND THEATRES

BOULÉE: ESSAI SUR L'ART DE CONSTRUIRE LES THEATRES

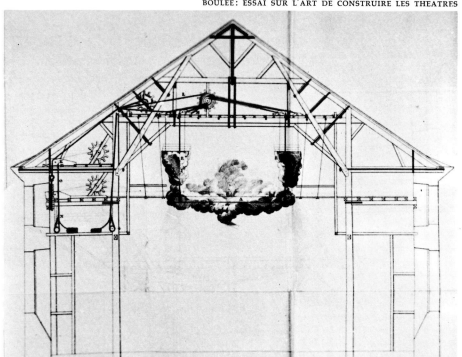

Fig. 280.
Rigging of a
cloud machine.

Fig. 282. Cutaway view of the construction of a nineteenth century French stage. Note the chariot in position and the stagehand rigging the "mast" to which wings are attached.

Fig. 283. Stagehands mounting a wing on a chariot mast.

Fig. 284. Changing the scenes on a nineteenth century stage.

Fig. 285. Machinery of a "glory" in its fully extended position, hanging from the flies. Additional masking pieces would be attached to cover actors seated within the "clouds."

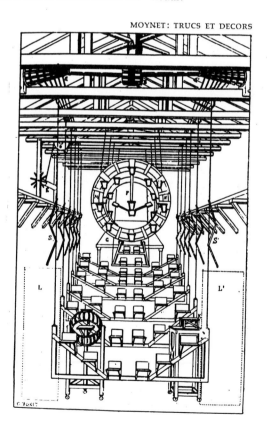

183

BOULÉE: ESSAI

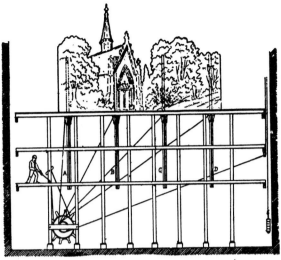

Fig. 286. Stagehand raising a bridge by releasing a line which lowers the counterweight.

Fig. 287. Stagehand raising a drop by releasing a line which lowers the counterweight.

BOULÉE: ESSAI

MOYNET: TRUCS ET DECORS

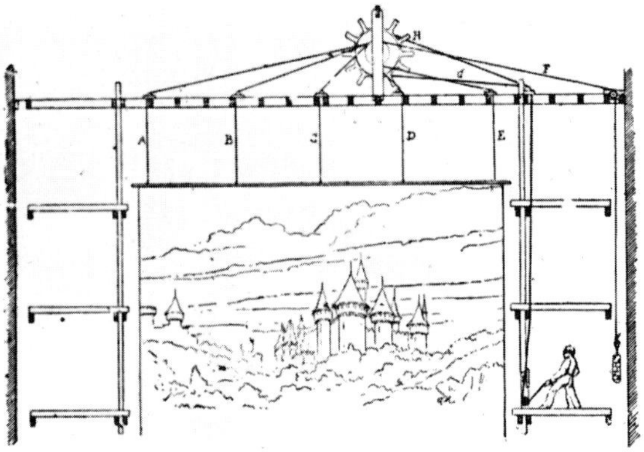

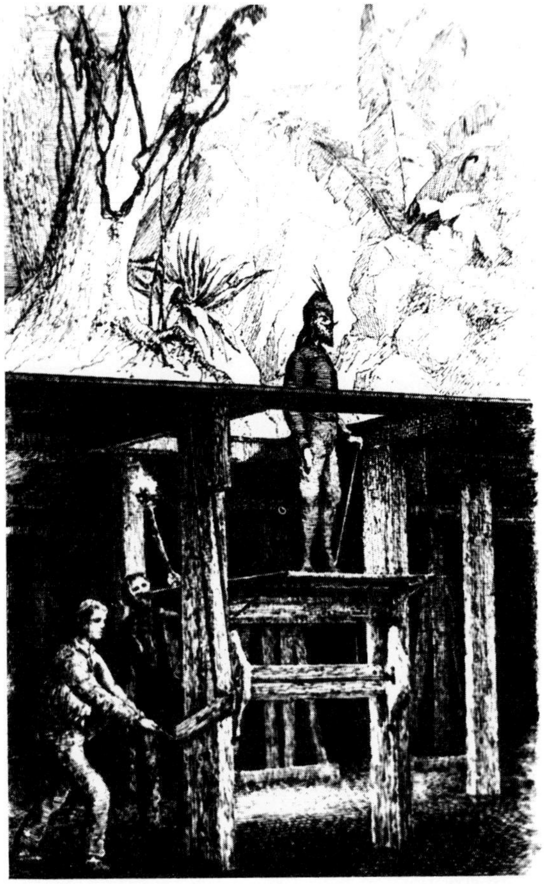

Fig. 288. The "opera trap" on a nineteenth century stage. The stagehand releases a counterweight and the figure on the platform is propelled upward.

Fig. 289. The maiden abandoned in an isolated tower as her tormenter sails away: the audience's view.

Fig. 290. The maiden, tower, and the ship sailing away: backstage view.

MOYNET: TRUCS ET DECORS

Fig. 291. Setting for one of the scenes of *l'Africaine* at the Paris opera, as seen from the audience. The gundeck and quarterdeck of a fully-rigged man-of-war which rolls with the waves.

Fig. 292. The ship from backstage, showing the elaborate cradle which permits the ship to rock realistically.

MOYNET: TRUCS ET DECORS

186

Reference Bibliography

These, listed by chapter, are the principal sources used for this book. Where the contents of a cited work are relevant for more than one chapter, the title is listed only under the chapter for which it proved most valuable as a reference. If one of several volumes is noted, then only that volume served as a reference. Standard general histories of the theatre have not been included, although some of them have been extremely helpful. The Bibliography is not exhaustive, but is designed as a guide for those who wish to pursue the subject further.

CHAPTER ONE

Alberti, Leone Baptista, *Della Architettura libri diece, traduzione Cosimo Bartoli*, Milan, 1833.

Barbaro, Danielo, *I diece Libri dell'Architettura de Vitruvio*, Venice, 1556.

Cesariano, Cesare, *De Lucio Vitruvio Pollione de Architettura Libri Dece Traducti de Latino in vulgare . . .* , Milan, 1521.

Chambers, E. K., *The Medieval Stage*, Oxford, 1903, vol. 2.

Kennard, Joseph, *The Italian Theatre*, New York, 1932, vol. 1.

Kernodle, George, *From Art to Theatre*, Chicago, 1944.

Serlio, Sebastiano, *Tutte l'Opere d'architettura et prospettiva*, 1619.

CHAPTER TWO

Campbell, Lily Bess, *Scenes and Machines on the English Stage During the Renaissance*, Cambridge, 1923.

Coppola, Giovanni Carlo, *Le Nozzi Degli Dei, favola . . .* , Florence, 1637.

Deierkauf-Holsboer, S. Wilma, *Le Théâtre de Marais*, Paris, 1954.

Donati, Paolo, *Descrizione del gran teatro Farnesiano di Parma*, Parma, 1817.

Furttenbach, Josef, *Architectura Civilis*, Ulm, 1628.

Hewitt, Bernard, ed., *The Renaissance Stage*, Coral Gables, 1958.

Holsboer, S. Wilma, *L'Histoire de a mise en scène dans le théâtre Français de 1600 a 1657*, Paris, 1933.

Institute Pédagogique Nationale, *La Vie Théâtrale au Temps de la Renaissance*, Paris, 1963.

Lawrenson, T. E., *The French Stage in the XVIIth Century: a study in the advent of the Italian order*, Manchester, 1957.

Leclerc, Helene, *Les Origines Italiennes de l'Architecture Théâtrale Moderne*, Paris, 1946.

Mayor, A. H., *Tempi e aspetti della scenografia*, Turin, 1954.

Mullin, D. C., "The Influence of Vitruvius on Theatre Architecture," *Educational Theatre Journal*, XVIII, 1 (March, 1966).

Nagler, Alois, *Theatre Festivals of the Medici*, New Haven, 1965.

———, "The Furtenbach Theatre in Ulm," *Theatre Annual*, 1953.

Niessen, Carl, *Das Buhnenbild*, Leipzig, 1924.

Ricci, Corrado, *La Scenografia Italiana*, Milan, 1930.

———, *I Teatri de Bologna nei Secoli XVII e XVIII*, Milan, 1888.

Scamozzi, Vicenzo, *The Mirror of Architecture, after the true principles of Vicenzo Scamozzi, Venetian*, translated by W. F., London, 1687.

Schrade, Leo, *La Représentation d'Edipo Tiranno au Teatro Olimpico*, Paris, 1961.

Sonrel, Pierre, *Traite de Scènographie*, Paris, 1943.

Strozzi, Giulio, *La Finta Pazza, feste theatrali . . .*, Paris, 1645.

Wiley, William, *The Early Public Theatre in France*, Cambridge, Massachusetts, 1960.

Worsthorne, Simon Townley, "Venetian Theatres 1637–1700," *Music and Letters*, July, 1948.

Reynolds, George, *The Staging of Elizabethan Plays at the Red Bull Theatre 1606–1625*, New York, 1940.

Simpson, Percy, and C. F. Bell, *Designs by Inigo Jones for Plays and Masques at Court*, Oxford, 1924.

Smith, Irwin, *Shakespeare's Globe Playhouse*, New York, 1936.

———, *Shakespeare's Blackfriars Playhouse*, New York, 1964.

Steele, Mary S., *Plays and Masques at Court*, New Haven, 1926.

Summers, Montague, *The Playhouse of Pepys*, New York, 1935.

Thorndyke, Ashley, *Shakespeare's Theatre*, New York, 1916.

Watkins, Ronald, *On Producing Shakespeare*, London, 1951.

Welsford, Enid, *The Court Masque*, Cambridge, 1927.

Wickham, Glynne William, *Early English Stages, 1300–1660*, New York, 1959, 2 vols.

CHAPTER THREE

Adams, John Cranford, *The Globe Playhouse*, Cambridge, 1942.

Adams, Joseph Quincy, *Shakespearian Playhouses*, Boston, 1917.

Beckerman, Bernard, *Shakespeare at the Globe*, New York, 1962.

Bell, Hamilton, "Contributions to the History of the English Playhouse, Part I: On a Plan by Inigo Jones," *Architectural Record*, XXXIII, 3 March, 1913).

Chambers, E. K., *The Elizabethan Stage*, Oxford, 1923, 2 vols.

Collier, John Payne, *Inigo Jones, the Life of an Architect*, London, 1848.

Gotch, John Alfred, *Inigo Jones*, London, 1928.

Harbage, Alfred, *Shakespeare's Audience*, New York, 1941.

Hodges, C. Walter, *The Globe Restored*, New York, 1954.

Hosley, Richard, "The Origins of the So-called Elizabethan Multiple Stage," *The Drama Review*, 12, 2 (Winter, 1968).

Lawrence, W. J., *The Physical Conditions of the Elizabethan Public Playhouse*, Cambridge, Massachusetts, 1927.

Mullin, D. C., "An Observation on the Origin of the Elizabethan Playhouse," *Educational Theatre Journal*, XIX, 3 (October, 1966).

Nagler, Alois, *Shakespeare's Stage*, New Haven, 1958.

Nicoll, Allardyce, *Stuart Masques and the Renaissance Stage*, New York, 1938.

Reyher, Paul, *Les Masques Anglais*, Paris, 1909.

CHAPTER FOUR

Baur-Heinhold, Margarete, *The Baroque Theatre*, New York, 1967.

Boydell, Peter, "The Manoel Theatre, Malta," *Theatre Notebook*, XII, 3 (Spring, 1958).

Decugis, Nicole, and Suzanne Reymond, *Le Décor de Théâtre en France*, Paris, 1953.

Giorgi, Felice, *Descrizione Istorica del Teatro di Tor di Nona*, Rome, 1795.

Gratiani, Girolamo, *Il Cromvele, tragedia . . .*, Bologna, 1671.

Lotti, Lotto, *L'Eta Dell'Oro, feste Teatrale . . .*, Piacenza, 1690.

Moniglia, Giovanni Andrea, *Ercole in Tebe, feste teatrale . . .*, Florence, 1661.

Nicoll, Allardyce, *The Development of the Theatre*, New York, 1938.

Noris, Mateo, *Il Greco in Troia, festa teatrale . . .*, Florence, 1688.

Pozzo, Andrea, *Perspectiva pictorum et architectorum*, Rome, 1693.

Ricci, Corrado, *I Bibiena, architette teatrale*, Milan, 1905.

Riccoboni, Luigi, *An Historical and Critical Account of the Theatre in Europe*, London, 1741.

Streit, Andreas, *Das Theater*, Vienna, 1903.

Touchard, Pierre-Aime, *Histoire Sentimentale de la Comédie Française*, Paris, 1955.

CHAPTER FIVE

Adam, Robert, *The Works in Architecture of Robert and James Adam*, London, 1778–1822, vol. 2.

Avery, Emmett L., *The London Stage*, Part II, Carbondale, Illinois, 1960.

———, "A Poem on Dorset Garden Theatre," *Theatre Notebook*, XVIII, 4 (Summer, 1964).

Boswell, Eleanore, *The Restoration Court Stage*, Cambridge, Massachusetts, 1932.

Brayley, Edward Wedlake, *Historical and Descriptive Account of the Theatres of London*, London, 1826.

Charlton, John, *The Banqueting House*, London, 1964.

Cibber, Colly, *An Apology for the Life of Mr. Colly Cibber*, London, 1822.

Daly, Augustin, *Woffington, a Tribute to the Actress and the Woman*, Philadelphia, 1888.

Defoe, Daniel, *A Review of the State of the British Nation*, facsimile edition, New York, 1938, vols. I and II.

Dent, E. L., *The Foundations of English Opera*, London, 1928.

Dibdin, Charles, Jr., *History and Illustration of the London Theatres*, London, 1826.

Dobrée, Bonamy, *The Complete Works of Sir John Vanbrugh*, London, 1928.

Doran, John, *Annals of the English Stage from Thomas Betterton to Edmund Kean*, New York, 1865, 2 vols.

Dutton, Ralph, *The Age of Wren*, London, 1951.

Eddison, Robert, "Capon, Holland and Covent Garden," *Theatre Notebook*, XIV, 1 (Autumn, 1959).

Genest, John, *Some Account of the English Stage*, Bath, 1832, vol. 2.

Godfrey, Walter, "The Apron Stage of the Eighteenth Century as Illustrated at Drury Lane," *Architectural Review*, 38, 1915.

Hotson, Leslie, *The Commonwealth and Restoration Stage*, Cambridge, Massachusetts, 1928.

Keith, William Grant, "John Webb and the Court Theatre of Charles II," *Architectural Review*, 57, 1925.

Langhans, Edward A., "Pictorial Material on the Bridges Street and Drury Lane Theatres," *Theatre Survey*, VII, 2 (November, 1966).

———, "Wren's Restoration Playhouse," *Theatre Notebook*, XVIII, 3 (Spring, 1964).

———, "Dorset Garden Theatre in Pictures," *Theatre Survey*, VI, 2 (November, 1965).

———, "The Vere Street and Lincoln's Inn Fields Theatres in Pictures," *Educational Theatre Journal*, XX, 2 (May, 1968).

Leacroft, Helen and Richard, *The Theatre*, London, 1958.

Leacroft, Richard, "Wren's Drury Lane," *Architectural Review*, CX (July, 1951).

Lynch, James J., *Box, Pit, and Gallery: Stage and Society in Jonson's London*, Berkeley, 1953.

Magalotti, Conte Lorenzo, *Travels of Cosimo the Third, Grand Duke of Tuscany, Through England, During the Reign of King Charles the Second, 1669*, London, 1821.

McAfee, Helen, *Pepys on the Restoration Stage*, New Haven, 1916.

Marton, Lee J., "From Forestage to Proscenium: A Study of Restoration Staging Techniques," *Theatre Survey*, IV, 1963.

Misson, Henri, *Misson's Memoirs and Observations in his Travels over England*, London, 1740.

Mullin, D. C., "The Queen's Theatre, Haymarket: Vanbrugh's Opera House," *Theatre Survey*, VIII, 2 (November, 1967).

———, "The Theatre Royal, Bridges Street: A Conjectural Restoration," *Educational Theatre Journal*, XIX, 1 (March, 1967).

Mullin, D. C., and Bruce A. Koenig, "Christopher Wren's Theatre Royal," *Theatre Notebook*, XXI, 4 (Summer, 1967).

Oulton, W. C., *A History of the Theatres of London*, London, 1818.

Phillips, Hugh, *Mid-Georgian London*, London, 1964.

Saunders, George, *Treatise on Theatres*, London, 1790.

Sitwell, Sacheverell, *British Architects and Craftsmen*, London, 1944.

Southern, Richard, *Changeable Scenery*, London, 1952.

———, *The Georgian Playhouse*, London, 1948.

———, *The Seven Ages of the Theatre*, London, 1962.

Stone, George Winchester, *The London Stage*, Part IV, Carbondale, Illinois, 1960.

Summers, Montague, *The Restoration Theatre*, New York, 1934.

Victor, M., *The History of the Theatres of London and Dublin from the year 1730 to the present time*, London, 1761, 2 vols.

Whistler, Laurence, *Sir John Vanbrugh, Architect and Dramatist*, London, 1938.

Wilkenson, George, *Londina Illustrata*, London, 1808–1825, vol. 2.

Wyatt, Benjamin, *Observations on the Design for the Theatre Royal, Drury Lane*, London, 1813.

CHAPTER SIX

Altman, Freud, Macgowan, and Melnitz, *Theatre Pictorial*, Berkeley, 1953.

Arnaldi, Conte Vincenzo, *Idea di un Teatro*, Vicenza, 1762.

Beauchamps, Pierre, *Récherches sur les Théâtres de France*, Paris, 1735, Part III.

Beijer, Agne, *Court Theatres of Drottningholm and Gripsholm*, Malmö, 1933.

Blondel, Jacques-Francois, *L'Architecture Françoise*, Paris, 1752–1756, vol. 4.

Croce, Benedetto, *I Teatri di Napoli*, Naples, 1891.

Doebber, Adolph, *Lauchstädt und Weimar: Ein theaterbau geschischtliche studie . . .* , Berlin, 1908.

Donnet, Alexis, *Architectonographie des Théâtres de Paris, ou parallel historique et critique de ces édifices*, Paris, 1821.

Dumont, M., *Parallel de plans des plus belles salles de spectacles d'Italie et de France avec details de machines théâtrales*, Paris, 1764.

Dumont, M., and M. Radel, *Recueil de planches sur les arts mechaniques avec leur explication*, Paris, 1777.

Ferrario, G., *Storie e descrizione de principali teatri antichi e moderni*, Milan, 1830.

Frenzel, Herbert A., *Brandenburg-Preussische Schloss-theater*, Berlin, 1959.

Giedion, Sigfried, *Spätbarocker und romantischer Klassisismus*, Munich, 1922.

Hammitzsch, Martin, *Das Moderne Theaterbau*, Berlin, 1907.

Hilleström, Gustaf, *Performances given at the Drottningholm Theatre*, Drottningholm, 1966.

Landriani, Paolo, *Osservazione su l'imp. r. Teatro alla Scala in Milano*, Milan, 1830.

Leclerc, Helene, "Au Théâtre de Basançon: Claude-Nicolas Ledoux; Reformateur des Moeurs et Prédurseur de Richard Wagner," *Revue d'Histoire du Théâtre*, 1958 II.

Louis, Louis-Nicolas (Victor), *Salle de Spectacle de Bordeaux*, Paris, 1782.

Lukomskii, G. J. K., *Les Théâtres Anciens et Modernes*, Paris, 1934.

Milizia, Francesco, *Trattato Completo, formale e materiale del teatro*, Rome, 1771.

——, *Lives of the celebrated architects, ancient and modern, with observations on their work and on the principles of the art*, translated by Mrs. Edw. Cresy, London, 1826, 2 vols.

Parfaict, Claude, *Histoire du Théâtre Français*, Paris, 1745.

Patte, Pierre, *Essai sur l'architecture théâtrale*, Paris, 1782.

Raval, Marcel, *Claude-Nicolas Ledoux*, Paris, 1950.

Rietdorf, Alfred, *Der Architekture von Gilly*, Berlin, 1940.

Schreyvogl, Friedrich, *Das Burgtheater*, Vienna, 1965.

Verlet, Pierre, "L'Opéra de Versailles," *Revue d'Histoire du Théâtre*, 1957, III.

Weichberger, A., *Goethe und das Komödienhaus*, Leipzig, 1928.

CHAPTER SEVEN

Dunlap, William, *History of the American Theatre*, New York, 1832.

Hewitt, Barnard, *Theatre U. S. A.*, New York, 1959.

Hornblow, Arthur, *A History of the Theatre in America*, Philadelphia, 1919, 2 vols.

Hughes, Glenn, *A History of the American Theatre*, New York, 1951.

Lewis, Stanley, "Classicism in New York Theatre Architecture: 1825–1850," *Theatre Survey*, VI, 1.

MacNamara, Brooks, "The English Playhouse in America," *Connoisseur*, December, 1967.

Pollock, Thomas Clark, *The Philadelphia Theatre in the Eighteenth Century*, Philadelphia, 1933.

CHAPTER EIGHT

Berliner Buhnen: Illustrierter Almanach, 1913.

Bierman, Franz, *Die Plane für Reform des Theaterbaues bei Karl Friedrich Schinkel und Gottfried Semper*, Berlin, 1924.

Booth, Michael, *English Melodrama*, London, 1965.

Bowman, Ned A., "Investigating a Theatrical Ideal: Wagner's Bayreuth Festspielhaus," *Educational Theatre Journal*, XVIII, 4 (December, 1966).

Brown, Alex, *The "Prinzregenten" Theatre in Munich*, Berlin, 1901.

Cavos, Albert, *Traite de la Construction des Théâtres*, St. Petersburg, 1847.

Chapman, John K., *Royal Dramatic Record*, London, 1849.

Contant, Clement, and J. de Philippi, *Parallele des principaux théâtres modernes de l'Europe et des machines théâtrales. . .* , Paris, 1870, 2 vols.

Daly, Cesar, *Les Théâtres de la Place de Chatelot*, Paris, 1865.

Garnier, Charles, *Le Theatre*, Paris, 1871.

Gosset, Alphonse, *Traite de la construction des théâtres*, Paris, 1886.

Hope-Wallace, Philip, *Picture History of Opera*, New York, 1960.

Hude, H. von der, and J. Hennicke, *Das Lessingtheater in Berlin*, Berlin, 1899.

Langhans, C. F., *Das Stadt-Theater in Leipzig*, Berlin, 1870.

Littmann, Max, *Die Königlichen Hoftheater in Stuttgart*, Darmstadt, 1912.

Mander and Mitcheson, *Picture History of the British Theatre*, London, 1957.

Moynet, G., *Trucs et Décors*, Paris, n.d. (c. 1881).

Sachs, Edwin Otho, *Modern Opera Houses and Theatres*, London, 1896–1898, 3 vols.

Sauvageot, Louis, *Considerations sur la construction des théâtres*, Paris, n.d. (c. 1885).

Semper, Gottfried, *Handbuch der Architektur: Theater*, Stuttgart, 1904.

Watson, Ernest Bradlee, *Sheridan to Robertson*, New York, 1963.

CHAPTER NINE

Fischel, Oskar, *Das Moderne Bühnenbild*, Berlin, 1923.

Gorelik, Mordecai, *New Theatres for Old*, New York, 1940.

Isaacs, Edith, *Architecture for the New Theatre*, New York, 1935.

Kranich, Friedrich, *Bühnentechnik der Gegenwart*, Berlin, 1929–1933, vol. 1.

Sayler, Oliver M., *Max Reinhardt and his Theatre*, New York, 1924.

Sexton, R. W., *American Theatres of Today*, New York, 1927–1930, 2 vols.

Shand, Philip M., *Modern Theatres and Cinemas*, London, 1930.

Urban, Joseph, *Theatres*, New York, 1930.

CHAPTER TEN

Aloi, Roberto, *Architetture per lo Spettacolo*, Milan, 1958.

Bentham, Frederick, "Theatre Design in Britain," *Tabs*, 24, 2 (June, 1966).

Burris-Meyer, Harold, and Edward C. Cole, *Theatres and Auditoriums*, 2d. ed., New York, 1964.

Correy, Percy, "Stages in America," *Tabs*, XIX, 2 (September, 1961).

Educational Facilities Laboratories, "Fine Arts Facilities: past, present, future," *Newsletter*, New York, 1965.

Glasstone, Victor, "Auditoria Galore," *Architectural Design*, November, 1963.

Johnson, Russell, "Acoustical Design of Multi-Purpose College Auditoriums," *American School and University*, 1962–63.

Joseph, Stephen, ed., *Adaptable Theatres*, Association of British Theatre Technicians, London, 1962.

Malmö Municipal Theatre, *Malmö Stadtsteater*, Malmö, n.d. (ca. 1945).

Schmertz, Mildred, "Better Architecture for the Performing Arts," *Architectural Record*, December, 1964.

Silverman, Max, and Ned A. Bowman, *Contemporary Theatre Architecture*, New York, 1965.

Werner, Eberhard, *Theatergebäude*, Berlin, (DDR), 1954, 2 vols.

ADDENDUM

A brief bibliography on theatre reform projects and competition projects.

American Federation of Arts, *The Ideal Theatre, Eight Concepts*, New York, 1962.

Bel-Geddes, Norman, "Design for a New Kind of Theatre," *New York Times Magazine*, November 30, 1947.

———, "Flexible Theatre," *Theatre Arts*, XXXII (June–July, 1948).

———, *Horizons*, Boston, 1933.

———, "Six Theatre Projects," *Theatre Arts Monthly*, September, 1930.

Bell, Hamilton, "Contributions on the History of the English Playhouse, Part II: On three plans of Sir Christopher Wren," *Architectural Record*, XXXIV, 1913.

Boulée, Louis-Etienne, *Essai sur l'art construire les théâtres, leurs machines et leurs movements*, Paris, 1801.

Chaumont, Chevalier de, *Exposition des principes que l'on suivre dans l'ordonnance des théâtres modernes*, Paris, 1769.

———, *Veritable construction d'un théâtre d'Opèra*, Paris, 1766.

Cochin, Charles Nicole, *Projêt d'un salle de spectacle*, Paris, 1765.

Hübsch, Heinrich, *Entwurf zu einem theater mit eisernen Dauhrüstung*, Frankfort, 1825.

Keith, William Grant, "A Theatre Project by Inigo Jones," *Burlington Magazine*, XXXI, 1917.

———, "John Webb and the Court Theatre of Charles II," *Architectural Review*, 57, 1 (1925).

Lamberti, Vincenzo, *Le Regolata construzione de teatri*, Naples, 1787.

Leclerc, Helene, "Louis-Etienne Boulée, architect visionnaire, et la competition pour une nouvelle salle d'opéra, 1781," *Revue d'Histoire du Théâtre*, II, 1965.

Milizia, Francesco, *Discorso sul Teatro*, Venice, 1773.

Noverre, Jean, *Observations sur la construction d'une salle de l'opera*, Paris, n.d. (c. 1760's).

Patte, Pierre, *Essai sur l'architecture théâtrale, où de l'Ordonnance le plus avantageuse à une salle de spectacle*, Paris, 1782.

Pozzo, Andrea, *Rules and Examples of Perspective proper for painters and architects*, translated by John James, London, 1707.

Rosenau, Helen, *Boulée's Treatise on Architecture*, London, 1953.

Saunders, George, *Treatise on Theatres*, London, 1790.

Wulliam and Farge, *Les Concours Publics*, Paris, 1896.

Index

Index